HIKING
WEST VIRGINIA

Mountain laurel

HIKING
WEST VIRGINIA

A GUIDE TO THE STATE'S GREATEST HIKING ADVENTURES

THIRD EDITION

Mary Reed

FALCONGUIDES

GUILFORD, CONNECTICUT

To all the West Virginians fighting to end mountaintop removal.

FALCONGUIDES®

An imprint of The Rowman & Littlefield Publishing Group, Inc.
4501 Forbes Blvd., Ste. 200
Lanham, MD 20706
www.rowman.com

Falcon and FalconGuides are registered trademarks and Make Adventure Your Story is a
trademark of The Rowman & Littlefield Publishing Group, Inc.

Distributed by NATIONAL BOOK NETWORK

British Library Cataloguing-in-Publication Information available

Library of Congress Cataloguing-in-Publication Data available

ISBN 978-1-4930-3573-1 (paperback)
ISBN 978-1-4930-3574-8 (e-book)

∞™ The paper used in this publication meets the minimum requirements of American National
Standard for Information Sciences—Permanence of Paper for Printed Library Materials, ANSI/
NISO Z39.48-1992.

Printed in the United States of America

The author and Rowman & Littlefield assume no liability for accidents happening to, or injuries
sustained by, readers who engage in the activities described in this book.

CONTENTS

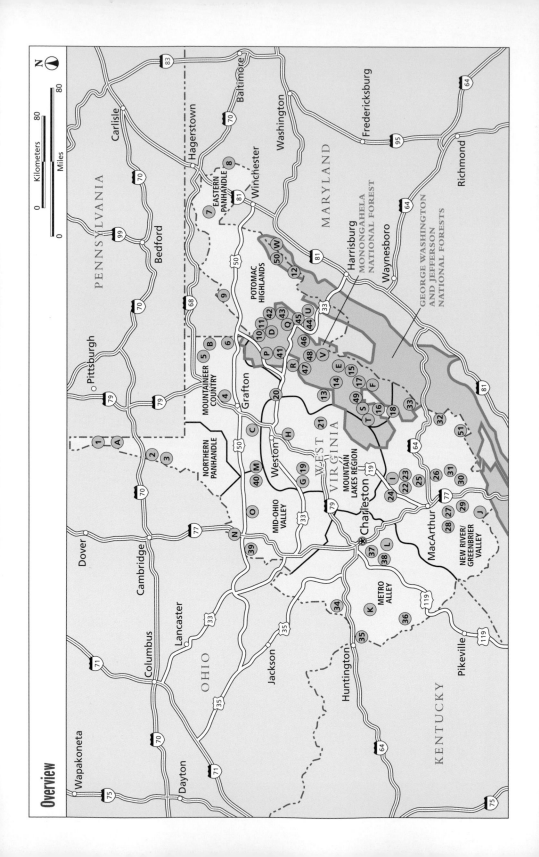

Overview

ACKNOWLEDGMENTS

Thank you to Steven Carroll and Mark Miller, authors of the first edition of *Hiking West Virginia;* this book is based on their considerable work. Thank you to all the employees at these destinations who reviewed entries, who are too many to name individually. Thanks also to Katie Benoit Cardoso and Julie Marsh at Globe Pequot Press for their work in readying this guide for publication. Many thanks to my hiking partners, porters, and models: Savanna Lyons, Jamie Fields, Chelsea Hindenach, Jonah Daw, Liz Migliore, Michael Boyes, Colin Donohue, Anna Gabritchidze, Kelee Riesbeck, Kim Landsbergen, Michelle Greenfield, Mara Giglio, the King-Cochran family—Lisa, James, Lucas, and Violet, and the Hitt family—Than, Mary Anne, and Hazel. Thanks to prAna for providing clothing that appears in many of the photos. Special thanks to trail angels who came

OUTDOOR PHOTOGRAPHY

West Virginia is such a beautiful state that you don't have to be Ansel Adams to get some good shots. However, following a few basic rules of photography will make your pictures worth the share button instead of the delete button. First, use a digital single-lens reflex (DSLR) camera. Then read the owner's manual, or at least the "getting started" section. Use a tripod; this will help you compose your shots and allow you to set the timer and get in the shot, and it will allow you to use a slow shutter speed (say, two seconds) to get an effect like silky white water from a waterfall.

As far as composition goes, sometimes that's a no-brainer: That mountain, waterfall, or bear is your subject. Other times, it's a little harder, in which case moving in closer on your subject or experimenting with a different perspective might work: Try shooting a rock in the river instead of the entire river, or try to fill the frame with a close-up of just one bright flower rather than the whole bunch from a distance. In general, avoid clutter. The so-called rule of thirds is also handy. Divide the space in your frame into thirds, both vertically and horizontally, then place your subject in a third of the frame that's right, left, up, or down, rather than dead center.

Light can be your best friend or your worst enemy, so befriend it. Plan to take landscape shots during the "golden hour" of warm light before sunset or shortly after sunrise. If you plan to have people in your shot, put them in open shade (outside in the shade of a tree, for example) so there are no harsh lights and shadows on them. If your only option is full sun, use "fill flash"—that is, use the flash on your camera to fill in those harsh shadows.

Finally, your job as a photographer isn't over once you return home. You must edit your photographs using Photoshop or another photo processing program. Crop the shots when necessary and adjust the contrast and color—most programs will automatically do this for you if you don't have the time or skills to do it yourself. And please don't share 300 photos from your last trip with the world; give us your best 30 and leave us asking for more.

through when needed, whether it was a ride, a place to stay, or whatever the immediate need was: Charlie Dundas, Mike Smith, and James and Karen Thibeault. A final thanks to my partner, Attila Horvath. He served as chauffeur, porter, hiking partner, model, photography assistant, copy editor, and number one supporter throughout the length of this project.

WEST VIRGINIA STATE SYMBOLS
State motto: *Montani Semper Liberi* (Mountaineers Are Always Free)
State bird: Cardinal
State wildflower: Rhododendron
State song: "The West Virginia Hills"

INTRODUCTION

Almost heaven. Wild and wonderful. West-by-God-Virginia. At some point you come to realize why the Mountain State inspires so many superlatives. There's an energy that lives here, and it only takes two steps to tap into that energy: one step away from the car and another step onto the trail. Experience the raw force of whitewater as the Gauley River hurtles its way through the mountains. Get a peak experience atop Seneca Rocks, reachable only under your own power. Hike the storied Appalachian Trail as it passes through Harper's Ferry. Wish—momentarily—that you hadn't taken that first step away from the car as you encounter a mother bear and her cubs in the Monongahela National Forest. This book is an invitation to discover West Virginia and to discover more about yourself. Are you ready to go that extra mile, both literally and figuratively?

LAND MANAGEMENT

Of West Virginia's 15.5 million acres, nearly 80 percent is covered by forests. Public lands total nearly 1.5 million acres. This is almost 10 percent of the total landmass of West Virginia. The state has preserved some of its natural heritage through the **West Virginia Division of Natural Resources,** which manages thirty-five state parks, seven state forests, and two long-distance trails—the Greenbrier River Trail and the North Bend Rail Trail. Parks offer various facilities, including day-use-only parks, year-round lodge parks, picnic tables, fine-dining restaurants, golf courses, and horseback riding. There are seven state forests, which are managed by the West Virginia Division of Forestry. State forest lands are used for wildlife management, industrial purposes (logging, mining, drilling), and recreational activities, such as hiking, biking, and horseback riding.

There are about one hundred wildlife management areas (WMAs) and public access areas (for boating and fishing) in the state, totaling more than 380,000 acres—far outstripping park and forest land in size. The land is managed by the state and federal governments and is primarily managed for game habitat.

Probably the most well known of the natural areas in West Virginia are

Trout lily in Kumbrabow State Forest

the national forests. The **USDA Forest Service** oversees the Monongahela National Forest—known locally as the Mon—and the George Washington and Jefferson National Forests, only a portion of which lies in West Virginia. The Mon covers more than 919,000 acres in eastern West Virginia and contains eight wilderness areas and one national recreation area, Spruce Knob–Seneca Rocks. With 874 miles of hiking trails to explore, this forest is a hiker's paradise.

The **National Park Service** is also in charge of land in West Virginia. The New River Gorge National River and the Bluestone National Scenic River provide a multitude of outdoor activities. Water sports like whitewater rafting, kayaking, canoeing, and fishing are by far the most popular. There are miles of hiking trails near steep cliffs, powerful whitewater, and babbling trout streams. The steep cliffs bring climbers to one of the premier climbing destination in the East, the New River Gorge.

The **US Fish and Wildlife Service** manages two national wildlife refuges (NWRs) in West Virginia: Canaan Valley NWR and Ohio River Islands NWR. National wildlife refuges are created to protect the nation's native wildlife by preserving and, when necessary, restoring natural habitats.

City and county parks make up still more public land in West Virginia. Some are small, some are large, and several are covered in this book. Grand Vue Park and Mountwood Park are both county parks with hiking opportunities.

Finally, **privately owned land** is sometimes open to the public for recreational use. For example, the Nature Conservancy holds land in preservation to protect biological diversity, while remaining open to the public for hiking. Snowshoe Resort, best known for its winter skiing opportunities, offers 40-plus miles of trails open to the public.

Trails cross the land, and hikers take to the hills. A proud state built on a rugged land has seen fit to preserve its natural heritage. But is it enough? Every day some of our "protected" lands are lost to the economic uses of mining and logging, and management of land is reevaluated. What is protected today may be gone tomorrow. To paraphrase a famous quote, we will only protect what we love and we can only love what we know. To know West Virginia's lands, it is necessary to experience them. Luckily, this is an enjoyable necessity.

GEOLOGY

The West Virginia Geological and Economic Survey breaks the state into two basic geologic areas: the ridges and hollows of the western two-thirds of the state that contain minable coal, and the eastern one-third of the state that is folded into steep mountains reaching nearly 4,000 feet that contain no minable coal. This is a rather simplistic economic view, but quite correct nonetheless. Processes that occurred millions of years ago set the "groundwork" for the beautiful topography and the mineral development that we observe today.

The economic value in the flatter, minable two-thirds of West Virginia was created relatively early in the state's geologic history. The vast resources of coal in West Virginia are the result of sedimentation and deposition. Approximately 500 million years ago, an inland sea covered much of the land that would become West Virginia. Sedimentation and marine deposition occurred, creating much of West Virginia's limestones. By 300 million years ago, the sea had retreated and the area was covered by swampland. Approximately 50 million years of growth and decay of plant matter deposited shales and the rich

organic coal seams. Sedimentation and deposition during this time produced a wealth of resources for the state. West Virginia has produced oil, gas, and high-quality coal. Mines in the state also extract limestone, sandstone, sand, gravel, salt, and iron.

The aesthetic value of West Virginia's beautiful landscape has been created and re-created throughout the state's geologic history. Shortly after the sediments were deposited, the process that lifted the eastern one-third of West Virginia began. Approximately 250 million years ago, the Appalachian Mountains were created as eastern West Virginia was folded and the high plateau was thrust upward. Today's landscape is a result of 250 million years of erosion. The New River and other waterways cut gorges on average 1,000 feet deep into the high plain. Rains washed away softer rocks from the ridges, leaving the harder, more resistant sandstones, such as the "fin" of Seneca Rocks.

The everyday result of West Virginia's geologic history is a state rich in landscape and minerals. The "flat" western two-thirds of the state actually has short but steep hills and hollows that give way to deep gorges and tall ridges as you go east. Hikers can enjoy various terrains in a single weekend, and often in a single day.

OUTDOOR ETHICS

Leave No Trace is a philosophy of outdoor use that has become the standard for responsibly enjoying the outdoors. The idea is to minimize human impact on the land and the natural flora and fauna. There are seven basic principles of Leave No Trace camping. By following these guidelines as closely as you can, you will help others to also have an enjoyable outdoor experience.

Plan and prepare ahead of time. Planning ahead and being prepared keeps you safe and will help limit impact to the environment. Hikers go out every weekend knowing

Mash Fork Falls (hike 28)

very little about the area, the terrain, or the trail they're hiking. They leave the trailhead without a map and without ever hearing a local weather report. To prepare, read hiking guides, park trail guides, and websites. Call the area contact to get current local conditions and area regulations, and study the contour lines on a map of the region.

Once you know about the area and conditions, you can plan your hike. Can you do that 20-mile loop or will 2,000 vertical feet in 2 miles slow you down a little? The dawn-to-dusk summer hike will take you until after dark in the winter. Knowing where you'll be at the end of the day will help you plan for a campsite and will keep you on the trail and away from bushwhacks. And remember, should something happen to you, mountain rescue involves a lot of staff and a lot of time. Impact to the environment will take a backseat to saving human life. Make sure accidents are truly accidents and not a result of being unprepared.

Hike on trails, and camp at campsites. The use of West Virginia's outdoor resources is increasing every year. Hiking on established trails and camping at established campsites concentrates impact to certain areas and minimizes impact to the whole. Trails generally travel to the most interesting landmarks, and many trails are dotted with campsites. When hiking a trail, do not cut switchbacks. This causes serious erosion problems, and saving a few steps out of several miles will not be noticeable.

Backcountry campsites are located throughout the wildlands, generally along streams, near vistas, and almost always near the trail. Camping in these previously used campsites benefits the hiker and the wilderness. These areas are usually the best spots around for camping: The ground is level, a stream is nearby, and there is room for a tent and a place to cook. Using established sites keeps impact from getting dispersed throughout the wilderness. If a site looks unused and is attempting to recover, don't camp in it. If you must camp in a new area, make sure the ecosystem is durable enough to recover. Pitch the tent on hard ground at least 200 feet away from streams. If camping in a meadow, move your tent every other day.

Use stoves whenever possible, and limit use of fires. In today's low-impact camping world, the era of the campfire is nearly over. Campfire rings scar the land, are slow to decay, and are eyesores to other hikers. Camp stoves, on the other hand, pack up clean and leave no evidence of their use. They also burn with higher, more controllable temperatures. Campers generally build campfires for aesthetics and not for cooking. Admittedly, the campfire has its place in the hearts of camping romantics. The light from a campfire, though, has a tendency to create a tiny "room" of light, effectively shutting you off from anything that lies outside that room. Spending an evening at camp without a fire allows one's eyes to adjust to the darkness, allows the creatures of the night to become alive, and allows the camper to be part of the environment.

Finally, and most obviously, fires can be dangerous to both humans and the wilderness. It takes years for a forest to recover from the damage of one forest fire. During dry times of the year, fires are often banned altogether. If a fire must be built, place it in an established campfire ring at an established campsite. Use only dead sticks on the ground for wood, and make sure there is a water source nearby for dousing the fire when you're done.

Dispose of waste properly. Pack out everything you pack in. The goal is fairly simple: Leave nothing behind. Before leaving, inspect your campsite to make sure you've gathered everything you brought in, including all trash and leftover food. There are entire books written on the subject of proper disposal of human waste. The basic idea

Tomlinson Run (hike 1)

is to dig a hole far from any water source. No backpacker, hiker, or any type of outdoor enthusiast should be without a small shovel. After doing your "business," stir it up and cover it. If it's not buried 6 to 8 inches, it's not properly disposed of. Some minimum-impact campers subscribe to the idea of packing out human waste, too. In some eco-systems, decay occurs at an extremely slow rate, making this philosophy appropriate. Although packing out human waste is a lower-impact way of camping, in most cases in the East, burying waste is acceptable.

Leave the area undisturbed. Part of the definition of wilderness contained in the Wilderness Act describes an area where "man himself is a visitor who does not remain." Think of yourself as a visitor to the outdoors. Leave the stones unturned and the flowers on the stems. Their beauty lies within the brief moment you experience them on the trail. Your goal is to slip in and out without the environment ever noticing.

Respect wildlife. This means to respect that they are wild and to respect their right to be wild. Do not feed the wildlife; it alters the animals' behavior and often makes them dependent on humans. Make sure all leftover food at your campsite is packed out. Do not approach wild animals; view them from a distance.

Respect other visitors. By respecting other visitors' rights to have an enjoyable out-door experience, we ensure the same for ourselves. Be courteous and treat others as you would like to be treated. Camp away from where others are camped. Keep noises and voices low. Yield to others on trails, especially to horses or other pack animals.

By keeping these seven principles in mind when you head out on a trip, you greatly increase the quality of your outdoor experience while minimizing the effect you have on the environment. These ethics are not a high mark to strive for, but rather a minimum of care that must be adhered to. For more information, visit LNT.org. With the use of outdoor resources ever increasing, it is everyone's responsibility to care for West Virginia's natural beauty.

PREPAREDNESS AND SAFETY

Hiking is a sport, and it requires the athlete participating to be responsible for his or her own preparedness and safety. There are no hikers' licenses and no hiker safety courses you must pass. Safety is directly related to preparedness; the two go hand in hand. A hiker who is prepared will avoid many of the problems an unprepared hiker will face. Unprepared and unsafe hikers put themselves and others at risk. To prepare for the sport of hiking, one must have the right equipment, one must practice, and one must have a knowledge of the sport.

As with any sport, you first need the right equipment. Too often hikers go into the woods without proper boots or clothing, or without enough food or water. A "short list" of essentials for all hikes includes:

- ❏ food and water
- ❏ a map and compass
- ❏ a first-aid kit, including insect repellent and sunscreen
- ❏ rain gear
- ❏ matches (preferably waterproof)
- ❏ a flashlight with fully charged batteries
- ❏ a knife
- ❏ a whistle

Second, a hiker must practice. Hiking is a physical activity. We have all heard of the desk jockey turned weekend warrior who hobbles into work Monday morning after being hurt in Saturday's softball game. Practice for hiking by exercising regularly and staying in good shape. Stay fit during the week by doing other aerobic activities like walking, running, biking, swimming, or weight lifting.

Third, knowledge of the sport is required. The participant must know the rules and the risks. Prepare for the hike by reading up on the rules and regulations that pertain to the area you will visit. Know what risks are involved, such as extreme weather conditions, dangerous cliff areas, poisonous plants, or potentially dangerous animals. The following sections list outdoor issues particular to West Virginia. Please remember that this list is not all-inclusive. Hiking is a sport, but the playing field is constantly changing.

Weather

There is one uncompromising truth: If we're going to be outside, we're going to be in the weather. Weather is part of the joy of the outdoors, part of the experience. Weather in West Virginia ranges from hot in the summer to frigidly cold in the winter. Sunny days can change to downpours in minutes. Knowing what weather to expect on a hike is a first step. Being prepared for changes in weather and knowing how to react to weather emergencies will keep a hiker safe and confident.

Hot and humid summer weather can be dangerous if the hiker is not aware of the risks of dehydration, which occurs when water intake does not keep pace with fluids expired as the body tries to cool itself. While hiking, body temperature rises and fluid is lost as perspiration. The evaporation of perspiration cools the body. If more fluids are lost than are ingested, the result is dehydration. The simple solution to this problem is to drink plenty of water. Drink before the hike, and drink while on the trail. Strenuous exercise often requires a liter or more of water per hour. With this type of intake, you will probably need several "refueling" stations. Before beginning a hike, determine where water will be available on the trail. Pack water according to the availability of filterable water sources on the trail. For example, a creek hike provides ample water; you may have to carry just a 1-liter bottle. A ridgeline hike, however, may travel for 10 miles before reaching a water source, thus requiring you to carry a bladder pack of 100 ounces or more.

Heat exhaustion and heatstroke are potentially life-threatening situations and are serious hazards of hiking in warm weather. Both ailments result when the body is not cooled properly. Heat exhaustion occurs first; if not treated, it can develop into the serious and sometimes fatal heatstroke. If extensive hiking is planned during warm weather, consult a first-aid guide on the symptoms and treatment of heat exhaustion and heatstroke.

Cold weather brings its own risks and dangers. Two cold-weather emergencies to be concerned about are hypothermia and frostbite. Hypothermia results when the body temperature drops below the normal temperature. If hypothermia is not treated, it can lead to death. As hypothermia worsens, it can cause disorientation and cause the hiker to make poor decisions, thus compounding an already bad situation.

Frostbite occurs when skin is exposed to cold, causing ice crystals to form in the body. Extremities such as fingers, toes, hands, and feet are at the greatest risk for frostbite. If hiking when the possibility of cold weather exists, consult a first-aid guide for the symptoms and treatment of frostbite and hypothermia.

Although not a guarantee of safety, both hypothermia and frostbite can be avoided by wearing proper clothing. This does not necessarily mean wearing *more* clothing. It is important to dress in layers that will keep you warm and wick away sweat and moisture. Clothing that becomes wet with sweat will rob the body of heat. As the hike becomes strenuous, remove layers to avoid becoming too hot. Add layers while resting to avoid becoming chilled. Always pack extra clothing for the worst-case scenario. Consider what you would need to be wearing to survive the night outside.

Jack-in-the-pulpit

Wind chill and wet weather can play a big role in both frostbite and hypothermia. Blowing wind and rain rob the body of heat. Frostbite and hypothermia can occur quickly when the wind or wetness is a factor. It is good idea to carry windproof and waterproof clothing while hiking, especially in areas with exposed ridges.

Storms are another weather risk of which to be aware. Especially in the higher elevations, storms can develop suddenly and become severe. During a thunderstorm, temperatures can drop 20 degrees and wind speed can increase by 20 miles per hour in less than an hour. Severe thunderstorms can bring with them driving rain, lightning, and hail. Any one of these conditions could be life threatening. If severe weather presents itself, find shelter from the storm. Move off exposed ridges and rock outcrops. Travel to the base of rocks, and look for overhangs to provide shelter. Do not take shelter under trees, especially on ridgetops. Be aware that heavy rains can cause flash flooding in narrow gorges.

On bright days, sunburn can be a problem in both summer and winter. Sunburn can be painful and can also significantly increase one's risk of developing skin cancer. The risk of sunburn exists even on partly sunny days. While hiking, wear a hat to protect the face, and a shirt to protect the back and arms. Shirts are not completely effective at blocking the sun's rays, especially when wet. Sunblock lotions above SPF 15 are also effective in preventing sunburn.

Plants

Several potentially harmful plants are found in West Virginia. Learning to identify such plants is the most effective way to avoid them. The most common of these is poison ivy, a climbing plant found along many trails. It grows best in sunny, open areas such as old clearings and paths. This plant has compound leaves of three leaflets. When touched, the plant leaves a residue that causes a skin rash, characterized by itchy redness and blistering. Treatment usually involves applying lotions to the affected areas to keep them dry and reduce the sensation of itching. In severe cases a doctor may need to be consulted. The best way to avoid the plant is to know what it looks like.

Stinging nettle is another type of plant that can be an annoyance while hiking. This plant stands about 24 inches high, with toothed leaves that grow in pairs opposite each other on the stem. The leaves have bristles that contain a watery juice. The juice can produce an intense but short-term itch. The best way to avoid problems with nettles is to wear long pants or gaiters while hiking.

There are many other plants in West Virginia that may cause allergic or toxic reactions. These include poison sumac and various species of mushrooms. Consult a field guide to educate yourself on their characteristics. Knowing the local flora is a pleasant way to enjoy the outdoors and the best way to keep safe.

Skunk cabbage in Cranberry Glades Botanical Area

Animals

It is important to remember the forest is the home of many animals and that we are visitors. Although most animals in the forest are small, even the smallest animal will defend itself when threatened. The best way to avoid unwanted problems with animals is to leave

A red eft newt

them alone. The rule of thumb is simple: Enjoy wildlife from a distance.

Animals like food and spend most of their time acquiring it. Over the years, many animals have learned that hikers represent a supply of food. To avoid problems with animals while on an overnight trip, place a rope over a high limb and suspend your food pack above the ground. By placing the pack in the air, animals will be unable to reach it and therefore not eat the food or destroy the pack. The mental image of a bear clawing through a tent wall to get to a pack should be enough to convince you to hang your food bag.

There are two types of poisonous snakes in West Virginia: rattlesnakes and copperheads. Both snakes will bite when threatened. Know what these snakes look like and where they are most likely to live. Both snakes prefer wooded hillsides, rock outcrops, and streams, ponds, and flooded areas (that is, everywhere a trail might go in West Virginia). If a copperhead or rattlesnake is encountered, stay away from it. If bitten by a snake, stay calm and seek medical help quickly. While hiking solo, it is advisable to carry a snakebite kit. Having a first-aid guide and knowing the procedure for dealing with snakebites is a must.

Insects can be a problem in the forest. The most notorious is the mosquito. In wet areas, these insects thrive and can make life miserable. When bitten by a mosquito, the area will swell slightly and itch. Try not to scratch the affected area. To avoid bug bites, wear extra layers of light clothing. Several brands of insect repellent are available. Ticks are also a concern. Inspect your skin for them periodically. If you find one, remove it with tweezers, taking care to pinch the head and not the body. Follow accepted first-aid procedures to minimize the risk of disease caused by a tick bite. Lyme disease, in particular, is a serious tick-borne illness. If, after hiking, you find a bullseye rash on your skin combined with flu-like symptoms, seek medical attention right away. Lyme disease is very treatable if you catch it early.

Heights

West Virginia is known for its sandstone cliffs. The eroded ridgetops are often lined with ever-repeating outcrops. Care should be taken to avoid injury in rocky environments. Be aware of high cliff areas, and be especially vigilant with children and pets. Night hiking in cliff areas can be extremely dangerous.

The view from Diamond Point shows how Endless Wall got its name.

Self-protection

This is a broad category and yet a very important one. There are many general precautions to take that will make a hike safer and more enjoyable. Let someone know where you will be hiking and when you expect to return. Know your travel route, its length, and the level of difficulty. Assess your ability to hike the trail.

Always carry a map and a compass. Before entering the wilderness, learn methods of outdoor orienteering. If you become lost, you will have the skills necessary to find your way out of the woods and back to your vehicle.

Clothing is another important consideration. Good boots are essential, protecting against turned ankles, wet feet, and a host of other minor problems that can make a hike miserable. As good as boots are, they are only as good as the socks worn inside them. Wool socks are good for hiking because they stay warm even when wet. There are also excellent brands of synthetic socks. Summer and winter versions of socks suit various thermal needs. A hat is important, too. A hat protects the head and face from sunburn, keeps the head dry when it's raining, and prevents blowing winds from cooling the body. A lightweight windbreaker should be carried in case of severe wind; a waterproof one can double for protection against the rain.

During the cooler months, hikers need to take additional precautions. Carry extra clothing, even on mild days. Many a day that began as clear morning has ended with a snowstorm. Dress in layers so that you can regulate your temperature by adding or removing a layer. Perspiration that soaks clothing will chill a hiker when he or she stops to rest. Gloves and a hat protect the extremities.

Hunting

The woods in West Virginia are open to hunting most of the year. Because the timing of hunting seasons varies from year to year, it is necessary to obtain a schedule from the Division of Natural Resources (304-558-2771; www.wvdnr.gov) and plan a hike accordingly. Deer and turkey seasons are probably the most dangerous, but be aware of any type of hunting activity. It is best to stay out of the woods during the general firearms season. If planning to hike during hunting season, wear blaze orange and bypass bushwhacks if possible. Blaze orange may not be much of a fashion statement, but it will reduce the chance of being involved in a hunting accident.

West Virginia's national forest, state parks and state forests are very popular among hunters. If you plan overnight trips to a park or forest during hunting seasons, advance reservations are recommended. Many parks and forests cater to the needs of hunters and adjust their schedules of operation accordingly. For example, many camping areas are open until the end of the deer rifle season, which typically ends on the first Saturday in December. For information regarding the availability of park or forest facilities during hunting seasons, call the management offices for the area in question. Remember, planning for your trip will ensure that it is both safe and enjoyable.

HOW TO USE THIS GUIDE

This guide is meant to provide accurate and concise information on some of the best hiking in West Virginia. Our goal is to answer the question, "Where should I go hiking this weekend?" The Overview map plots hiking destinations in relation to geographic regions and major roads.

The guide groups hikes into the following ten geographic regions: Northern Panhandle, Mountaineer Country, Eastern Panhandle, Potomac Highlands, Mountain Lakes Region, New River/Greenbrier Valley, Metro Valley, Mid-Ohio Valley, Monongahela National Forest, and George Washington and Jefferson National Forests. Hikes within a region are similar in ecology, habitat, flora, fauna, and geology.

Use the map to decide on a hike in the part of the state you would like to visit, then read the appropriate entry to begin more detailed planning of your trip. Each entry contains the following information:

Start: This is where the hikes begins; the trailhead.

Distance: The total distance in miles that the hike travels is listed here.

Hiking time: This is an estimate of how long it will take to hike the trail. Note, this is just an estimate and can vary widely according to hiking pace and stops along the way.

Difficulty: A subjective opinion made by the author of the difficulty of the hike. Hikes are classified as easy, moderate, or difficult.

Trail surface: This indicates what type of surface you will be hiking on, such as dirt trail, boardwalk, paved path, etc.

Best season: A suggested best time of year in which to hike the trail.

Other trail users: This section lists other trail users you might expect to see during your hike, such as hunters, mountain bikers, horseback riders, etc.

Canine compatibility: This tells you if it is legal to bring your dog on the trail.

Land status: This indicates who owns or manages the land on which the trail passes, for example, national forest or private resort.

Nearest town: The closest city or town with basic amenities is listed here.

Mountain laurel blooms throughout West Virginia in the spring.

Fees and permits: This self-explanatory entry will ensure that you have enough cash or that you have obtained proper paperwork if required.

Schedule: Hours the trail and visitors centers, offices, etc. are open to the public.

Maps: This section provides a listing of maps particular to the hike. Maps listed will include park maps and USGS 1:24,000 quad maps. (A detailed map is provided for each hike, showing trailheads, parking, trails, peaks, and other landmarks. These maps are not, however, meant for orienteering or compass work.)

Trail contact: The address and phone number for acquiring up-to-date local information is included here.

Special considerations: Specific trail hazards or warnings such as when hunting season occurs, when there might be ice on the trail, or a lack of water.

Finding the trailhead: Directions to the trailhead are provided. Often, two or more sets of directions are listed to get you to different trailheads or to guide you from different starting points. This information should be used in conjunction with the maps in this guide, USGS maps, and state road maps. Abbreviations used in this section include:

- I—interstate
- US—US highway
- WV—West Virginia state route
- CR—county road
- FR—forest road

The hike: Generally, the hike described is the most interesting or most scenic hike in the park or area. Alternate routes or suggestions for other nearby hikes may also be included here.

Local information: Contact information for the local convention and visitor bureau or similar organization.

Camping: Information regarding campgrounds and camping rules are provided in this section.

Local events/attractions: Information about other hiking or non-hiking events or attractions in the area.

Hike tours: Information about organized hike tours, if available.

Organizations: Local nonprofit or friends groups affiliated with the destination.

TRAIL FINDER

	BEST HIKES FOR CHILDREN	BEST HIKES FOR WATERFALLS	BEST HIKES FOR GREAT VIEWS	BEST SHORT HIKES	BEST RIVERSIDE HIKES	BEST HIKES FOR BIG TREES	BEST HIKES FOR BACKPACKING
NORTHERN PANHANDLE							
1. Laurel to White Oak Trail Loop, Tomlinson Run State Park							
2. Hardwood Ridge and Falls Vista Trails, Oglebay Resort	•						
3. 4 Mile Loop Trail, Grand Vue Park							
MOUNTAINEER COUNTRY							
4. Rocky to Rhododendron Trail Loop, Valley Falls State Park		•					
5. Virgin Hemlock Trail, Coopers Rock State Forest					•	•	
6. Cathedral to Giant Hemlock Trail Lcop, Cathedral State Park						•	
EASTERN PANHANDLE							
7. Laurel to Ziler Loop Trail, Cacapon Resort State Park							
8. Appalachian Trail to Loudoun Heights Trails, Harpers Ferry National Historical Park			•				
POTOMAC HIGHLANDS							
9. High Timber to Sunset Trail, Jennings Randolph Lake Project			•				
10. Elakala to Yellow Birch Trail Loop, Blackwater Falls State Park		•					

	BEST HIKES FOR CHILDREN	BEST HIKES FOR WATERFALLS	BEST HIKES FOR GREAT VIEWS	BEST SHORT HIKES	BEST RIVERSIDE HIKES	BEST HIKES FOR BIG TREES	BEST HIKES FOR BACKPACKING
11. Beall Trails Loop, Canaan Valley National Wildlife Refuge							
12. White Oak to Big Ridge Loop, Lost River State Park			•				
13. Meat Box Run to Raven Rocks Trail Loop, Kumbrabow State Forest							
14. Cheat Mountain Ridge to Shavers Lake Trail Loop, Snowshoe Mountain Resort	•		•				
15. Thorny Creek Trail, Seneca State Forest							
16. Minie Ball to Overlook Trail Circuit, Droop Mountain Battlefield State Park	•		•				
17. Arrowhead Trail to Jesse's Cove Trail Loop, Watoga State Park					•		
18. Beartown Boardwalk, Beartown State Park	•			•			
MOUNTAIN LAKES REGION							
19. Park View to Fishermen's Trail Loop, Cedar Creek State Park	•						
20. Alum Cave Trail, Audra State Park	•			•	•		
21. Reverie to Tramontane Trail Loop, Holly River State Park							
NEW RIVER/GREENBRIER VALLEY							
22. Island in the Sky Trail, Babcock State Park	•			•			
23. Skyline Trail, Babcock State Park			•				

	BEST HIKES FOR CHILDREN	BEST HIKES FOR WATERFALLS	BEST HIKES FOR GREAT VIEWS	BEST SHORT HIKES	BEST RIVERSIDE HIKES	BEST HIKES FOR BIG TREES	BEST HIKES FOR BACKPACKING
24. Long Point Trail, New River Gorge National River	•		•				
25. Glade Creek Trail, New River Gorge National River					•		
26. Grandview Rim Trail to Turkey Spur Overlook, New River Gorge National River							
27. Cliffside Trail, Twin Falls Resort State Park	•		•				
28. Falls Trail, Twin Falls Resort State Park	•	•		•			
29. Farley Ridge to Mash Falls Trail Loop, Camp Creek State Park		•					
30. River to Farley Loop Trail, Pipestem Resort State Park							
31. Bluestone Turnpike Trail, Bluestone National Scenic River							
32. Kates Mountain Loop, Greenbrier State Forest							
33. Greenbrier River Trail					•		
METRO VALLEY							
34. Kanawha Trace Trail							•
35. Sensory to Tulip Tree Trail Loop, Huntington Museum of Art	•			•			
36. Sleepy Hollow Trail, Cabwaylingo State Forest							

	BEST HIKES FOR CHILDREN	BEST HIKES FOR WATERFALLS	BEST HIKES FOR GREAT VIEWS	BEST SHORT HIKES	BEST RIVERSIDE HIKES	BEST HIKES FOR BIG TREES	BEST HIKES FOR BACKPACKING
37. Overlook Rock Trail, Kanawha State Forest			●				
38. Polly Hollow Trail to Wildcat Ridge Trail Loop, Kanawha State Forest							
MID-OHIO VALLEY							
39. Island Road, Blennerhassett Island Historical State Park	●					●	
40. North Bend Rail Trail, North Bend State Park	●						
MONONGAHELA NATIONAL FOREST							
41. Otter Creek Trail, Otter Creek Wilderness		●			●		●
42. Dolly Sods North Circuit, Dolly Sods Wilderness			●				●
43. Sods Circuit, Dolly Sods Wilderness			●				●
44. North Fork Mountain Trail, Spruce Knob–Seneca Rocks National Recreation Area			●				
45. Seneca Rocks Trail, Spruce Knob–Seneca Rocks National Recreation Area			●				
46. Seneca Creek Trail to Spruce Knob Summit, Spruce Knob–Seneca Rocks National Recreation Area			●				●
47. High Falls Trail, Monongahela National Forest		●					

	BEST HIKES FOR CHILDREN	BEST HIKES FOR WATERFALLS	BEST HIKES FOR GREAT VIEWS	BEST SHORT HIKES	BEST RIVERSIDE HIKES	BEST HIKES FOR BIG TREES	BEST HIKES FOR BACKPACKING
48. Laurel River Trail South, Laurel Fork South Wilderness					•		•
49. Middle Fork to Big Beechy Trail Loop, Cranberry Wilderness							•
GEORGE WASHINGTON AND JEFFERSON NATIONAL FORESTS							
50. Rock Cliff Lake to Trout Pond Trail Loop, Trout Pond Recreation Area							
51. Allegheny Trail to Hanging Rock Raptor Observatory	•		•	•			

Map Legend

Transportation

≡🛡81🛡≡ Interstate Highway

≡⬡2⬡≡ US Highway

≡⬭105⬭≡ State Road

≡[CR 71]≡ Local/County Road

==== Unpaved Road

├──┼──┤ Railroad

▮───▮ Tunnel

─ ·· ─ State Boundary

Trails

▬▬▬▬ Featured Trail

▬ ▬ ▬ Trail

───── Paved Trail

Water Features

⬭ Body of Water

Marsh

〜〜 River/Creek

Symbols

▲ Backcountry Campground

⚎ Bridge

■ Building/Point of Interest

⛺ Campground

� Cliff

! Gate

🅿 Parking

⚍ Pass

▲ Peak/Elevation

🎋 Picnic Area

🚻 Restroom

🔭 Scenic View

⟃ Spring

🐎 Stable

▥▥ Steps/Boardwalk

🏛 Tower

○ Town

⑳ Trailhead

❓ Visitor/Information Center

≋ Waterfall

A great hiking map resource from the state of West Virginia is www.mapwv .gov/trails.

NORTHERN PANHANDLE

The cartographically obvious Northern Panhandle comprises the extreme north portion of West Virginia. Tucked in against the Ohio River, the Northern Panhandle occupies a narrow sliver of land between Pennsylvania and Ohio. Barely 5 miles wide in some places, this region is characterized by lazy rivers, rolling hills, and shallow stream-cut valleys.

Hiking in the Northern Panhandle is more of a pleasurable jaunt than an expedition. Trails here tend to be well manicured and easy to follow. Because there are no national parks or national forests in the area, hikes travel state parks and municipal parks. After your hike is done, you can check out museums, zoos, and golf courses. Overnight stays are equally indulging. Camping can be found in campgrounds rather than backcountry campsites; because the car will carry the load, you have the luxury of taking anything and everything you might desire.

If campgrounds aren't suitable, you can find fine hotels in Wheeling, the picturesque metro center of the Northern Panhandle and a city steeped in history. In 1862 the city's Independence Hall witnessed the birth of the state when West Virginia split from Virginia. Wheeling's Victorian heritage is evident in the beautiful architecture throughout the town. River culture abounds along the Ohio River, where towns made their living on the currents of the water.

Dogwoods from the elevated walk, Oglebay Resort (hike 2)

1 LAUREL TO WHITE OAK TRAIL LOOP

Tomlinson Run State Park

WHY GO?

Tomlinson Run, which is named after early European settlers to the area, was once home to several grist mills. The stream was perfect for this use, since it drops roughly 100 feet per mile as it makes its way down to the Ohio River. Today, the run is dammed to create Tomlinson Run Lake. The Laurel and White Oak Trails are in the wilderness area of the park. The White Oak Trail follows an old nineteenth-century turnpike, which is further evidence of early settlement here. Aside from the road grade, you can see rock walls that line the old road-turned-trail. Belying this former development is the wilderness feel of this section of the park, where Tomlinson Run cuts a gorge surrounded by sandstone and shale walls, second-growth forest, and quiet surroundings.

THE RUNDOWN

Start: Laurel Trail trailhead, off Washington School Road
Distance: 4.4-mile loop with out-and-back
Hiking time: About 2 hours
Difficulty: Moderate due to some steep sections and loose terrain from landslides
Trail surface: Dirt trail
Best season: Spring
Other trail users: Mountain bikers, horseback riders

Canine compatibility: Leashed dogs permitted
Land status: State park
Nearest town: New Cumberland
Fees and permits: None
Schedule: Open year-round for hiking, 6 a.m.–10 p.m.
Maps: Tomlinson Run State Park trail map; USGS quad: East Liverpool South
Trail contact: Tomlinson Run State Park, (304) 564-3651 or www.tomlinsonrunsp.com

FINDING THE TRAILHEAD

At the intersection of WV 2 and WV 8 on the north side of New Cumberland, head north on WV 8. Proceed 3.3 miles to the park entrance. Turn left into the park and continue 1.7 miles to a T intersection at Washington School Road (CR 3). Turn right and proceed 0.1 mile to a small parking pullout on the right. The signed trailhead is on the left side of the road. There is more parking available if you take a left at the T intersection with Washington School Road and park at the Old Mill Scout Camp, then walk 0.1 mile north along the road to the trailhead. **GPS:** N40 32.95′ / W80 35.73′

THE HIKE

The Laurel and White Oak Trails are in the wilderness area of Tomlinson Run State Park, which lies west of Washington School Road. This area is largely undeveloped

Tomlinson Run

and has no roads. The Laurel Trail, marked with blue blazes, begins with an easy climb through a stand of second-growth hardwoods. Near the top of the rise, the trail begins to meander along the edge of a steep bluff that overlooks Tomlinson Run, most visible late fall through early spring. The Laurel Trail parallels the bluff and descends gradually to the old turnpike approximately 0.2 mile from the trailhead. Hardwoods dominate the canopy here, and the forest floor is full of mayapple and other spring flowering plants, including phlox and trillium.

After a junction, the White Oak Trail descends gradually to Tomlinson Run, with large beech and maple trees lining the trail. At the creek, the trail begins to hug the left bank. Large flat rocks occupy the bed of the shallow creek. Towering hemlock and cove hardwoods dominate the canopy. Small cliffs line the side of the creek. At a creek junction, the trail bends right and begins following another small creek upstream. The White Oak Trail ends before crossing this side creek. (If you cross the creek and see a metal deer stand, you've gone too far. You will soon see park boundary signs.)

Turn around and follow the White Oak Trail back to the Laurel Trail. Turn right on the Laurel Trail, which makes a moderate descent back to Tomlinson Run. The rock face of the bluff is on the right. Near the creek is an old sandstone bridge abutment with a view upstream of the riffling creek, large boulders, and trees hanging over the water. This is your best bet for a lunch spot. After this abutment, the trail becomes a rugged path, passing through a narrow, steep-walled canyon. Rhododendron thickets crowd the trail,

In the park is ELPO Rock—that stands for East Liverpool Post Office. It's a rock that once apparently served as a formal mail drop. Go to www.geocaching.com and search for ELPO ROCK. You'll see a photo of the rock and GPS coordinates.

Laurel to White Oak Trail Loop

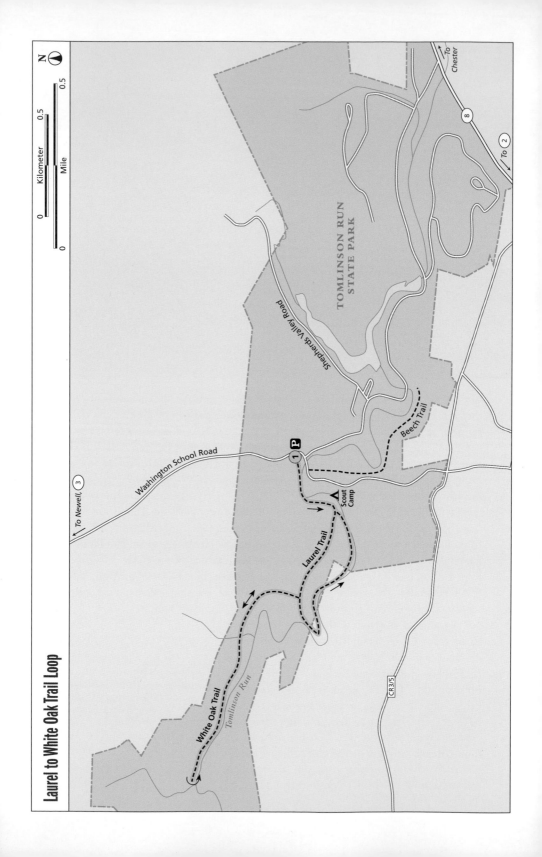

which hugs the left side of the canyon wall. There is a small waterfall cascading off the canyon wall on the opposite bank.

Shortly after passing through this rough section, the trail again follows an old road and the hike becomes easier. There is some trail confusion in this area. As the picnic area comes into view across the stream, the trail turns sharply uphill. You can follow the trail uphill and bushwhack another 50 feet or so to a parallel trail—this is the one you began on. Turn right and backtrack to the parking area. Alternately, you can ford the creek and cross over to the camp area. Take the camp area access road back to Washington School Road and take a left. Walk the last 0.1 mile on the road back to the trailhead and parking pullout.

MILES AND DIRECTIONS

0.0 START at the Laurel Trail trailhead along Washington School Road, marked with a sign. Walk into the woods, ascending the slope.

0.9 Come to a junction with the White Oak Trail. Take a right and begin the White Oak Trail, marked with white blazes.

2.0 After the trail curves right, following a side run to Tomlinson Run, stop before crossing the side run. You can see a metal deer stand across the creek. This is near the state park boundary. Turn around and return to the junction with the Laurel Trail.

3.1 At the junction with the Laurel Trail, take a right, following the blue blazes.

3.3 Come to an old sandstone bridge abutment and continue straight, paralleling Tomlinson Run. (**FYI:** This is a good lunch spot.)

4.1 As the scout camp comes into view across the run, the trail takes a sharp turn uphill. Walk uphill and the trail peters out. Bushwhack another 50 feet or so, continuing directly upslope. You will soon see blue blazes for the beginning section of the Laurel Trail. Hit the trail and turn right, returning to the trailhead. (**Option:** Ford Tomlinson Run to the scout camp. Walk through the scout camp to Washington School Road and take a left. Walk the last 0.1 mile back to the trailhead.)

4.4 Arrive back at the trailhead.

HIKE INFORMATION

Local information: The Top of West Virginia Convention and Visitors Bureau, (877) 723-7114 or (304) 797-7001, www.topofwv.com

Camping: The park has a 54-site campground that is open Apr to Oct; yurts and primitive cabins are also available for rental.

Local events/attractions: There is a swimming pool and waterslide at the park, open Memorial Day weekend to Labor Day weekend. A fee is charged.

Hike tours: The Tomlinson Run State Park Foundation puts on programming during the summer months; check with the park for up-to-date information.

Organizations: Tomlinson Run State Park Foundation, PO Box 500, New Manchester, WV 26056

2 HARDWOOD RIDGE AND FALLS VISTA TRAILS

Oglebay Resort

WHY GO?

The best thing about environmental education is the classroom. Case in point: the Oglebay Institute's 3.1-mile A. B. Brooks Discovery Trail System, which begins from the green-designed Schrader Environmental Education Center and includes a forest canopy walkway, a butterfly garden, and interpretive stations to help you better appreciate your surroundings. Those surroundings include a hardwood and hemlock forest, rhododendron-lined streams, and a double-decker waterfall. Add in a regular calendar of environmental education events, and you'll find yourself ready to go back to school.

THE RUNDOWN

Start: Trailhead behind the Schrader Center

Distance: 2.2-mile out-and-back

Hiking time: About 1 hour

Difficulty: Easy

Trail surface: Mulch and dirt trail

Best season: Winter Festival of Lights in Nov to early Jan

Other trail users: Mountain bikers

Canine compatibility: Leashed dogs permitted

Land status: Municipal park

Nearest town: Wheeling

Fees and permits: None for hiking

Schedule: Trails open year-round from dawn to dusk.

Maps: Oglebay Resort map; USGS quad: Wheeling

Trail contacts: Oglebay Resort and Conference Center, (304) 243-4000 or (800) 624-6988, www.oglebay .com; Schrader Environmental Center, (304) 242-6855 or www .oionline.com

FINDING THE TRAILHEAD

 Take I-70 to exit 2A and turn north on WV 88. Travel 0.4 mile and turn left at the light to remain on WV 88. Continue 2.9 miles and turn right at the sign for the zoo and Schrader Environmental Education Center. Proceed 0.7 mile and park at the Schrader Center. Pick up the trailhead behind the center, at the bottom of the stairs. It is marked by a trailhead kiosk with a map and brochures. **GPS:** N40 05.78' / W80 39.73'

THE HIKE

Begin or end your hike with a visit to the Schrader Center, home to Oglebay Institute's environmental education programming and the trailhead for all of the hiking paths. The building itself is made from 97 percent recycled materials, including tires, newspapers, plastic bottles, and aluminum cans. The trails are open dawn to dusk daily for a hike on your own, but if you plan ahead, you might be able to join one of the many programmed activities sponsored by the Oglebay Institute.

Oglebay Falls

The A. B. Brooks Discovery Trail System is named after Alonzo Beecher Brooks, who came to Oglebay in the 1920s to develop nature programming. His first hike, on April 14, 1928, was attended by three people. Things have grown quite a bit since then: Oglebay Institute now serves more than 40,000 people a year with its environmental and natural history programming, which includes astronomy, nature scavenger hunts, senses hikes, and bird watching, among many others.

The trailhead is located behind the Schrader Center. On the north side of the trailhead is a 120-foot-long elevated walkway that is 40 feet above the ground at its end. In May, this is a great place to watch migrating warblers from a canopy-level view of the forest. Interpretive signs and mounted binoculars help you further appreciate the forest ecosystem here. To the south of the trailhead is the butterfly garden, complete with a wrought-iron gate in the shape of a butterfly and plant species that attract butterflies in the summer months.

Start on the mulched trail and begin a moderate descent. You will soon pass an amphitheater on your left and then come to Hemlock Run. Walk over the bridge and parallel the creek downstream. At a fork for the Hardwood Ridge and Falls Vista Trails, take the right fork and walk along the well-maintained Hardwood Ridge Trail, blazed green. As the name says, you're on a ridge with hardwood trees as well as hemlocks and rhododendrons. Several side trails come in and out to overlooks, a memorial to A. B. Brooks, and a section of woods where the maple trees are tapped for sap every year. The trail ends

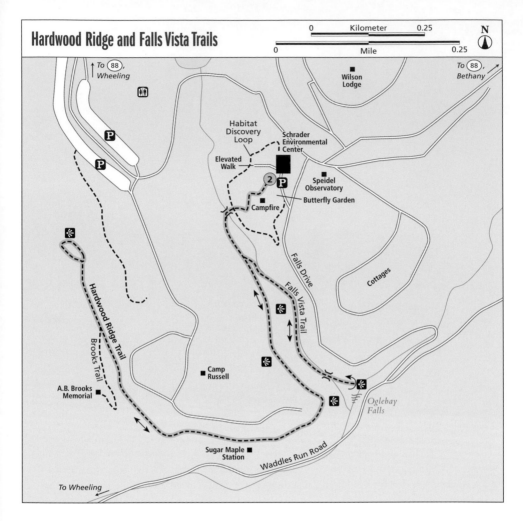

Kilometer

Mile

N

To 88,
Wheeling

Wilson
Lodge

To 88,
Bethany

Habitat
Discovery
Loop

Schrader
Environmental
Center

Elevated
Walk

2

Speidel
Observatory

Campfire

Butterfly Garden

Falls Drive

Cottages

Falls Vista Trail

Hardwood Ridge Trail

Brooks Trail

Camp
Russell

A.B. Brooks
Memorial

Oglebay
Falls

Sugar Maple
Station

Waddles Run Road

To Wheeling

at an overlook of a very small waterfall and returns to the junction with the Falls Vista Trail, blazed blue.

Taking a right switchback, descend the Falls Vista Trail to Oglebay Falls, a double-decker cascade near the road. There is an overlook deck from which you can view the falls. Return the way you came to the trailhead by the Schrader Center. A 0.3-mile Habitat Discovery Loop also begins and ends at the Schrader Center. You can tack this onto your hike to further explore nature here at Oglebay.

At the end of the day, you can take in some of the activities Oglebay Resort is most known for: its spa, golf course, zoo, ski resort, and winter festival of lights (seasonally, of course). Lodging includes the Wilson Lodge and cottages.

MILES AND DIRECTIONS

0.0 START behind the Schrader Center. Steps lead down to a trailhead kiosk with a map and brochures. To your right is the elevated walkway, and to your left is the butterfly garden. The mulched trail, on the left of the kiosk, leads down the slope into the woods.

0.1   Arrive at the junction with the Habitat Discovery Loop, blazed red. Continue straight, crossing the footbridge over the creek, to begin the Hardwood Ridge Trail, blazed green. (This is also the beginning of the Falls Vista Trail, blazed blue.)

0.3   Come to a fork. Take the right fork to continue on the Hardwood Ridge Trail.

0.5   Pass several sets of stairs on the left. Stay straight and level to continue on the main Hardwood Ridge Trail. It's easy to follow; look for green blazes.

0.9   Come to a wooden overlook platform. This is the end of the trail. From here, take a right and walk up wooden stairs to a T intersection. Take a right and return the way you came from the junction with the Falls Vista Trail.

1.6   Arrive at the junction with the Falls Vista Trail. Take a right switchback to continue on the Falls Vista Trail, blazed blue.

1.8   Arrive at Oglebay Falls. After enjoying the falls, return the way you came from the junction with the Hardwood Ridge Trail.

2.0   Arrive at the junction with the Hardwood Ridge Trail. Continue straight back to the Schrader Center.

2.2   Arrive back at the trailhead.

HIKE INFORMATION

Local information: Wheeling Convention and Visitors Bureau, (800) 828-3097 or www.wheelingcvb.com

Camping: Camping is not available, but you can spend the night at the lodge or cottages, (800) 624-6988 or www.oglebay.com.

Local events/attractions: Oglebay Resort is home to a zoo, conference center, spa, and ski resort; programming includes the winter festival of lights. For more info call (304) 243-4000 or (800) 624-6988, or go to www.oglebay-resort.com.

Hike tours: Oglebay Institute has regular programming throughout the year. Find a calendar of events at www.oionline.com/calendar or call (304) 242-6855.

Organizations: Brooks Bird Club, www.brooksbirdclub.org; Oglebay Astronomy Club, www.oionline.com/astronomy

3 4 MILE LOOP TRAIL

Grand Vue Park

WHY GO?
Join zipliners, mountain bikers, cross-country runners, disc golfers, and other fun-seekers who congregate at Grand Vue Park, a 650-acre county park that packs in about as many activities as possible in one small outdoor space. Just outside of Moundsville, Grand Vue sits high on a ridge overlooking the Ohio River Valley. The 4 Mile loop trail wraps around the ridge and passes through early successional forest and open meadows. From the trailhead area, you can get the namesake view of the Ohio River Valley and the nearby town of Moundsville.

THE RUNDOWN
Start: Trailhead between main office and zipline station
Distance: 3.6-mile loop
Hiking time: About 2 hours
Difficulty: Easy
Trail surface: Mowed grass and dirt trail
Best season: Spring through fall
Other trail users: Mountain bikers
Canine compatibility: Leashed dogs permitted

Land status: County park
Nearest town: Moundsville
Fees and permits: None
Schedule: The park is open daily year-round from dawn to dusk.
Maps: Grand Vue Park map; USGS quad: Moundsville
Trail contact: Marshall County Parks and Recreation, (304) 845–9810, www.grandvuepark.com

FINDING THE TRAILHEAD

At the intersection of US 2 and US 250 in Moundsville, turn south on US 250. Proceed 0.8 mile to a stoplight and turn left on First Street. Continue 0.2 mile and turn left on Fostoria. Continue straight as Fostoria becomes Oak and then Grandview Road. Proceed 1.4 miles, turn left at an intersection with a sign marked TRAILS, and drive to the second parking area on the right. The trailhead is also on the right, where the mowed area meets the woods. Look for the trailhead sign. **GPS:** N39 56.76' / W80 43.84'

THE HIKE
Grand Vue is named for the view of the Ohio River Valley afforded from the high ridgetops in the park. Much of the park is mowed, which allows for enough of a clearing in the forest to see not only the river valley but also the town of Moundsville below. The park's two main hiking trails—the 4 Mile loop and the 2 Mile loop—wind mostly through the woods but also through some meadow areas as well. Once the location of the county home, GrandVue became a park in 1974. Since then it has steadily built up its infrastructure to include many outdoor adventure opportunities, from hiking and mountain biking to disc golf and geocaching, along with a new zipline canopy tour.

The park buzzes with activity, and you will see this throughout your hike. Begin near one of the zipline canopy tour stations and enter the woods. Unblazed, the 4 Mile Trail is a wide, mowed, mostly level path. Side trails come in and out throughout your hike, but as long as you stay mostly level and on the wide path, you will be on the 4 Mile Trail. Soon after entering the woods, a mountain bike trail, blazed orange, comes in on the left. Continue straight. The trail enters a grassy area near the cabins, and an access trail joins at this point. The trail takes a U-turn just before mile 1.0, and then at mile 1.3 you'll see a steep trail to the left known to local high school cross-country runners as Cardiac Hill.

Continue walking below the ridgeline, and at mile 2.5 you'll come to The Point, a three-way junction where the ridge descends to the Ohio River. Stay on the outermost trail as it turns sharply to the left. In another 0.1 mile, arrive at the Sacred Cairn, built with stones and topped with dreamcatchers. This cairn was built in honor of the Native Americans who called today's Grand Vue and Moundsville home. Moundsville was named for the many prehistoric Adena Indian mounds that dotted (and still do dot) the area. The Grave Creek Mound, at Tomlinson and Ninth Streets, is listed on the National Register of Historic Places. It's estimated to be more than 2,000 years old.

The trail continues much as it has before—level, in and out of the woods. At mile 3.5, you will finally leave the main trail for a spur that takes you through a disc golf hole and back to the parking lot where you parked. From this end of the trail, you'll also see a barn—the park was also once a farm—and basketball courts. Check on park programming before your visit, and you may be able to tag along on an organized hike that will help you learn more about the park's history and nature.

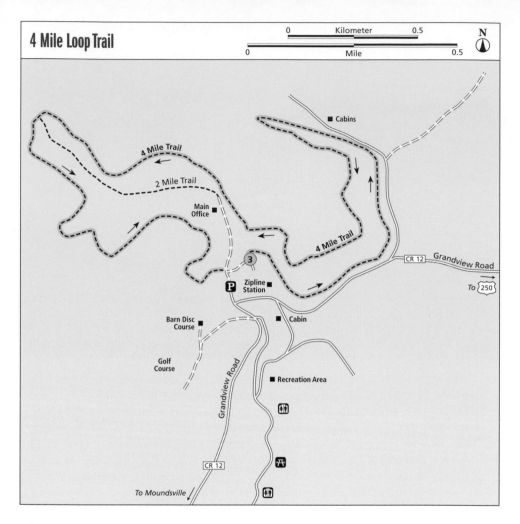

4 Mile Loop Trail

Cabins

4 Mile Trail

2 Mile Trail

Main Office

4 Mile Trail

CR 12   Grandview Road

To 250

3

P   Zipline Station

Barn Disc Course

Cabin

Golf Course

Grandview Road

Recreation Area

CR 12

To Moundsville

MILES AND DIRECTIONS

0.0 START at the trailhead, which is east of the second parking area between Grandview Road and the park office. It is below the ridgetop, past a steep dirt road, where the mowed area meets the forest, and is marked with a sign. Walk into the woods.

0.2 Pass a mountain bike trail on the left, blazed orange. Continue straight.

0.8 Come to a T intersection with an access trail from the cabins. Turn left. In another 50 yards, hit another T intersection. Take a right.

1.0 The trail takes a U-turn to the left.

1.1 Come to a four-way intersection. Continue straight.

1.3 Come to another four-way intersection. Continue straight.

1.4 The trail forks. Take the right fork.

2.1 A side trail comes in from the left. Continue straight.

2.25 Arrive at a three-way intersection by a bench. Continue straight.

2.5 Come to The Point, a three-way junction. Take the second left, staying on the outermost part of the trail as it curves left.

2.6 Pass a side trail on the right, near the Sacred Cairn. Continue straight.

2.7 Pass a trail on the left. Continue straight.

2.8 Pass a mountain bike trail coming in from the right, blazed orange. Continue straight.

2.9 The mountain bike trail leaves the main trail to the left. Continue straight.

3.0 Pass an access road on the left and a trail on the right. Continue straight as the 4 Mile loop continues straight, going along the edge of the woods and the grass.

3.5 As you see the barn come into view, arrive at a connector trail on the left. Leave the main trail at this point and walk uphill to disc golf basket 16. Continue walking uphill to the road, where you will take a left back to your car.

3.6 Arrive back at the parking lot.

HIKE INFORMATION

Local information: Greater Moundsville Convention and Visitors Bureau, www.visit moundsville.com/

Local events/attractions: Grand Vue Park has a canopy zipline tour, (304) 845-9810 or www.grandvuepark.com. For something completely different, visit the nearby Hare Krishna Palace of Gold, (304) 843-1600 or www.palaceofgold.com.

Camping: Tent camping is not available, but the park does rent cabins and treetop villas, (304) 845-9810 or http://grandvuepark.com/lodging/treehouse-village/.

Hike tours: Grand Vue Park has regular programming, (304) 845-9810 or www.grand vuepark.com/events/.

Honorable Mention

A PANHANDLE TRAIL, HARMON CREEK TO COLLIERS

The Panhandle Trail is less hiking trail and more rail trail—its crushed gravel surface is suitable for bikes and is even wheelchair accessible. But at nearly 39 miles, the trail offers plenty of hiking opportunities between Weirton, West Virginia, and Carnegie (near Pittsburgh), Pennsylvania. You can even keep going from there, as the Panhandle Trail connects with Pittsburgh's Montour Trail, which in turns connects to the Great Allegheny Passage and then the C&O Canal Towpath all the way to Washington, DC. Now that's a hike! Try the section in West Virginia between Harmon Creek and Colliers for a 7.2-mile out-and-back hike. It's mostly in full sun, so this trail is a good late-fall, winter, and early spring option. For information go to www.panhandletrail.org.

The Panhandle Trail near Harmon

To find the Harmon Creek trailhead, start from WV 2 and US 22 south of Weirton. Travel east on US 22 for 2.3 miles to Harmon Creek Road (exit 3). At the end of the ramp, take a right and go 0.1 mile to McColl Road. There's a sign here for the Panhandle Trail. Take a right switchback and go another 0.1 mile to a parking area behind some trailer homes. GPS: N40 23.63'/W80 34.12'

MOUNTAINEER COUNTRY

Mountaineer Country occupies seven counties between the northern and eastern panhandles in the rugged foothills of West Virginia's mountain region. Early settlers worked hard and lived off the land mining coal, timbering forests, and building railroads to carry goods across America. Development of the region was far from total, however, and many natural wonders exist throughout.

Hikes in this region are contained in some of West Virginia's most beautiful state parks and forests. There are trails for all ability levels here. Cathedral State Park has many short scenic trails through virgin hemlock forest. Camping is found in campgrounds only (that is, there is no backcountry camping in this region), and many area parks are day-use only.

Amenities abound in Morganton, a hip college town and the largest city in the region, which bustles with students and commerce alike. When the day's hike is done, take a trip into town and enjoy the college nightlife. One word of warning: Be aware of crowds on Saturdays in the fall. Football at WVU is very important, and it seems as though the entire state of West Virginia converges on the city on game days. If you plan to visit Morgantown in the fall, check a schedule and plan for crowds if the Mountaineers are playing at home.

Raven Rock overlook at Coopers Rock State Forest

4 ROCKY TO RHODODENDRON TRAIL LOOP

Valley Falls State Park

WHY GO?

When you hear waterfalls a half mile away, you know they're worth a look. Indeed, the centerpiece of Valley Falls State Park is the Tygart Valley River and its multiple waterfalls, chutes, and whitewater rushing around an obstacle course of boulders. The hike begins at the centerpiece set of falls, the first on a 500-foot-wide river, falling 14 feet, followed shortly downstream by a 200-foot-wide cascade tumbling another 18 feet. This loop begins and ends near the falls, but takes you away from them in the meantime as it transects the park's ridges and valleys in second-growth hardwood forest. A number of trails crisscross, allowing you to create a hike of whatever length you please.

THE RUNDOWN

Start: Rocky Trail trailhead, at the upper parking lot near the falls
Distance: 4.4-mile loop
Hiking time: About 2 hours
Difficulty: Moderate due to length and elevation gain
Trail surface: Dirt trail
Best season: Spring
Other trail users: Mountain bikers
Canine compatibility: Leashed dogs permitted

Land status: State park
Nearest town: Fairmont
Fees and permits: None
Schedule: Open daily year-round 7 a.m. to dusk
Maps: Valley Falls State Park map; USGS quad: Fairmont East
Trail contact: Valley Falls State Park, (304) 367-2719 or www.valley fallsstatepark.com

FINDING THE TRAILHEAD

Take I-79 to exit 137 and head south on WV 310. Travel 7.6 miles to CR 31/14 (Valley Falls Road) and turn right (there is a sign for the state park). At the next two forks, bear left. Pass the park office and continue on the park road to mile 2.7 to the parking area on the right. The Rocky Trail trailhead sign is between two sets of wooden steps. The trail begins at the top of the first set of steps. **GPS:** N39 23.36' / W80 5.28'

THE HIKE

Natural and human history meet at Valley Falls. The natural history of the Tygart Valley River and these two-tiered falls—a 500-foot-wide band of 15-foot falls, followed shortly downstream by a second set of 18-foot falls—can be told in geologic time. Over millennia, water eroded not only the river valley but also the softer stone that gave way under the harder Connoquenessing sandstone that makes up the rim of the falls.

The centerpiece falls at
Valley Falls State Park

The human history of this spot is drawn from its natural history. In the mid-1800s this location became home to a grist mill and whip mill (a mill that used a two-man whipsaw; whose remnants are visible near the falls), a B&O railroad station, and even a post office and shops. The timber industry boomed. The good times were not to last, however. In 1886 a fire destroyed most of the community, and then a flood two years later destroyed what was left. The state of West Virginia acquired the land in 1964 to create a state park. Today, the old mill workers have long been replaced by picnickers, hikers, mountain bikers, and photographers.

Start by checking out the waterfalls—there's plenty of rock-hopping, picnicking, and picture-taking to do here. There is no swimming or wading, however, and for good reason. As you walk near the falls, you might notice bolts holding eye hooks into the rock. These are used to attach a safety rope when trying to save someone from drowning, a fate that has met more than 150 people in the documented history of this spot. There have been eight deaths since 1993, when it was made illegal to swim, wade, or consume alcohol here. In addition to very swift water, there are still pieces of narrow-gauge railroad steel below the surface.

To begin this loop, walk back to the upper parking area, the one farthest from the falls. The signed trailhead for the Rocky Trail is located at the top of the first set of stairs in the parking lot. The trail is yellow blazed and is marked by a series of stones laid along the path. After approximately 0.1 mile of moderate grade, the Rocky Trail intersects the Red Cardinal Trail. Turn right on the Red Cardinal Trail and follow the red blazes. For a shorter hike, continue straight on the Rocky Trail and climb the ridge to the intersection with the Dogwood Trail and the Wild Turkey Trail, then descend to join the Rhododendron Trail.

The Red Cardinal Trail passes through a forest of second-growth hardwoods. At 0.25 mile there is a left bend and the trail begins a short, steep climb. The Red Cardinal Trail contours along the ridge for about 1.0 mile and then descends gradually to the park road after passing a pawpaw patch. Cross the road to the trailhead for the Deer Trail, marked with white blazes. About 0.25 mile from the road, the Deer Trail intersects the Red Fox Trail. To hike a shorter loop (3.2 miles) by way of paralleling the river, stay on the Deer Trail and follow it back to the parking area.

Turn left on the Red Fox Trail and begin a short, steep climb up the ridge to the park road. Turn right on the park road and walk past the office. The trailhead for the Wild Turkey Trail and the Dogwood Trail is located on the left side of the road past the park office. Turn left off the park road and make a short descent, followed by a short, steep climb. At the top of the climb, the Wild Turkey and Dogwood Trails diverge. Take the right fork and follow the Dogwood Trail, marked with orange blazes. This might be more appropriately named the Barberry Trail, as this invasive shrub has choked out about everything else in the understory.

The trail follows a wide old road into the woods on an easy grade. After 0.5 mile, the trail bends left. Tall, straight cove hardwoods give the forest a parklike feel. The trail then makes a short, moderate descent to a small meadow. In the meadow, signs point to the Dogwood Trail and the Wild Turkey Trail. Continue straight. About 75 feet past these signs is a sign for the Rhododendron Trail.

Turn left and begin a moderate descent. The Rhododendron Trail follows an old rocky road that soon gives way to a rocky footpath. When the path forks at an unmarked intersection, take the left fork, which takes you in the direction of the Tygart River and

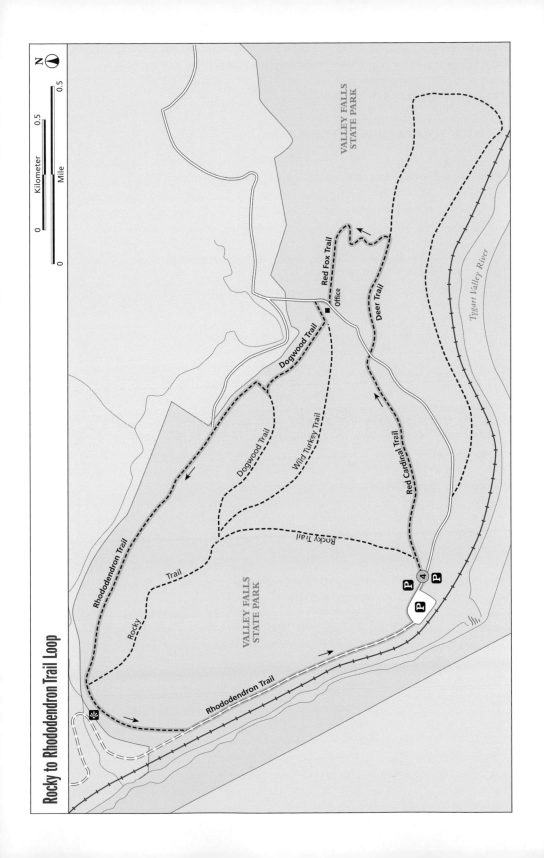

Rocky to Rhododendron Trail Loop

Valley Falls State Park

Valley Falls State Park

Red Fox Trail

Office

Deer Trail

Dogwood Trail

Dogwood Trail

Wild Turkey Trail

Red Cardinal Trail

Rocky Trail

Rhododendron Trail

Rocky

Trail

Rhododendron Trail

Tygart Valley River

N

Kilometer
0   0.5

Mile
0   0.5

P 4 P

P

the parking lot. Remain on the Rhododendron Trail, which begins to parallel the river about 0.3 mile past the intersection with the Rocky Trail. The trail now follows a wide gravel road. On the right is a rock outcrop and an obscured view of the river. The trail continues its easy descent to the parking lot.

MILES AND DIRECTIONS

0.0 START at the Rocky Trail trailhead, at the top of the first set of wooden steps in the upper parking lot. Walk into the woods, ascending slightly.

0.1 Come to the junction with the Red Cardinal Trail, marked with a sign. Take a right and begin the Red Cardinal Trail.

1.0 Cross the park road. Trend left about 50 feet to pick up the Deer Trail, also marked with a sign.

1.25 Come to a junction with the Red Fox Trail. The sign here only marks the Deer Trail. Take a left and walk uphill.

1.6 Ascend to the park road, near the office. Take a right and walk past the park office about 200 feet and pick up the Wild Turkey Trail on the left side of the road.

1.7 After crossing under power lines, come to a junction with the Dogwood Trail. Take a right and reenter the woods on an old road grade.

2.5 The signed Dogwood Trail turns left at a junction. Continue straight here, and in about 75 feet take a left on the signed Rhododendron Trail.

2.9 An unmarked trail joins from the right. Continue straight.

3.5 The trail forks. Take a left at this fork, walking uphill.

3.6 Pass the Rocky Trail on the left, marked with a sign. Continue straight.

3.8 A trail comes in from the right. Continue straight on the road grade, descending.

4.0 The Tygart River is now within earshot; a spur trail on the right leads to an obscured view of the river.

4.4 Arrive back at the parking lot.

HIKE INFORMATION

Local information: Convention and Visitors Bureau of Marion County, (304) 368-1123 or (800) 834-7365, www.marioncvb.com

Camping: Valley Falls is day-use only; camping is available at Tygart Lake State Park with 40 sites open mid-Apr through Oct, (304) 265-6144 or www.tygartlake.com.

Organizations: Valley Falls State Park Foundation; contact the park for info.

5 VIRGIN HEMLOCK TRAIL

Coopers Rock State Forest

WHY GO?

Coopers Rock State Forest is a vortex of outdoor adventure possibilities. Just 20 minutes from Morgantown (home of West Virginia University) Coopers Rock draws everyone from picnickers to "drive by" hikers from I-68 to rock climbers to photographers snapping pictures of the Cheat River valley. The section of forest north of I-68 sees significantly less traffic than the southern section, so much so that you might get the Virgin Hemlock Trail to yourself. Get ready to crane your neck upward as you gaze at a stand of mature hemlocks along this loop. The trail takes you along the rhododendron-choked Little Laurel Run, through stands of mountain laurel, and on singletrack trail through a forest floor carpeted in ferns. When you're done, head back to Motown where you can enjoy an après-hike brew or meal.

THE RUNDOWN

Start: At the Hemlock Trail, off of County Route 73
Distance: 1.5 miles
Hiking time: 1 hour
Difficulty: Easy
Trail surface: Dirt trail
Best season: Year-round
Other trail users: Hikers only
Canine compatibility: Leashed dogs permitted
Land status: State forest, leased and managed by West Virginia University

Division of Forestry and Natural Resources
Nearest town: Morgantown
Fees and permits: None
Schedule: Open daily year-round 6 a.m. to 10 p.m. for day use
Maps: Coopers Rock State Forest map and trail guide; USGS quads: Bruceton Mills, Masontown, Lake Lynn
Trail contact: Coopers Rock State Forest, (304) 594-1561 or www.coopersrockstateforest.com

FINDING THE TRAILHEAD

Take I-68 to exit 15 (CR 73-12) and turn north at the end of the ramp. Come right away to a stop sign (CR 73/73). Turn right at the stop sign and proceed 2.4 miles to the trailhead. There is parking on both sides of the road. The trail is marked with a sign that reads HEMLOCK TRAIL that's parallel to the road, so it's easy to miss. **GPS:** N39 39.29' / W79 44.22'

THE HIKE

The Hemlock Trail is a great hike any time of year, offering shade and cool water in the summer, as well as color in the winter, thanks to the evergreen hemlocks, rhododendrons, and mountain laurels. As with all West Virginia State Forests, Coopers Rock is multi-use, meaning that it is managed for recreation, timber, forest research, and other uses. The northern portion of the forest, known as West Virginia University Research Forest, is

Walking among the hemlocks on the Virgin Hemlock Trail

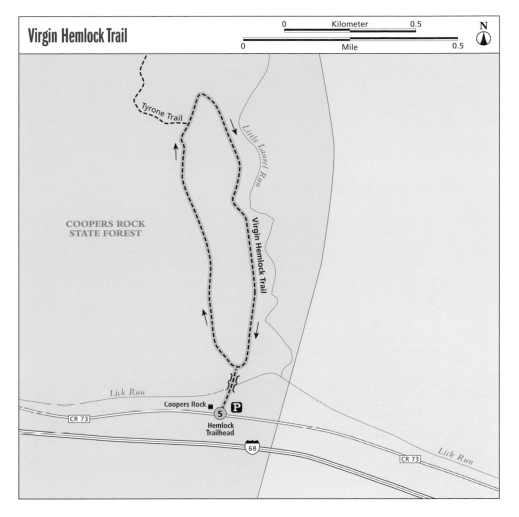

managed by the West Virginia University Division of Forestry and Natural Resources. The portion of WVU Research Forest that holds virgin hemlocks is essentially "unmanaged," or simply left in its natural state. Many of the oldest hemlocks here have already died a natural death.

The Virgin Hemlock Loop begins on the north side of the road. A sign marks the trailhead as Hemlock Trail. There are no blazes for this trail; the white blaze is a boundary marker. The trail begins with a short descent through a mixed hardwood forest. Rhododendron thrives in the understory. The trail is easy to follow as it weaves through boulders that dot the landscape. After 0.1 mile, the trail drops down to and crosses Lick Run on a set of footbridges, then bends left and parallels the run. This begins a loop.

The creek to your left is a series of small shelf riffles and low falls. The forest is a palette of greens, with ferns, rhododendrons, hardwoods, and hemlocks providing different shades. Walk a tidy singletrack footpath to a junction near another side run to Laurel Run. This junction is marked with a large rock cairn. Go straight at this junction and

> Coopers Rock is named after a legendary—as in, this is probably a legend—cooper (barrel maker) who hid from the law at what is now Coopers Rock. He continued making the barrels from his hideout to sell them, presumably, to moonshiners.

complete the loop without ever crossing Little Laurel Run. Parallel Little Laurel Run downstream and keep an eye out across the stream—soon a dense stand of mature hemlocks comes into view. This is the virgin hemlock section of forest. Just after this spot, the trail curves to the right and returns to the junction where the loop began. Take a left, cross the footbridges and return to the trailhead.

MILES AND DIRECTIONS

0.0 START at the Hemlock Trail trailhead, off of CR 73/73. Walk north, descending into the woods.

0.1 Descend stairs and cross over two footbridges. Just after the second footbridge, come to a T-intersection. Take a left and begin a clockwise loop.

0.75 Pass a big rock cairn and then come to a second rock cairn at a trail junction. Continue straight at this junction. Do not cross Little Laurel Run.

1.3 Look across Little Laurel Run to see a stand of mature hemlock trees. After this, the trail curves around to the right and ends the loop. Take a left and retrace your steps from the beginning of the hike by crossing back over the two footbridges and ascending to the road.

1.5 Return to the trailhead.

HIKE INFORMATION

Local information: Greater Morgantown Convention and Visitors Bureau, (800) 458-7373 or www.tourmorgantown.com

Camping: There are twenty-five campsites with electric hookups, open April 1 through November 30. There is no backpack camping allowed within the forest boundaries.

Local Events/Attractions: The traveling Banff Mountain Film and Book Festival comes to Morgantown, www.banffcentre.ca/mountainfestival/worldtour/usa; there's a seasonal lineup of trail running and mountain biking events at nearby Big Bear Lake, (304) 379-4382 or www.bigbearwv.com.

6 CATHEDRAL TO GIANT HEMLOCK TRAIL LOOP

Cathedral State Park

WHY GO?

Cathedral State Park is indeed a place to worship at the altar of the natural world. It's so magical that as you take in the hemlock forest with a canopy reaching nearly 100 feet, walk atop a carpet of moss, squeeze through rhododendron thickets, and walk along a clear, trickling stream, you half expect to see a fairy jump out from behind one of the trees. The largest hemlock in the state (along with its large cousins) is located within the park boundaries, along with more than 170 types of vascular plants, 30 tree species, and more than 50 species of wildflowers.

THE RUNDOWN

Start: Trailhead on north side of parking area
Distance: 1.8-mile lollipop
Hiking time: About 1 hour
Difficulty: Easy
Trail surface: Dirt trail with a road crossing
Best season: Spring
Other trail users: Mountain bikers
Canine compatibility: Leashed dogs permitted

Land status: State park
Nearest town: Aurora
Fees and permits: None
Schedule: Open daily year-round 6 a.m. to 10 p.m. for day use
Maps: Cathedral State Park map and trail guide; USGS quad: Aurora
Trail contact: Cathedral State Park, (304) 735-3771 or www.cathedral statepark.com

FINDING THE TRAILHEAD

Take US 50 1.1 miles east of Aurora and 2.8 miles west of the Maryland border. The park entrance is on the north side of US 50. After entering the park, turn left and continue 150 feet to the parking area. The wooden steps on the north side of the parking area with a Cathedral State Park sign is the beginning of the hike. **GPS:** N39 19.58' / W79 32.19'

THE HIKE

The Cathedral Trail is a short, easy loop trail that takes you through an old-growth hemlock forest. Once on the trail, the sheer immensity of the trees will dwarf you—happily. Past the picnic shelter, the Cathedral Trail splits; take the left fork. Just past this junction, turn left on the Wood Thrush Trail, which almost immediately crosses US 50. Be careful of traffic when crossing the road. The trail climbs gradually and then begins an easy descent among hemlock, fern, mountain laurel, and downed logs covered with moss. The crowns towering high overhead give the distinct impression of being in a cathedral.

The Wood Thrush Trail crosses a small spring creek and begins to parallel US 50 a short distance. After crossing US 50 again, the Cathedral Trail comes in from the right

Giant hemlocks tower in Cathedral State Park.

to join the Wood Thrush Trail. Turn left here and cross Rhine Creek. Soon the trail splits; take the Partridge Berry Trail to the left. The Partridge Berry Trail is an easy stroll through towering hemlocks. Not far from this intersection, the Cardinal Trail turns off to the left. Remain on the Partridge Berry Trail and make an easy descent to a clearing near the park boundary, where the trail switches back to the right and begins to parallel Rhine Creek.

Just before a creek crossing, turn right on the Giant Hemlock Trail. Along this section of trail, you'll see the largest grouping of the bigger hemlocks in the forest. (The largest tree, located behind the park office, fell due to lightning in 2004.) Note this is a natural forest where snags and downed trees ("nurse logs") stay right where they are, providing habitat for bird, insect, and plant species. At the end of Giant Hemlock Trail, turn left on the Cathedral Trail. The trail, crowded by rhododendron, parallels the creek closely. At the junction with the Partridge Berry Trail, turn right to remain on the Cathedral Trail. The trail leaves the creek and reaches a T intersection. Turn right and continue 25 yards, then turn left. At the first intersection, take a left again to complete the loop by passing the shelter and returning to the trailhead.

HEMLOCK WOOLLY ADELGID

When you hike at Cathedral State Park, you might notice metal tags hanging from some of the largest hemlock trees in the park. These trees are being chemically treated for hemlock woolly adelgid, a nonnative, invasive insect that literally sucks the life out of hemlock trees by feeding on the sap at the base of the needles. At this point, there is no effective treatment to halt the damage these pests are inflicting on hemlocks throughout the Mountain State. As you hike, you will probably notice how many hemlocks throughout the state are already dead.

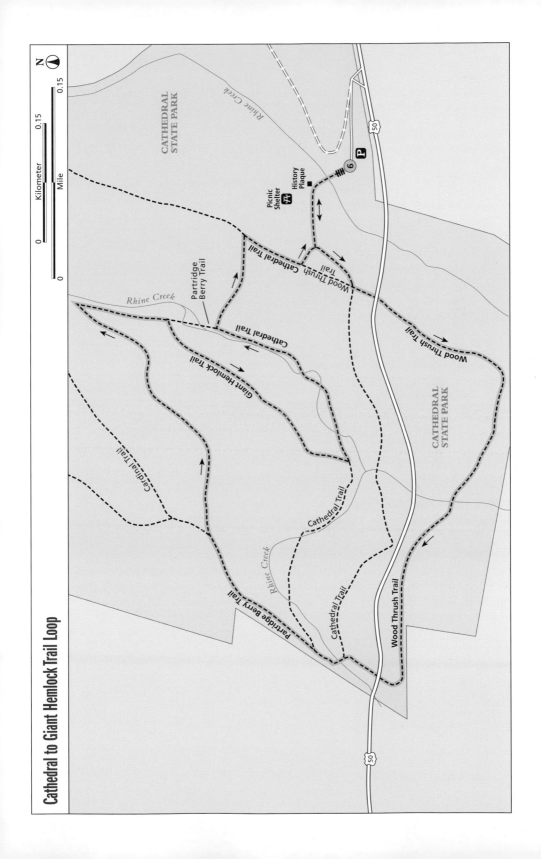

Cathedral to Giant Hemlock Trail Loop

MILES AND DIRECTIONS

0.0 START at the stairs next to a Cathedral State Park sign, visible on the north side of the parking area. Descend the stairs, cross the creek, and bear left on the trail. Pass the picnic shelter, which is on your right.

0.1 Come to a T intersection with the Cathedral Trail, blazed red. Take a left. Within about 50 feet, come to a junction with the Wood Thrush Trail. Continue straight on the Wood Thrush Trail. In another 50 feet or so, cross US 50 to the south.

0.6 The trail takes a sharp right and then crosses US 50 again, this time to the north. Angle to the right, crossing the road in order to pick up the trail again. After crossing the road, walk about 100 yards to a T intersection with the Cathedral Trail. Turn left.

0.7 Arrive at the junction with the Partridge Berry Trail. Take a left and follow the blue blazes.

0.9 Pass the Cardinal Trail on the left. Continue straight.

1.1 Come to the Partridge Berry Trail sign at a junction. This is before the creek. Take a right and parallel the stream to continue on the Partridge Berry Trail.

1.2 Come to the junction with the Giant Hemlock Trail. Take a right, following the white blazes.

1.4 Come to a T intersection marked with a Giant Hemlock Trail sign. Take a left and continue on the Cathedral Trail.

1.6 Arrive at a junction with the Partridge Berry Trail, before crossing the creek again. Take a right.

1.7 Arrive at a junction with the Wood Thrush Trail. Take a left. In about 100 feet, return to the initial Cathedral Trail junction. Take a left and pass the picnic shelter again, this time on your left.

1.8 Arrive back at the trailhead.

HIKE INFORMATION

Local information: Preston County Visitors' Center, (800) 571-0912 or www.tour preston.com

Camping: The park is day-use only; a lodge, cabins, and camping are all available at nearby Blackwater Falls State Park, (304) 259-5216 or www.blackwaterfalls.com.

Restaurants: Melanie's Family Restaurant is very reasonably priced and right across the street, (304) 735-3219.

Honorable Mentions

B RAVEN ROCK TRAIL, COOPERS ROCK STATE FOREST

The calling card of Coopers Rock State Forest is the Cheat River Canyon and the spectacular rock bluffs located high above the river. Most people take a few steps to the Coopers Rock overlook. But you can get a full hike in—plus a chance at some solitude—if you opt for the 2.5-mile round-trip Raven Rock Trail to this overlook. The trail has seen its share of insults over the years, including a high-tension-wire tower at the rocky overlook and, more recently, a logging operation quite visible from the trail. Still, the view from the overlook can't be beat. Although the area is beautiful year-round, from mountain laurel and rhododendron blooming in the spring to a blanket of snow covering the forest in the winter, perhaps the best time to hike this trail is late September to early October, when the fall colors are at their peak. The host of colors on the opposite mountainside at the end of the trail is truly a sight to behold. For more information, contact Coopers Rock State Forest at (304) 594-1561 or go to www.coopersrockstate forest.com.

To get there, take I-68 to exit 15 and turn south on State Forest Road. Proceed 2.1 miles to the trailhead. Parking is on the right. The trail is across the road from the parking, next to a gate that spans a gravel road. GPS: N39 38.21'/W79 48.08'

C DOGWOOD TO WHITE OAK TRAIL LOOP, WATTERS SMITH MEMORIAL STATE PARK

It's easy to keep driving on I-79 right past Watters Smith, in pursuit of more well-known and popular hiking destinations. But with more than 11 miles of trails, this park is worth a stop along the way. Take to the Dogwood Trail in April to see its namesake trees, plus redbuds, in full bloom. Connect with the White Oak Trail to a narrow ridgetop and descend the ridge alongside nearby farm fields, then end up walking through a small cove of virgin forest. On summer weekends you can also visit the museum and a replica of the hand-hewn log Smith House, built by the family that settled this former farm. For more information, contact Watters Smith Memorial State Park at (304) 745-3081 or go to www.watterssmithstatepark.com.

Take I-79 to exit 110 and head west on WV 270. Travel 5.3 miles and turn left on Duck Creek Road (CR 25/6). Continue 2.5 miles to the park office road. Turn left and travel 0.3 mile to the parking area next to the park activity building. GPS: N39 10.34'/W80 24.37'

EASTERN PANHANDLE

The Eastern Panhandle covers the three counties of Morgan, Berkeley, and Jefferson in the extreme northeast portion of West Virginia. The Eastern Panhandle is bordered to the south and southeast by Virginia, and to the east and north by Maryland. Very rural and characterized by wide valleys and tall, flat ridges, the region is a symbolic gateway linking West Virginia to the metropolitan areas of the East.

The hikes here are often a small part of a much larger whole. The Eastern Panhandle is home to the famed Appalachian Trail, which travels nearly 2,200 miles on its course from Georgia to Maine. From Harpers Ferry, it is possible to hike the path nearly 1,000 miles in either direction.

Harpers Ferry National Historical Park is a must-see in the Eastern Panhandle. Home to the Appalachian Trail and its governing body, the Appalachian Trail Conference, Harpers Ferry is also an important part of American history. The fuel that ignited the Civil War was fanned here in 1859 when abolitionist John Brown overtook the US arsenal. Brown eventually lost his battle, and his life, but not before figurative lines had been

The Shenandoah River at Harpers Ferry

drawn between North and South. The geographic location of Harpers Ferry made it a frequent battleground during the heat of the Civil War. The town was alternately controlled by Confederate and Union troops throughout the war. Today the town is operated by the National Park Service as a reminder of life as it used to be. The entire town is a working museum that highlights a difficult time in our nation's history.

7 LAUREL TO ZILER LOOP TRAIL

Cacapon Resort State Park

WHY GO?

Hiking to the top of 2,300-foot Cacapon Mountain proves that the journey is as important as the destination. You will not be rewarded with a vista from the top, but along the way you'll walk through a rock-studded forest thick with blueberries and mountain laurels, and a trail dotted with pink lady's slippers. Expect to encounter wildlife that may include birds, amphibians, reptiles, deer, and black bears.

THE RUNDOWN

Start: Laurel Trail trailhead, by cabin 25
Distance: 6-mile loop
Hiking time: About 3 hours
Difficulty: Moderate due to length and elevation gain
Trail surface: Dirt trail
Best season: Spring
Other trail users: Horseback riders, mountain bikers
Canine compatibility: Leashed dogs permitted

Land status: State park
Nearest town: Berkeley Springs
Fees and permits: None
Schedule: Open daily year-round 6 a.m. to 10 p.m. for day use
Maps: Cacapon Resort State Park map and trail guide; USGS quads: Great Cacapon, Ridge
Trail contact: Cacapon Resort State Park, (304) 258-1022 or www.cacaponresort.com

FINDING THE TRAILHEAD

From I-81 in Virginia, take US 522 north 27 miles to the park entrance on the left side of the road. From I-70 in Maryland, take US 522 (exit 82A) south 16 miles; the park entrance is on the right (west), just after the town of Omps. From the park entrance, follow the signs 0.7 mile to the lodge. Park at the lodge and walk the road back to the cabin area. The trailhead starts from cabin 25. **GPS:** N39 30.20' / W78 18.08'

THE HIKE

According to park literature, the word *Cacapon* comes from the Shawnee Indian language, meaning "medicine waters." Evidence of mineral waters in this area is most prominent at nearby Berkeley Springs, but a hike to the top of Cacapon Mountain gives you a glimpse of this, too. What are normally storm-water drainages coming down a steep mountain slope are spring-fed runs here, flowing with water year-round.

The Ziler Trail is part of an old trail used by pioneers to walk between communities in this area. Unlike those pioneers, you have all the comforts of the resort—a lodge, restaurant, horseback riding, swimming—to return to when you're done hiking up and down the mountain.

From the trailhead by cabin 25, follow the green-blazed trail past the white-blazed Cabin Loop Trail. The Laurel Trail travels uphill at a moderate slope, reaching Middle Fork Road within the first mile. Across Middle Fork Road, the red-blazed Central Trail begins near a small stream. Follow the trail past a rental cabin. The trail is rocky as it

Pink lady's slippers line the Central Trail at Cacapon Resort State Park.

travels downward through a forest of oak and maple. Pass some spring-fed runs and wet areas along the trail. Look for pink lady's slippers in late May.

Reach the blue-blazed Ziler Loop Trail and follow it uphill. (A left at the intersection leads to the Batt picnic shelter.) The trail has difficult uphill sections as it ascends Cacapon Mountain. At 3.25 miles from the trailhead, the trail crests the mountain.

The Ziler Loop Trail travels the crest of Cacapon Mountain for approximately 0.75 mile before beginning the descent of the ridge. The ridge crest is wide and grassy, and there is very little middle canopy. At 3.5 miles from the trailhead, the Ziler Loop Trail heads off the mountain to the right for a steep 2.5-mile hike to the cabin area. To continue the hike, stay on the Ziler Loop Trail as it crosses the ridgetop, passing a shelter to the left. Finally, at 4.0 miles, the Ziler Loop Trail begins to descend the ridge.

Another 0.75 mile of hiking completes much of the descent of Cacapon Mountain and leads you to the Central Trail. In late May and early June, this section of the hike is gorgeous with blooming mountain laurel. The trail becomes rocky and leads through switchbacks. When the angle becomes easy and the trail widens, come to the junction with the Ziler Loop and Central Trails. Go straight to follow the lone Central Trail. The

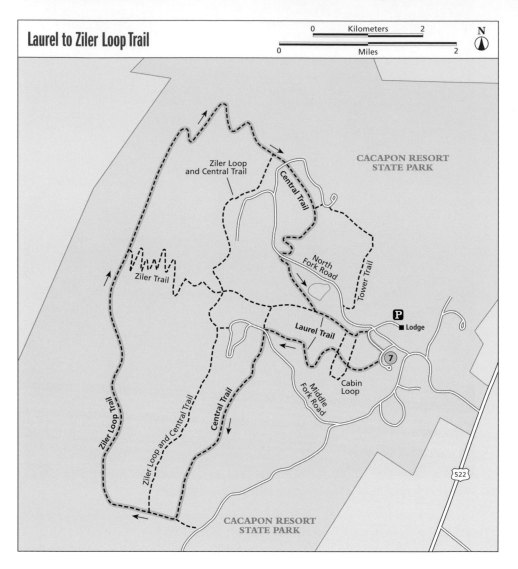

Laurel to Ziler Loop Trail

Central Trail leaves the Ziler Loop Trail and crosses a gravel road. The trail hikes through a stand of pine, and mountain laurel fills the middle canopy. Thick blueberry covers the ground, causing the trail to become very narrow. After passing some large boulders, stone stairs lead to a paved road.

Cross the paved road and follow the trail across a grassy area to the banks of the park lake. At 5.9 miles, the Central Trail passes a bench overlooking the lake. The Central Trail travels moderately uphill to the intersection with the Laurel Trail. Turn left onto the Laurel Trail and hike downhill to the trailhead between cabins 21 and 22. Follow the paved road back to the lodge parking lot.

MILES AND DIRECTIONS

0.0 START at signed trailhead for the Laurel Trail, near cabin 25. The trail is marked with green blazes.

0.1 Pass a trail joining from the left and come to a four-way intersection with the Cabin Loop Trail. Continue straight on the Laurel Trail.

0.25 Pass the second junction with the Cabin Loop Trail. Continue straight.

0.4 The trail switches back to the right; look for the blazes.

0.8 Come to an intersection next to Middle Fork Road. Take a left and cross the road, then pick up the Central Trail, marked with a trailhead sign and red blazes.

1.8 Come to a T intersection with a spur to the Ziler Loop Trail. Take a right.

1.9 Come to the junction with the Ziler Loop Trail, blazed blue. Go straight, ascending the mountain.

3.2 After walking along the crest of Cacapon Mountain, arrive at the junction with the Ziler Trail, which goes right. Continue straight on the Ziler Loop Trail.

4.75 After beginning the descent of the mountain, come to the junction with the Ziler Loop and Central Trail, marked with a sign. Continue straight, following the blue and red blazes for the Central Trail. In about 75 feet, pass another trail on the right, continuing straight. In about 150 feet, cross a gravel road, continuing straight again.

5.1 Come to a fork. A spur marked Tower Trail goes left; take the right fork to continue on the Central Trail, marked with a sign.

5.4 Cross North Fork Road.

5.7 Come to the junction with the Laurel and Ziler Trails. Take a left, following the green blazes.

5.9 The Cabin Loop Trail joins from the right. Continue straight.

6.0 Come to a four-way intersection, marked with Laurel and Cabin Loop Trail signs. Take a left and walk about 200 feet to the road between cabins 21 and 22. Take a right and walk the road back to the lodge.

GYPSY MOTHS

If you are hiking in the Cacapon area in the summer and notice few leaves on the trees or the ground covered with green leaf pieces, look on the branches for a medium-size, lightly fuzzy caterpillar with red spots. The oaks in the area have been attacked by gypsy moths, a species brought to the United States in the late 1860s to produce silk. The moth escaped, and by the 1890s defoliation was occurring. Although gypsy moth larvae will feed on many tree species, oaks are their favorite. In areas with severe infestation, trees may be totally defoliated. According to the USDA Forest Service, several years of gypsy moth defoliation plus other stresses can cause trees to die. Some areas have been aerially sprayed in an attempt to combat this pest.

HIKE INFORMATION

Local information: Berkeley Springs, (800) 447-8797 or www.berkeleysprings.com

Camping: There is no camping at Cacapon Resort State Park, but a 47-room lodge and 25 rental cabins are on-site.

Local events/attractions: Berkeley Springs State Park, (304) 258-2711 or www .berkeleyspringssp.com

Hike tours: The nature center offers year-round nature and recreation programs.

Organizations: Cacapon State Park Foundation; contact the park for information.

8 APPALACHIAN TRAIL TO LOUDOUN HEIGHTS TRAILS

Harpers Ferry National Historical Park

WHY GO?

The mother of all long-distance trails in North America, the Appalachian Trail extends 2,180 miles from Georgia to Maine. If you can't take six months to tackle the whole thing, take a day to jump on this section of the trail, which travels near the historically significant and picturesque small town of Harpers Ferry—the unofficial halfway point along the AT. The town itself is located at the confluence of two wide, riffling mountain rivers, the Shenandoah and the Potomac. This hike takes you across the Shenandoah and up a ridge crest with a great view of the confluence and the town.

THE RUNDOWN

Start: River Access parking lot off Shenandoah Street

Distance: 5.9-mile out-and-back with a loop

Hiking time: About 3 hours

Difficulty: Moderate due to length and elevation gain

Trail surface: Dirt trail plus a paved highway bridge crossing over the river

Best season: Fall

Other trail users: Hikers only

Canine compatibility: Leashed dogs permitted

Land status: National park and national scenic trail

Nearest town: Harpers Ferry

Fees and permits: National Park Service access fee or annual pass required; fee envelopes provided at River Access parking lot

Schedule: Appalachian Trail is open for hiking dawn to dusk year-round; Harpers Ferry National Historical Park buildings are open 9 a.m. to 5 p.m. daily, except Thanksgiving, Christmas, and New Year's Day.

Maps: Harpers Ferry Official Map and Guide; Appalachian Trail guide maps; USGS quads: Charles Town, Harpers Ferry

Trail contact: Harpers Ferry National Historical Park, (304) 535-6223 or www.nps.gov/hafe

Special considerations: The River Access parking lot fills early on weekends. Alternate parking is at the park entrance, about 1.5 miles west of the River Access parking lot on US 340. Look for the park entrance sign at the stoplight. A shuttle bus runs daily from 8 a.m. to 6:45 p.m. during summer (5:45 p.m. the rest of the year) from the park entrance to information center in Harpers Ferry. From the information center, pick up the AT and walk west 0.75 mile to the trailhead described above. This section of the AT takes you past the view from Jefferson Rock. It is a good alternate starting point.

FINDING THE TRAILHEAD

From the junction of WV 230 and US 340, west of Harpers Ferry, travel east 2.5 miles on US 340 to Shenandoah Street. Take a left onto Shenandoah Street and then an immediate right into the River Access parking lot. Walk on the

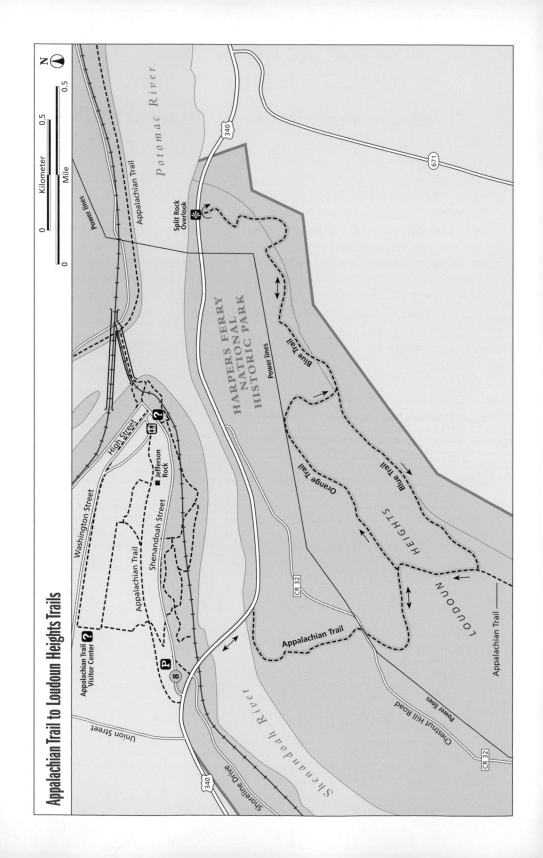

Appalachian Trail to Loudoun Heights Trails

sidewalk from the parking lot back to US 340 to pick up the Appalachian Trail, which crosses the river over the highway bridge. **GPS:** N39 19.30′ / W77 44.58′

THE HIKE

Harpers Ferry is known for many things, most prominently for John Brown's raid, in which the white abolitionist organized an armed rebellion of slaves, which took over the US Armory and Arsenal at Harpers Ferry for thirty-six hours. The 1859 raid is credited as one of the events that incited the Civil War. During the war, control of Harpers Ferry alternated between Union and Confederate troops eight times. But Harpers Ferry goes back further in America's history. George Washington passed through the town twice on surveying expeditions; Thomas Jefferson deemed Harpers Ferry worth a trip across the Atlantic to visit; and Harpers Ferry was where Lewis and Clark outfitted for their expedition.

Yesterday's politicians, explorers, and abolitionists have given way to today's history buffs, water-sport enthusiasts, and hikers—which include both day hikers and AT thru-hikers. Harpers Ferry is home to the Appalachian Trail Conservancy offices and is the unofficial halfway point along the famous trail.

Set out in the morning to take advantage of the best light conditions for photographing Harpers Ferry from the overlook. Walk from the parking area off Shenandoah Street and begin by crossing the Shenandoah River on a highway bridge. You are already officially on the AT. After crossing the river, the sidewalk crosses under the bridge and the pavement ends, then the dirt trail begins. Almost immediately you will begin ascending Loudoun Heights by way of switchbacks and steep climbing. The highway noise barely dissipates.

Cross CR 32 and continue the ascent of the mountain. Upon reaching the junction with the Orange Trail, leave the AT and continue to ascend to the ridgetop. At that point, join the Blue Trail, take a left, and walk to Split Rock. This overlook gives you a clear view of the town of Harpers Ferry and the confluence of the Shenandoah and Potomac Rivers. The morning light is best for photos, and this is, of course, your best lunch spot. To make a loop of the hike, take the Blue Trail all the way to the junction with the AT. This junction is marked with an AT sign; take a right here and follow the trail downhill back to the river and the trailhead.

MILES AND DIRECTIONS

0.0   START at the River Access parking lot at the junction of US 340 and Shenandoah Street. From the parking lot, take the sidewalk to US 340 and turn left, crossing the Shenandoah River on the bridge. There is a sidewalk here. White blazes mark the Appalachian Trail. (**FYI:** Don't forget to display a daily or yearly National Park Service pass in your car or you could get ticketed.)

0.4   Cross under the bridge and enter the woods on the obvious path. Begin to ascend the mountain.

0.9   Cross CR 32. (**FYI:** Be careful at this road crossing—it's near a curve and traffic is fast here.)

1.25   Come to a junction with the Orange Trail. Take a left, walking northeasterly.

1.9   Come to a T intersection with the Blue Trail. Take a left.

Overlooking Harpers Ferry from Split Rock

2.9 Arrive at a fork in the trail. Take the left fork and descend to Split Rock on a steep trail with some wooden steps. The rocks are only about 25 feet from the fork. After checking out the views from Split Rock, retrace your steps. (**FYI:** The trail ends here. You cannot take the right fork and continue past Split Rock; the trail is closed.)

3.9 Arrive back at the junction of the Blue and Orange Trails. Continue straight, following the Blue Trail back.

4.4 Come to a junction with the Appalachian Trail, marked with a sign. Take a right, walking downhill.

4.6 Return to the junction of the AT and the Orange Trail. Stay on the AT, following the white blazes, and retrace your steps to the trailhead.

5.9 Arrive back at the parking lot.

JEFFERSON ROCK

Along the AT in Harpers Ferry is Jefferson Rock, named after Thomas Jefferson, who found the view from the rock noteworthy. In his 1785 book, *Notes on the State of Virginia* (remember, this was Virginia then), he wrote, "The passage of the Patowmac through the Blue Ridge is perhaps one of the most stupendous scenes in Nature. . . . It is as placid and delightful as that is wild and tremendous." He added that the scene was worth a voyage across the Atlantic, which, of course, took considerably more effort back then.

HIKE INFORMATION

Local information: Harpers Ferry Historic Town Foundation, (304) 535-6955 or http://historicharpersferry.com

Camping: Overnight backpacking is allowed on the Appalachian Trail but not in the national park.

Local events/attractions: C&O Canal Towpath, www.nps.gov/choh

Hike tours: Contact Harpers Ferry National Historical Park for programming info, which includes shorter hikes, or River and Trail Outfitters, (301) 695-5177 or www.rivertrail.com.

Organizations: Appalachian Trail Conservancy, (304) 535-6331 or www.appalachiantrail.org

POTOMAC HIGHLANDS

Rising abruptly in eastern West Virginia, the peaks and ridges of the Allegheny Mountains create an outdoor playground for the hiker. The same geologic events that pushed the high plain of western West Virginia straight up also tilted and folded the ground of the Potomac Highlands, creating majestic mountains and deep valleys. As the name suggests, the watersheds in the region give rise to the mighty Potomac River, which flows north toward Harpers Ferry. Great expanses of resistant Tuscarora sandstone line ridgetops and provide breathtaking vistas at nearly every turn.

Hiking the Potomac Highlands is very rewarding. Walks range from short, easy boardwalk paths to difficult, extended day hikes. Trails in the area reach altitudes of 4,000 feet, and ecosystems vary greatly as altitude changes. Creek bottoms are lined with birch and hemlock, while spruce dominates the ridgetops. Trails here are managed by state parks or

The view from Cranny Crow Overlook (hike 12)

state forests. Camping is permitted in campgrounds, and it is advisable to make reservations. Although much of the land in this region is owned by the federal government and managed as the Monongahela National Forest, trails in the forest itself are described in a separate section of this guide.

In addition to hikers, the Potomac Highlands attracts many other outdoor athletes. Canaan Valley, Timberline, and Snowshoe ski resorts bring both downhill and cross-country skiers from all over the East Coast. Summertime sees the ski resorts catering to mountain bikers. Rock climbers enjoy the sandstone cliffs, while whitewater enthusiasts flock to the stream banks.

9 HIGH TIMBER TO SUNSET TRAIL

Jennings Randolph Lake Project

WHY GO?

Jennings Randolph Lake is a US Army Corps of Engineers project; the lake was created in 1981 when the dam was built to make a freshwater reservoir and to control floodwaters on the North Branch of the Potomac River. Recreation, however, is hardly an afterthought. In addition to ample water-sport opportunities, you can head out on this trail loop in the morning or evening and likely return with photos of the Jennings Randolph Lake overlook or the wind turbines that line the eastern horizon along Green Mountain, and perhaps stories of your own wildlife sightings, which might include anything from a snapping turtle to a bald eagle to a black bear.

THE RUNDOWN

Start: High Timber Trail trailhead, between campsites 69 and 71
Distance: 2.6-mile loop
Hiking time: About 1 hour
Difficulty: Easy
Trail surface: Dirt and mowed grass trail with a section along a road
Best season: Spring or fall
Other trail users: Mountain bikers
Canine compatibility: Leashed dogs permitted
Land status: US Army Corps of Engineers land
Nearest town: Keyser

Fees and permits: None
Schedule: Hiking trails are accessible only when the campground is open, generally late Apr to early Oct. Campground gate is closed between 10 p.m. and 7 a.m.
Maps: Robert W. Craig Campground hiking trails map; USGS quads: Kitzmiller, Westernport
Trail contact: Reservoir Manager, Jennings Randolph Lake, (304) 355-2346 or www.nab.usace.army.mil/Missions/Dams-Recreation/Jennings-Randolph-Lake/

FINDING THE TRAILHEAD

At the intersection of US 50 and WV 42, turn north on WV 42 and travel 4.8 miles to WV 46 in Elk Garden. Turn right on WV 46 and continue 5.2 miles to the campground entrance. Turn left and proceed to the entrance station. Parking is available on the right for the trailhead for the Sunset Trail, which you can access even when the gate is closed. To reach the High Timber Trail, follow the campground road. There is trailhead parking between sites 69 and 71. **GPS:** N39 7.70' / W78 31.03'

THE HIKE

Timing is everything when it comes to the trails at Jennings Randolph Lake. Tackle this forest-and-meadow loop midday in midsummer, and you might end up complaining about sunburn and ticks. However, head out in the morning or evening and you'll have perfect conditions for photographing the Jennings Randolph Lake overlook to the west or the wind turbines that line the horizon atop Green Mountain to the east.

Wind turbines along an eastern ridge, viewed from Jennings Randolph Lake

Wear long pants to ward off ticks, and begin from the Robert Craig Campground. There is a trailhead with parking for the orange-blazed High Timber Trail between sites 69 and 71. Begin a gradual descent to a small stream, where you'll find a bench to relax and enjoy the forest made up of maples, serviceberries, and other hardwoods. Cast your eyes downward and you might see red eft newts, wild mushrooms (look for morels in the spring), and wildflowers.

Cross a stream on a footbridge and begin a gradual climb. At a right bend, the 0.5-mile Connector Spur leads to the Sunset Trail and is also marked with orange arrows. Turn left on the Connector Spur and descend gradually to the intersection with the Sunset Trail. At the trail junction, a right provides a shortcut back to the parking area.

To continue the loop, stay straight on the Sunset Trail. The trail crosses the road and heads toward the big meadow. This meadow is actually a reclaimed quarry, the source of the stone used to build the dam. It's now covered with grasses and a few small trees, like autumn olive. In addition, summer wildflowers here include black-eyed Susans and daisies. Climb to the summit of a small knoll. Actually, it is worth the climb to the top, as the view of the meadow is spectacular. Drop down to some picnic tables and a fence at 1.25 miles for a good view of Jennings Randolph Lake and the mountains that ring it.

Continue past the wooden fence, following a mowed trail. Skirt along the steep escarpment a short distance and then begin to cross the meadow. The trail leaves the meadow and becomes a footpath as it enters the woods; watch for red and orange arrows. The

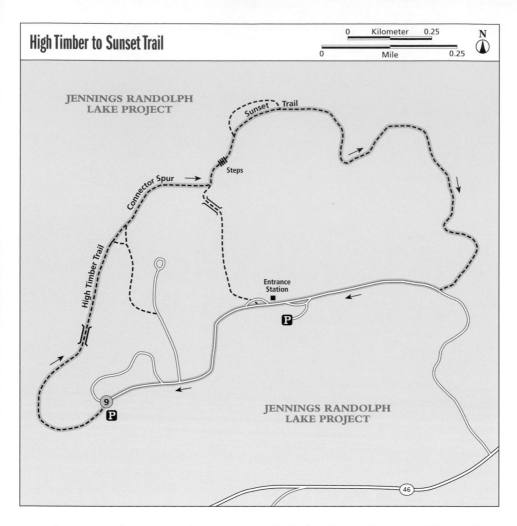

grade increases after entering the woods, then climbs the ridge to the road and the guard-rail. Turn right on the road and walk a short distance back to the parking area. Along the way, you should stop at an overlook along the roadside, where below you can see much of the trail you just hiked.

MILES AND DIRECTIONS

0.0 START at the High Timber Trail trailhead, between campsites 69 and 71. Walk into the woods under the High Timber Trail sign. The trail is marked with orange blazes.

0.5 Come to the junction with the Connector Spur, marked with blue arrow blazes. This portion of the High Timber Trail can be difficult to find. Continue generally straight; follow any blaze you see, which may be blue, orange, or brown.

0.75 Walk slightly downhill toward the power-line cut and a bench. There is a sign here for the Sunset Trail. Take a right and begin walking on a mowed path.

0.8 Come to a T intersection with a doubletrack road. Go left, following the sign for the Sunset Trail.

1.0 Arrive at a fork in the mowed path; a hiker sign points right. Take the right and descend a few wooden steps. In about 200 feet, come to a four-way mowed intersection. To the east are wind turbines on a distant ridgetop. Continue straight at this intersection, toward the wooden fence that over-looks Jennings Randolph Lake.

1.7 Enter the woods and follow red arrow blazes and some orange arrows.

1.8 Ascend stairs to the campground road. Take a right and follow the road back to the campground.

2.0 A mountain meadow overlook is on the right, just off the road. There is a bench here.

2.6 Arrive back at the trailhead.

HIKE INFORMATION

Local information: Mineral County Convention and Visitors Bureau, (304) 788-2513 or www.visitmineral.com

Camping: Robert W. Craig Campground has 84 sites. There is primitive riverside camping along the North Branch of the Potomac just a few miles away. From the campground, return to WV 46 and take a left. Go 1.2 miles to Barnum Road (46/2), marked with a Barnum Whitewater Area sign. Take a left and descend the mountain 2.1 miles and enter the Barnum Whitewater Area, marked with a sign. Drive past the restroom and cabins to tent campsites along the river.

Local events/attractions: Scheduled dam releases allow for whitewater rafting and kayaking on the North Branch of the Potomac; for information, go to www.nab-wc.usace.army.mil/northBranch.html.

Organizations: Friends of Jennings Randolph Lake sponsors interpretive talks at the campground, www.nab.usace.army.mil/Missions/Dams-Recreation/Jennings-Randolph-Lake/Friends-of-Jennings-Randolph-Lake/.

10 ELAKALA TO YELLOW BIRCH TRAIL LOOP

Blackwater Falls State Park

WHY GO?

The first rule of real estate is location, location, location—and Blackwater Falls State Park is hard to beat in that department. Its centerpiece is the state's most well-known cascade, Blackwater Falls, and the 1,000-foot-deep Blackwater River Canyon. To the south spreads the rest of the Canaan Valley, an alpine valley that's home to vast freshwater wetlands and boreal forest plant and animal communities more commonly found in Canada. This loop hike allows you to experience a little bit of everything the area has to offer: upland hardwoods and lush marshy bogs in addition to views of the Falls of Elakala, Balanced Rock, and Blackwater Canyon. At the end of the day, there are nearby lodging, food, and drinking options to satisfy the tastes of everyone from the devoted penny-pincher to the comfort seeker.

THE RUNDOWN

Start: Elakala Trail trailhead
Distance: 3.6-mile loop with out-and-back
Hiking time: About 2 hours
Difficulty: Easy
Trail surface: Dirt trail that can get quite muddy
Best season: Spring
Other trail users: Horseback riders, mountain bikers on Yellow Birch Trail
Canine compatibility: Leashed dogs permitted
Land status: State park

Nearest town: Davis
Fees and permits: None
Schedule: Park and lodge are open year-round, 24/7 for campers and lodge guests; 6 a.m. to 10 p.m. for day use.
Maps: Blackwater Falls State Park map and trail guide; USGS quad: Blackwater Falls
Trail contact: Blackwater Falls State Park, (304) 259-5216 or www.blackwaterfalls.com

FINDING THE TRAILHEAD

From WV 32 on the north side of Davis, turn left on CR 29 (Blackwater Falls Road). Travel 1.2 miles to a crossroad (29-1), turn left, and continue 1.5 miles to a fork. Take the right fork to the lodge and the Elakala Trail trailhead. **GPS:** N39 06.46' / W79 29.89'

THE HIKE

Blackwater Falls, voluminous and nearly 60 feet tall, is the most famous—and arguably the most beautiful—waterfall in West Virginia. The waterfall marks the start of the Blackwater Canyon, up to 1,000 feet deep in places. This park lies in contrast to Canaan Valley, where the Blackwater River cuts a gentle path northward through this open valley,

Falls of Elakala

ringed by mountains that rise up another 1,000 feet. The name *Blackwater* is attributed to the dark color of the river water, created by tannins from the peaty soil of hemlock and spruce stands as well as bogs along its course.

This hike begins downstream from Blackwater Falls, at the lodge. Enter the woods on the Elakala Trail and in moments you will hear the water from the Falls of Elakala crashing into the rock at the bottom of the 35-foot cascade. The falls are generally running at their highest volume in the spring. Walk for a few minutes and come to a bridge that crosses over the top of the falls. Continuing along the trail, you can follow the informal trail to the bottom of the waterfall. Exercise caution here, as the slope is steep and the rocks are wet.

Continuing on, there are occasional overlooks of Blackwater Canyon, beautiful year-round but especially striking in the fall due to colorful foliage. The hemlocks and red spruce, combined with rhododendrons and mountain laurels, create a year-round green component of forest. Soon the Elakala Trail ends at Park Road 29-1. Cross the road and begin the Balanced Rock Trail.

The Balanced Rock Trail, blazed orange, leads away from Blackwater Canyon and into deeper woods. An informal pastime of hikers along this trail is to build rock cairns all over the place. Please remember that this violates Leave No Trace principles. After arriving at Shay Run (upstream from the Falls of Elakala), the Balanced Rock Trail crosses the Red Spruce Riding Trail and takes a right. The trail ascends here into a clearing where few canopy trees exist among the rhododendrons. Arrive at Balanced Rock, which is about 15 feet tall, and return the way you came to the junction of the Balanced Rock Trail and Red Spruce Riding Trail.

At the Red Spruce Riding Trail, turn right to continue the loop, which now follows a wide road. A short climb is followed by an S-turn descent to a feeder creek. Cross the creek on a footbridge and begin a steady climb. There is an elevation gain of approximately 260 feet.

You will eventually arrive at a barn that has been used for horseback riding stables and for a petting zoo. The loop continues past this barn by turning left onto the Yellow Birch Trail, which is blazed yellow. The trail climbs a small hill, but the grade is easy. Moss, fern, and rhododendron dominate the understory. The trail ends at the park road, near the lodge. Cross the road and walk along the entrance road back to the lodge.

MILES AND DIRECTIONS

0.0 START at the Elakala Trail trailhead on the west end of the lodge parking lot.

0.1 Cross a wooden footbridge over the Falls of Elakala.

0.25 Pass a junction and a sign for the park road. Continue straight.

0.4 The Elakala Trail ends at the park road. Cross the road and pick up the Balanced Rock Trail directly across the road.

0.5 Come to a junction with the Shay Trace Trail. Continue straight on the Balanced Rock Trail. Keep an eye on the orange blazes to make sure you stay on the trail.

0.9 Cross Shay Run and come to the junction with the Red Spruce Riding Trail. The Balanced Rock Trail, marked with a sign, is to the right. Take the right and begin the Balanced Rock Trail.

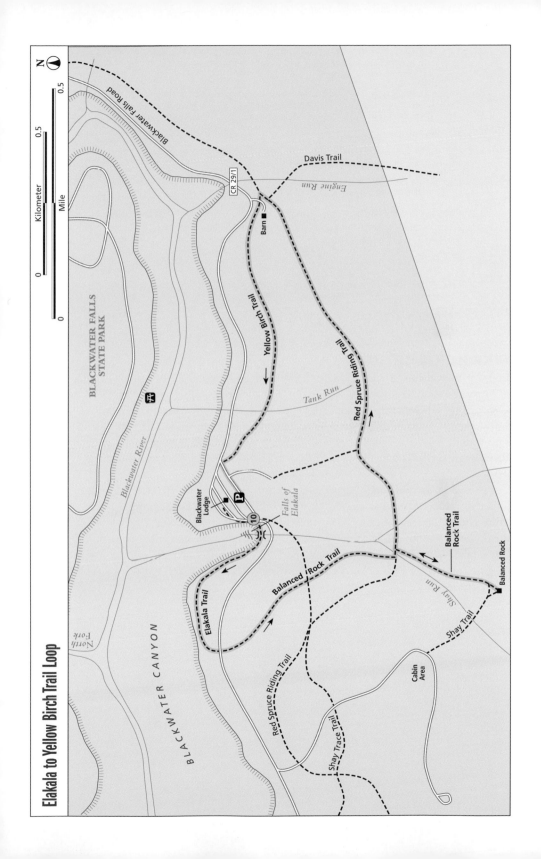

Elakala to Yellow Birch Trail Loop

N

Kilometer
0   0.5

Mile
0   0.5

BLACKWATER FALLS
STATE PARK

Blackwater Falls Road

CR 29/1

Davis Trail

Engine Run

Barn ■

Yellow Birch Trail

Tank Run

Red Spruce Riding Trail

Blackwater River

Blackwater Lodge

P

10

Falls of Elakala

Elakala Trail

Balanced Rock Trail

BLACKWATER CANYON

North Fork

Red Spruce Riding Trail

Shay Run

Balanced Rock Trail

Balanced Rock ■

Shay Trace Trail

Shay Trail

Cabin Area

1.2   You might see a faint side trail to the right, also marked orange that is part of a loop around Balanced Rock and a continuation of the trail to Southside Cabin Area. Continue straight.

1.3   Arrive at Balanced Rock. Although the trail continues from here to the Southside Cabin Area and Rhododendron Trail, and is blazed orange, it's best to avoid the confusion beyond and turn around here. Go back the way you came.

1.7   Return to the junction with the Red Spruce Riding Trail. Take a right to follow the trail, which is an old road at this point.

2.0   Come to a junction with the Water Tank Trail to the lodge on the left. Continue straight.

2.7   The Red Spruce Riding Trail ends at a barn and a junction with the Davis Trail, blazed yellow. After passing the barn, take a left and walk to the paved driveway. In about 100 yards, the Yellow Birch Trail crosses the driveway. Take a left and reenter the woods. The trail is also marked with a yellow blaze.

3.5   The Yellow Birch Trail ends at the park road. Cross the road and walk along the entrance road to the lodge.

3.6   Arrive back at the lodge parking lot.

HIKE INFORMATION

Local information: Tucker County Convention and Visitors Bureau, (800) 782-2775 or http://canaanvalley.org

Camping: Blackwater Falls State Park has a 65-site campground open from the last weekend of Apr through Oct 31. Cabins and rooms in the lodge are available year-round.

Restaurants: Blackwater Brewing Company, (304) 259-4221; blackwaterbrewingwv .com

Local events/attractions: Canaan Valley Institute's nearby property is open to the public for nonmotorized recreation, (304) 259-4739 or www.canaanvi.org.

Hike tours: The nature center is open daily Memorial Day to Labor Day. It is open at the discretion of the naturalist the rest of the year. The nature center has programming that includes nature hikes year round.

Organizations: Friends of Blackwater Canyon, (877) WVA-LAND or www.saveblack water.org

11 BEALL TRAILS LOOP
Canaan Valley National Wildlife Refuge

WHY GO?
Go on a snipe hunt in Canaan Valley National Wildlife Refuge. It's not a practical joke this time; rather, the refuge is home to some 200 bird species, including Wilson's snipe, bobolink, and northern saw-whet owl. Forest, wetlands, meadows, and the Blackwater River provide habitat for an estimated 580 plant species. Listen and look for ever-present birdlife, expect to see deer, and hope for a black bear sighting, which is not uncommon around here. But in Canaan Valley, the whole is greater than the sum of its parts: The scenery is ever-changing, yet always exceptional.

THE RUNDOWN

Start: Beall Trail North trailhead
Distance: 5.4-mile figure eight plus spur trails
Hiking time: About 2 to 2.5 hours
Difficulty: Easy
Trail surface: Grass and dirt; trails can be muddy
Best season: May and June for nesting birds, like bobolinks
Other trail users: Horseback riders and mountain bikers on the Beall Bridge Trail
Canine compatibility: Leashed dogs permitted on pedestrian trails
Land status: National wildlife refuge

Nearest town: Davis
Fees and permits: None
Schedule: Refuge lands are open year-round to the public an hour before sunrise to an hour after sunset. Visitor center hours are 10 a.m. to 4 p.m. daily; 10 a.m. to 4 p.m. Wed through Sat in winter, generally Dec. 1 to Memorial Day.
Maps: Canaan Valley National Wildlife Refuge maps; USGS quads: Blackwater Falls, Davis
Trail contact: Canaan Valley National Wildlife Refuge, (304) 866-3858 or www.fws.gov/canaanvalley

FINDING THE TRAILHEAD
From WV 32 in Davis where it crosses over the Blackwater River, travel 3.5 miles south to Cortland Road. Take a left (east) and go 2.2 miles to Coffmans Lane Road and a blue national wildlife refuge sign. Take a left and go 0.5 mile to the trailhead parking lot. **GPS:** N39 03.82' / W79 25.09'

THE HIKE
As the name suggests, expect to encounter wildlife at Canaan Valley National Wildlife Refuge, which lies in the heart of the Canaan Valley, the highest valley of its size east of the Rockies. The valley floor lies at about 3,200 feet above sea level, and the mountains that ring it, including Cabin Mountain, rise up another 1,000 feet. The gently moving Blackwater River runs northward through the valley, which is 13 miles north to south and 3 miles east to west. The refuge is home to deciduous and red spruce forests, managed open grasslands, and five—count 'em, five—types of wetlands (if you must know: muskeg, alder, wet meadow, swamp forest, and spirea thicket).

A female bluebird perches on a trail sign along the Beall Trail in Canaan Valley.

What is today an environmental showcase could have been an opportunity lost, had history gone the other way. Allegheny Power Systems purchased land in the valley during the 1920s and in the '70s made plans to build a pumped storage hydroelectric power facility, which would have flooded one-third of the valley floor. The US Army Corps of Engineers did not issue a permit, due to its impact on the wetlands. Despite years of appeals, the hydroelectric project was never built. While the refuge was established with the purchase of 86 acres in 1994 (it is the 500th refuge in the system), the power company eventually sold 12,000 acres of land in 2002. The refuge is now up to just over 16,000 acres.

Stop at the informative kiosk before beginning the Beall (pronounced "bell") Trail North. Walk into a stand of woods and then back into a meadow. This is former farmland, and today the national wildlife refuge manages the grasslands for habitat through mowing and controlled burning. May and June see a number of nesting birds, including ground-nesting grassland birds such as the eastern meadowlark, bobolink, Henslow's sparrow, American woodcock, and the aforementioned Wilson's snipe.

Return to the woods and continue along the northern loop trail until you arrive at the Hemlock Spur Trail to the Blackwater River. Take that trail to get your first view of the Blackwater, named for the dark color created by tannins. Meadows, forests, wetlands, and the riparian (river) areas all provide habitat for wildlife, and in combination, these edge habitats are ripe for wildlife sightings, particularly at dawn and dusk. Returning to the main loop, continue south to the Beall Bridge Trail, which is multiuse. Another side trip will take you directly to the Blackwater River, where you might see signs of beaver activity, and your chances are good to spot a great blue heron or belted kingfisher. You would be lucky to glimpse a mink, but they do call this area home.

After returning to the main trail, take the Shortcut Trail to the Beall Trail South loop. At this point, you'll enter a meadow that can be measured in square miles. This section of trail provides expansive views of the Canaan Valley and of the ski slopes at Timberline

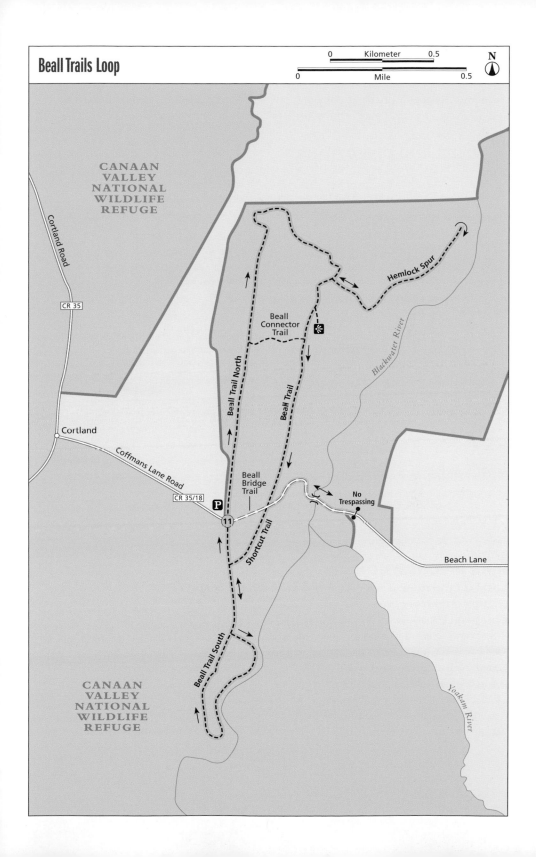

Beall Trails Loop

0   Kilometer   0.5

0   Mile   0.5

N

CANAAN
VALLEY
NATIONAL
WILDLIFE
REFUGE

Cortland Road

CR 35

Cortland

Coffmans Lane Road

CR 35/18

P

11

Beall Trail North

Beall Trail

Beall Connector Trail

Hemlock Spur

Blackwater River

Beall Bridge Trail

Shortcut Trail

No Trespassing

Beach Lane

Beall Trail South

CANAAN
VALLEY
NATIONAL
WILDLIFE
REFUGE

Yoakum River

and Canaan Valley ski resorts. The trail drops down to parallel the Blackwater River for a stretch. Enjoy the sights and sounds of this narrow strip of trail between the riffling river to the east and a steep slope to the west. Moss–covered rocks dot the ground here and deciduous trees dominate the canopy, but look also for the native red spruce. Finish this loop to make a general figure eight of the Beall Trails, north and south.

MILES AND DIRECTIONS

0.0 START at the Beall Trail North trailhead at the north end of the parking lot, next to the large kiosk with information pamphlets and interpretive panels.

0.5 Pass the Beall Connector trail on the right. Continue straight.

1.1 Come to the junction with the Hemlock Spur. Take a left and descend toward the river.

1.7 Reach the end of the Hemlock Spur at a sign for the refuge boundary and the river. Turn around from here to return to the main trail.

2.3 Return to the Beall Trail and take a left.

2.7 Pass the Beall Connector trail on the right. Continue straight.

3.2 Come to the junction with the unmarked Beall Bridge Trail. It's a gravel road. (There's a sign ahead for the Shortcut Trail.) Take a left to gain quick access to the river. The Beall Bridge Trail goes over an at-your-own-risk bridge.

3.5 The Beall Bridge Trail ends at private property. Return to the junction with the Beall Trail.

3.8 At the junction with the Beall Trail, take a left and begin the Shortcut Trail, marked with a sign.

4.0 Arrive at the junction with the Beall Trail South. Take a left.

4.25 Come to the beginning of the loop of the Beall Trail South and a brown trail marker. Take a left and descend to the river.

5.0 After completing the loop, return to the junction and brown trail marker where you started the loop and continue straight, toward the parking lot.

5.4 Finish at the south end of the parking lot.

HIKE INFORMATION

Local information: Tucker County Convention and Visitors Bureau, (800) 782-2775 or http://canaanvalley.org

Camping: Canaan Valley Resort State Park has a 34–site campground, 2- and 4-bedroom cabins, and a lodge, (304) 866-4121 or (800) 662-4121, www.canaanresort .com.

Local events/attractions: Canaan Valley Birding Festival, www.canaanresort.com/ events/canaan-valley-birding-festival

Hike tours: The refuge hosts hiking, bird–watching, and snowshoeing tours on an irregular basis; check the website for information.

Organizations: Friends of the 500th, www.facebook.com/Friendsofthe500th.

12 WHITE OAK TO BIG RIDGE LOOP

Lost River State Park

WHY GO?

Just two and a half hours from Washington, DC, Lost River State Park is a place to put the city life behind you. Take the White Oak Trail to the Cranny Crow Overlook, and you'll know just how far you are from civilization: The overlook provides a vast view into Virginia of nothing but mountain ridges folding into the horizon and the occasional bucolic farm. Lest you think you're completely deprived of civilization, know that Lost River is also home to CCC-era infrastructure that includes log cabins and deluxe cabins, a horse stable, and a gift shop showcasing West Virginia–made arts and crafts.

THE RUNDOWN

Start: White Oak Trail trailhead, near the stable
Distance: 5.2-mile lollipop
Hiking time: About 3 hours
Difficulty: Moderate due to the steep slopes
Trail surface: Dirt trail and gravel road
Best seasons: May and June for mountain laurels and rhododendrons; Sept and Oct for colorful vistas
Other trail users: Horseback riders

Canine compatibility: Leashed dogs permitted
Land status: State park
Nearest town: Lost City
Fees and permits: None
Schedule: Open daily year-round 6 a.m. to 10 p.m. for day use
Maps: Lost River State Park map and trail guide; USGS quad: Lost River State Park
Trail contact: Lost River State Park, (304) 897-5372 or www.lostriversp.com

FINDING THE TRAILHEAD

At the intersection of WV 259 and CR 12 in Mathias, turn west on CR 12. Proceed 4.1 miles and turn right (north) on Dove Hollow Road, marked with a sign for the stable. Continue 0.3 mile and park at the stable on the right. If the stable parking lot is full, continue on the road to a pullout on the left prior to the sign that says LEAVING LOST RIVER STATE PARK. **GPS:** N38 54.19' / W78 55.10'

THE HIKE

After the Revolutionary War, it was a fairly common practice to reward military leaders for their service with land. This is how "Light Horse Harry" Lee, a Revolutionary War officer and later Virginia governor, came to own the land that is today Lost River State Park. Lee's family—which included his son, who would become General Robert E. Lee—had a summer cabin at Howard's Lick. The cabin is now on the National Register of Historic Places and is located near the park office, across from the swimming pool. Lee Sulphur Springs is named after the family.

Cranny Crow Overlook

The more recent history of the park continues with the advent of the Civilian Conservation Corps. The 1930s work project brought young men to the area who built and rebuilt many of the buildings that still exist today, from the springhouse that covers Lee Sulphur Springs to the superintendent's residence to the cabins that are available for rent.

You can see the junction of natural and human history when you visit Lost River State Park. The White Oak to Big Ridge Loop is the best way to take in the nature of the park and features the well-known vista from the Cranny Crow Overlook. A solidly built stone shelter that was constructed by CCC workers marks your arrival at the Cranny Crow Overlook. The trailhead, at an elevation of 1,960 feet, is on the east side of the road past the stable. The trail begins with a short climb up the road embankment. After crossing a small feeder creek, the trail passes the stable and begins a gradual climb up the side of the finger ridge. The beginning of the trail suffers from severe erosion.

The forest is composed of pine and chestnut oak. Blueberry and mountain laurel fill the understory. After a left bend, the trail climbs the actual ridge. Cross a road and pass under a power line. The trail is now on the side of the ridge again. Halfway up the mountain is a small shelter with a view. The trail really begins to climb the ridge after the shelter. There are several bends and switchbacks during the climb, which is long and difficult.

Near the crest of the ridge is the junction with the Millers Rock Trail, a long trail that extends from one end of Big Ridge to the other. The distance from the trailhead to this junction is 1.7 miles, and the elevation is 2,800 feet. Turn right on the yellow-blazed Millers Rock Trail and head south to the Cranny Crow Overlook, a stone shelter with an expansive view of the forested mountains of Virginia. The trail descends rapidly to Cheeks Rock, an outcrop that offers another vista to the southeast. Continue descending to the Virginia View Trail. Another rock outcrop is visible just beyond the junction with this trail.

Turn left on the Virginia View Trail and begin climbing back up Big Ridge. The trail is marked with red blazes and the grade is easy, climbing gradually for 0.4 mile to the Big Ridge Trail. At the junction with the Big Ridge Trail, there's an option to turn left and climb up to the meadow, which has a small shelter, picnic tables, a privy, and a log cabin built in the 1840s. The added distance (0.6 mile) is worth the effort.

> The Lost River is so named because it sinks under the ground and emerges again a couple of miles downstream. Despite it being Lost River State Park's namesake, the river does not go through the park, though it does go through the nearby town of Mathias.

The Big Ridge Trail is a heavily used trail marked with yellow blazes. It begins with a steep descent and then levels out for a short distance, followed by another steep descent down to a fork. Take the right fork and follow the trail as it bends around the base of Cheeks Rock. The grade near this rock face is easy. Past the rock face, the trail begins a moderate descent to the gravel road. Turn right on the gravel road and make an easy climb about 0.4 mile to the junction with the White Oak Trail. Turn left on the White Oak Trail and descend to the parking area.

MILES AND DIRECTIONS

0.0 START at the White Oak Trail trailhead, located past the horse stable on Dove Hollow Road. Walk along an old road grade, ascending into the woods. In about 100 yards, pass an access trail from the stable and then walk straight through a four-way intersection, under the power-line cut.

0.4 The trail forks. Take the left fork, up the ridge, following orange blazes.

0.7 Cross a gravel road. Continue straight.

0.9 The trail forks and then rejoins in about 50 feet. Watch for the orange blazes.

1.0 Come to an old wooden shelter. The trail takes a left by the shelter, up the hill.

1.7 Come to the end of the White Oak Trail at a T intersection with the Millers Rock Trail, blazed yellow. Take a right.

1.75 Pass a road joining from the left and arrive at the Cranny Crow Overlook, with a stone shelter. (**FYI:** This is your best bet for a lunch spot.)

2.1 Come to a junction with a big rock cairn. Take a left to begin the Virginia View Trail, blazed red. (**FYI:** There is another overlook straight ahead.) (**Option:** This ends the most scenic section of trail. You can turn around here for a 4.2-mile out-and-back hike.)

2.5 Arrive at the junction with the Big Ridge Trail, marked with a sign. Take a right.

2.9 The trail, which is now an old road grade, forks. Keep right. (The left is blocked with a sign.)

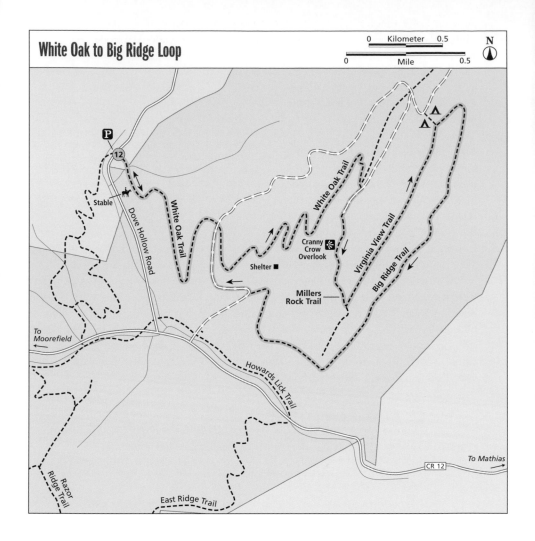

White Oak to Big Ridge Loop

0 — Kilometer — 0.5

0 — Mile — 0.5

N

P

12

Stable

Dove Hollow Road

White Oak Trail

White Oak Trail

Virginia View Trail

Big Ridge Trail

Cranny Crow Overlook

Shelter

Millers Rock Trail

To Moorefield

Howards Lick Trail

Razor Ridge Trail

East Ridge Trail

CR 12

To Mathias

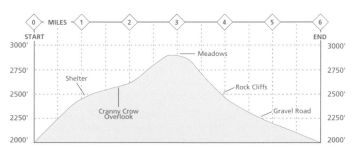

MILES

0 START   1   2   3   4   5   6 END

3000'

2750'

2500'

2250'

2000'

Shelter

Cranny Crow Overlook

Meadows

Rock Cliffs

Gravel Road

4.0 The Big Ridge Trail ends at a gravel road. Take a right.

4.4 Come to the junction with the White Oak Trail. Take a left and retrace your steps from the beginning of the hike.

5.2 Arrive back at the trailhead.

HIKE INFORMATION

Local information: Hardy County Convention and Visitors Bureau, (304) 897-8700 or www.visithardy.com

Camping: There are two hike-in campsites along the White Oak Trail; park cabins are available year-round.

Local events/attractions: Lost River Artisans Cooperative, (304) 897-7242 or www .lostrivercrafts.com

Hike tours: A naturalist leads hikes and other programming during the summer.

13 MEAT BOX RUN TO RAVEN ROCKS TRAIL LOOP

Kumbrabow State Forest

WHY GO?

It's a testament to both the quantity and quality of hiking in West Virginia that Kumbrabow State Forest is largely overlooked by hikers. The upside is that Kumbrabow offers a chance for some real seclusion. The forest is wild and rugged with steep slopes and tall stands of cove hardwoods. This 4-mile loop parallels the run up to the top of the mountain and then loops back down, with a stop at the Raven Rocks overlook on the way.

THE RUNDOWN

Start: Meat Box Run Trail trailhead

Distance: 4-mile loop

Hiking time: About 2 hours

Difficulty: Moderate due to the steep slope

Trail surface: Dirt trail

Best season: Spring

Other trail users: Hunters during hunting season; bicyclists on the forest roads

Canine compatibility: Leashed dogs permitted

Land status: State forest

Nearest town: Huttonsville

Fees and permits: None

Schedule: Open daily year-round 6 a.m. to 10 p.m. for day use

Maps: Kumbrabow State Forest map and trail guide; USGS quads: Adolph, Pickens, Samp, Valley Head

Trail contact: Kumbrabow State Forest, (304) 335-2219 or www.kumbrabow.com

Special considerations: Deer rifle season is usually late Nov to early Dec.

FINDING THE TRAILHEAD

About 18 miles south of Elkins, at the intersection of CR 219-55 and CR 250-92, head south 7.5 miles to the intersection of CR 219-55 and CR 219-16. Turn west on CR 219-16. Travel 3.7 miles to the Y intersection and bear left. The Mill Creek camping area is 2.1 miles on the right. The Meat Box trailhead (on the right) and picnic area (on the left) are at mile 2.7. **GPS:** N38 39.64'/W80 21.50'

THE HIKE

Try this loop hike in the spring, when the lightly traveled Meat Box Run Trail is an uninterrupted sea of wildflowers, dominated by trout lily and false hellebore. Wet portions of the trail are home to skunk cabbage. Like most West Virginia forests, invasives are a problem—think multiflora rose—but the trails are generally kept clear here.

The Meat Box Run Trail, marked with red blazes, parallels Meat Box Run as the climb up the mountain begins. The trail follows an old road up the left side of the hollow. A short, steep climb through an area of yellow birch is followed by an easy walk through a stand of hemlock and red spruce. Ferns thrive in the moist understory. After crossing a dry feeder stream, the trail passes through an area of significant storm damage on an

Raven Rocks overlook in Kumbrabow State Forest

easy grade. This is followed by a short, moderate climb into a wet area. The trail crosses many small feeder streams, followed by a hard push to the ridge crest at 1.5 miles. The trail is steep and the slopes are covered with tall, straight hardwoods. On the crest is the junction with the Rich Mountain Fire Trail.

Turn right on the fire road and proceed to a T intersection. Turn right again and follow the fire road to the Raven Rocks Trail. Take this trail along the descending ridgeline to the Raven Rocks overlook, where you get a view of the Mill Creek valley and Mill Ridge across the way. The mountains are covered with a

> No, Kumbrabow is not a Native American word for *neat place to hike*. The state forest is named after three prominent families involved in purchasing the land: KUmp, BRAdy, and BOWers.

mix of deciduous trees and conifers. Raven Rocks is an excellent lunch spot. To return to the trailhead, make a steep descent to CR 219-16, turn right, and follow the road about 0.3 mile to the picnic area.

MILES AND DIRECTIONS

0.0 START at the Meat Box Run trailhead, across from the Meat Box Run Picnic Area. Walk up the hill on an old logging road grade, paralleling Meat Box Run.

1.4 Come to the end of the Meat Box Run Trail at a junction with a doubletrack dirt road. Take a right. In about 100 yards, come to the junction with the Rich Mountain Fire Trail, marked with a sign. Take a right.

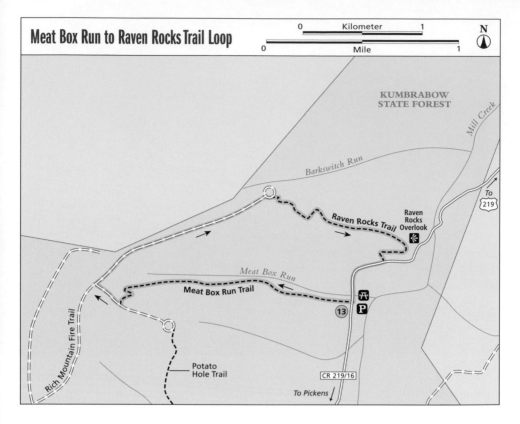

Meat Box Run to Raven Rocks Trail Loop

0   Kilometer   1

0   Mile   1

N

KUMBRABOW STATE FOREST

Mill Creek

Barkswitch Run

To 219

Raven Rocks Trail

Raven Rocks Overlook

Meat Box Run

Meat Box Run Trail

Rich Mountain Fire Trail

13

P

Potato Hole Trail

CR 219/16

To Pickens

2.6   Come to the junction with the Raven Rocks Trail, marked with a sign. Take a right.

3.5   Arrive at a side trail to the Raven Rocks overlook on the left. Check out the overlook and return to this spot to continue. (**FYI:** This would make a good lunch spot.)

3.7   The trail ends at the road and the Raven Rocks trailhead. Take a right on the road and walk back to the picnic area.

4.0   Arrive back at the trailhead.

HIKE INFORMATION

Local information: Randolph County Convention and Visitors Bureau, (304) 636-2780 or (800) 422-3304, www.randolphcountywv.com

Camping: Kumbrabow State Forest operates a 13-site campground, open from Apr 15 through deer rifle season, usually late Nov or early Dec. The forest also has 4- to 8-person cabins for rent.

Local events/attractions: The nearby Swiss-settled town of Helvetia hosts a Mardi Gras–like festival called *Fasnacht* every Tues before Lent, www.helvetiawv.com.

14 CHEAT MOUNTAIN RIDGE TO SHAVERS LAKE TRAIL LOOP

Snowshoe Mountain Resort

WHY GO?

If you've ever visited the nearly mile-high Snowshoe Resort, it was probably in the winter. Take advantage of the "off-season" here and hit some of the 40-plus miles of trails Snowshoe offers. Snowshoe Resort is located on the top of the mountain (most ski resorts are located at the bottom), so start on the ridgetop of Cheat Mountain and follow it to the fire tower, which you can climb for a 360-degree view. Then descend the mountain to Shavers Lake and walk around it to pick up the chairlift—allowing you to hike in the mountains, but never up one. This unique West Virginia hiking experience begins and ends at a mountaintop village full of dining, lodging, and entertainment options.

THE RUNDOWN

Start: Cheat Mountain Ridge Trail trailhead, located at South Mountain
Distance: 6.4-mile loop
Hiking time: About 3 hours
Difficulty: Moderate
Trail surface: Gravel and dirt access road and dirt trail
Best season: Spring through fall
Other trail users: Service vehicles, mountain bikers, Green Zebras (not the animals, the ATVs)
Canine compatibility: Leashed dogs permitted
Land status: Private resort
Nearest town: Snowshoe
Fees and permits: None required to hike at Snowshoe; fee for lift ticket

back to the top of the mountain (purchase at the Depot before hiking)
Schedule: The Ball Hooter chairlift runs from 10 a.m. to 4:30 p.m. on weekends Memorial Day to July, daily July through Labor Day (until 6 p.m. on Sat in July and Aug), weekends after Labor Day through first full weekend of Oct, and daily in the winter.
Maps: Snowshoe Mountain Resort trail map, available at the Depot at Village Center; USGS quad: Cass
Trail contact: Snowshoe Mountain Resort, (877) 441-4386 or www.snowshoemtn.com

FINDING THE TRAILHEAD

From Elkins, take US 219 South/WV 55 West 42.2 miles to WV 66 East. Take a left and drive 0.7 mile to Snowshoe Drive, marked with an entrance sign. Take a left and drive up the mountain 6.8 miles to South Mountain parking (mountaintop check-in). From the parking lot, walk past the southeast corner toward Sawmill Village on the road. The road forks; take the right fork (gravel) to a gate and the trailhead. **GPS:** N38 23.95'/W79 59.64'

THE HIKE

Located at 4,848 feet, Snowshoe receives an average of 180 inches of snow every winter, making it an ideal location for a West Virginia ski resort. Lesser known are the resort's summertime offerings, from downhill mountain biking to concerts to the trails that lead you through the red spruce forests found at this elevation.

The early part of the twentieth century saw massive logging operations in these mountains; the logs were then carried out by rail. Today's names at Snowshoe reflect this logging and railroading past, from Ball Hooter lift (a ball hooter was a person who rolled logs down especially steep slopes) to Powder Monkey lift (a powder monkey was the person who carried explosives) to Gandy Dancer run (a gandy dancer was a worker who laid railroad tracks). In the 1970s, Thomas "Doc" Brigham founded Snowshoe as a ski resort, and today it is the largest ski resort in the Mountain State.

Before heading out on this suggested loop, go to the Depot at Village Center and purchase a "fun pass," which will serve as your lift ticket to get back to the top of the mountain. You can opt for a hike that doesn't require a chairlift back up, but you'll be hiking up either way if you don't purchase your lift ticket beforehand; you can't buy it at the bottom of the mountain.

Begin the hike from the South Mountain area, and walk along Cheat Mountain Ridge Trail—this isn't so much a trail as an access road for service vehicles. More appropriately a cross-country skiing trail or mountain biking trail, hiking along Cheat Mountain Ridge doesn't give you the scenic coziness of a proper trail, but it does afford some views of

The sun sets over the rim of fire at Snowshoe Resort.

the surrounding mountains and gets you where you want to go: to the backcountry hut (complete with an Adirondack chair made of old skis, a picnic table, and views to the south) and then to the fire tower. Climb the fire tower to get a 360-degree view, which includes Snowshoe Resort and its 2-by-5-mile bowl to the west (you can hear the bells ringing from Saint Bernard Chapel) and the Greenbrier River Valley to the east (you can hear the whistle from the Cass Scenic Railroad train). There are also picnic tables here, and it's a good spot for lunch.

After checking out the views from the fire tower, retrace your steps about 100 yards to the Bail Out Trail, marked with a trailhead sign. Descend Cheat Mountain on this trail, which begins in a spruce forest and gives way to a spruce and deciduous forest. The trail goes over roots and rocks, and the open forest floor is largely covered in fern.

> Snowshoe Mountain Resort is named for the snowshoe hare; this area is the southernmost part of its range. This 20-inch animal's coat is brown in the summer and white in the winter.

About halfway down the mountain, the sound of a babbling mountain run becomes your companion for the rest of the trip down to Shavers Lake. Arriving at the lake, you can walk around it in a clockwise or counterclockwise direction. Going clockwise, the trail takes you through the forest some more. You'll see wildlife interpretive signs (and signs of beaver) as well as irises and other wildflowers.

Continue to the other side of the lake, where you can pick up the Ball Hooter lift back to the mountaintop and Village Center. At this point, you're just a few steps away from restaurants, bars, shopping, and other activities in Village Center. Stick around for the sunset—the view is great from the Rimfire Lodge, named for the view of the mountain sunset from here. From Village Center, take a left on Snowshoe Drive and walk a half mile back to South Mountain, where you parked your vehicle.

MILES AND DIRECTIONS

0.0 START at the Cheat Mountain Ridge Trail, located past the southeast corner of the South Mountain parking lot. Walk on a road toward Sawmill Village; the road forks. Take the right fork to the trailhead, which is at the gate across the road. Pass the gate and walk on the road. In about 200 feet, the Main Loop leaves the road to the left. Continue straight on the road.

0.1 The road forks. Take the left fork, following signs for the campsites and backcountry hut.

0.25 Come to a junction with the Snowshoeing Route, which is a grassy lane to the right. Continue straight on the road. (**FYI:** Backcountry campsites are located along the Snowshoeing Route. You can reserve them for a fee.)

0.3 The Main Loop crosses the road, as do other side trails. Continue walking along the road.

2.0 Arrive at the backcountry cabin. This is an option for a rest or lunch, with views to the south.

3.1 After passing some unmarked bulldozer trails, come to the junction with the 6,000 Steps Trail, on the left. It is marked with a trailhead sign. Continue straight, on the road.

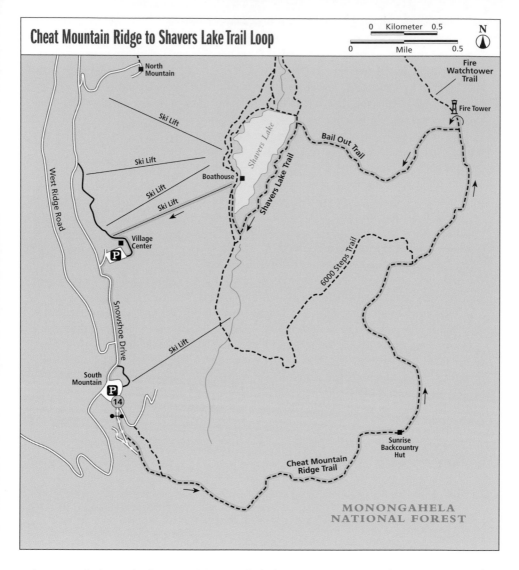

Cheat Mountain Ridge to Shavers Lake Trail Loop

0   Kilometer   0.5

0   Mile   0.5

N

North Mountain

Ski Lift

Ski Lift

Ski Lift

Ski Lift

Boathouse

Shavers Lake

Shavers Lake Trail

Bail Out Trail

Fire Watchtower Trail

Fire Tower

West Ridge Road

Village Center

P

6000 Steps Trail

Snowshoe Drive

Ski Lift

South Mountain

P

14

Sunrise Backcountry Hut

Cheat Mountain Ridge Trail

MONONGAHELA NATIONAL FOREST

3.9 Arrive at the fire tower. You can climb the tower to get a 360-degree view of Snowshoe Mountain Resort to the west and the Greenbrier River Valley to the east. This is a good lunch spot, with picnic tables.

4.0 About 100 yards south of the fire tower (the way you came), take a right onto the Bail Out Trail, marked with a trailhead sign.

5.0 The Bail Out Trail ends at Shavers Lake and the junction with the Shavers Lake Trail. Take a left and walk along the lakeside trail in a clockwise direction. (**Option:** Take a right and circle the lake in a counterclockwise direction.)

5.6 Come to what looks like a T intersection. This is actually a left turn in the trail, away from the lake.

5.7 Cross over Shavers Fork on a footbridge and come to a junction, marked with a Shavers Fork Trail sign. Take a right and follow Shavers Fork downstream, toward the lake.

5.9 The Shavers Lake Trail ends near the bottom of the Ball Hooter chairlift. Take the lift to the top of the mountain. At the mountaintop, walk through Village Center to Snowshoe Drive. Take a left and walk south to the South Mountain parking lot where you began.

6.4 Return to the South Mountain parking lot.

HIKE INFORMATION

Local information: Pocahontas County Convention & Visitors Bureau, (800) 336-7009 or www.pocahontascountywv.com/

Camping: Backcountry camping is available near the Cheat Mountain Ridge Trail. There is also a backcountry cabin along this trail and a wide array of lodging options at the resort, (877) 441-4386 or www.snowshoemtn.com/lodging.

Local events/attractions: Spring through fall, Snowshoe is home to downhill mountain biking, golf, horseback riding, swimming, bungee jumping, and more. It also hosts several festivals, including the Fire on the Mountain Chili Cook-off. In the winter, Snowshoe is a ski resort.

Organizations: Snowshoe Foundation, (304) 572-8500 or www.snowshoefoundation .org

15 THORNY CREEK TRAIL

Seneca State Forest

WHY GO?

Seneca State Forest's 23 miles of trails include sections of the 80.7-mile Greenbrier River Trail and the 330-mile Allegheny Trail. The Thorny Creek Trail loops through the heart of the forest. This trail climbs easily along Thorny Creek through rhododendron tunnels. The sheltered creek bottom along the Thorny Creek Trail is home to a thriving stand of towering white pine and small hemlock and cove hardwoods. Seneca State Forest's campground is considered among the best car camping in West Virginia, so plan more than a day trip.

THE RUNDOWN

Start: Parking lot by boat docks
Distance: 7.3-mile loop, with a 3.9-mile loop option
Hiking time: About 3 to 4 hours
Difficulty: Moderate
Trail surface: Dirt trail with sections along a gravel road
Best season: Spring
Other trail users: Mountain bikers, hunters during hunting season
Canine compatibility: Leashed dogs permitted
Land status: State forest
Nearest town: Marlinton
Fees and permits: None

Schedule: Hiking is available year-round, but the road may be impassable due to snow in the winter.
Maps: Seneca State Forest trail map; USGS quads: Clover Lick, Paddy Knob
Trail contact: Seneca State Forest, (304) 799-6213 or www.senecastateforest.com
Special considerations: Park maps show this loop at 6.0 miles, but it is actually 7.3 miles; deer rifle season late Nov to early Dec

FINDING THE TRAILHEAD

From the intersection of US 219 and US 39 in Marlinton, go east on US 39. Travel 5.4 miles and turn north on WV 28. Proceed 10.3 miles to the Seneca State Forest entrance and office. Continue 1.7 miles to the parking area on the left, just beyond the bridge that passes over the lake spillway. **GPS:** N38 18.36' / W79 56.62'

THE HIKE

Seneca State Forest is named for the Native America tribe that inhabited the area, or at least used it for hunting purposes. Europeans settled the area in the eighteenth century, and a booming logging business was established in the late nineteenth and early twentieth centuries. Today, logging continues in Seneca State Forest as part of its state-mandated mission. However, most timber operations exist far from trails (and must take place at least 200 yards from a trail).

The Thorny Creek Trail, marked with blue circles, begins at the boat docks. A sign marks the trailhead. The trail parallels the left bank of Seneca Lake under a canopy of hemlock trees. From the lake portion of the trail, you can see some of the cabins built in the 1930s by the CCC. These "pioneer cabins" are designed to allow guests to have a quasi-pioneer experience, complete with wood-burning cookstoves and gas lamps, and no electricity or running water (there are hand-pumped water wells).

At the end of the lake (about 0.3 mile), the Fire Tower Trail climbs the ridge to the left. The Thorny Mountain fire tower was built in 1935 and was still in use as late as the 1980s. The Thorny Creek Trail continues in the valley, then ascends the ridge to Loop/Lake Road, which turns south and continues all the way to the park road. Taking a right at the park road and returning directly to Seneca Lake makes for a 3.9-mile hike.

Walking through rhododendrons on the Thorny Creek Trail, Seneca State Forest

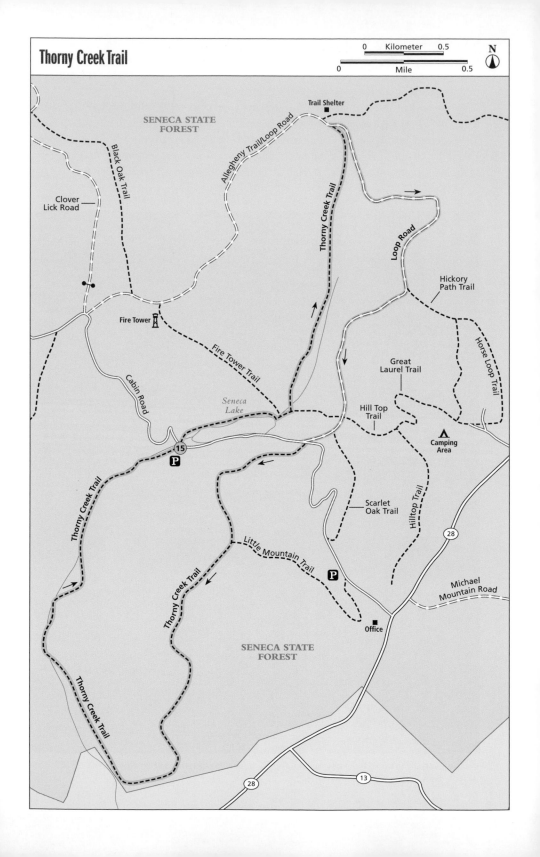

Thorny Creek Trail

0 Kilometer 0.5
0 Mile 0.5

N

SENECA STATE FOREST

Trail Shelter

Allegheny Trail/Loop Road

Black Oak Trail

Clover Lick Road

Thorny Creek Trail

Loop Road

Hickory Path Trail

Fire Tower

Fire Tower Trail

Horse Loop Trail

Cabin Road

Seneca Lake

Great Laurel Trail

Hill Top Trail

Camping Area

15

P

Scarlet Oak Trail

Hilltop Trail

Thorny Creek Trail

Little Mountain Trail

P

28

Thorny Creek Trail

Michael Mountain Road

Office

SENECA STATE FOREST

Thorny Creek Trail

28

13

Continuing south on the Thorny Creek Trail, the path stays atop the ridge until finally descending to Thorny Creek, downstream of Seneca Lake. The final miles of trail parallel the babbling Thorny Creek, which is socked in by lush rhododendron thickets and shaded by hemlock and hardwood trees above.

MILES AND DIRECTIONS

0.0 START at the Thorny Creek Trail trailhead across from the parking lot by the boat docks; there is a trailhead sign. Parallel the lake's edge.

0.3 Pass the Fire Tower Trail on the left, blazed orange. Continue straight.

0.4 Come to a fork with the Hill Top Trail. Take the left fork, following the blue blazes. Soon cross a rickety bridge with caution.

1.6 Come to an old gravel doubletrack road with signs for the Thorny Creek Trail, Lake Road, and fire tower. Take a right and begin walking along the road.

2.5 Pass the Hickory Path Trail on the left. Continue straight.

3.2 Pass the Hill Top Trail on the left and the Lake Trail on the right. Continue straight.

3.3 Pass the Scarlet Oak Trail on the left. Continue straight.

3.4 The gravel road you've been walking is now Loop Road (marked with a sign) and ends here at the park road. Cross the park road. Across the park road, pick up the Thorny Creek Trail again, marked with a sign. (**Option:** You can shorten the hike by taking a right on the park road and walking along the road 0.5 mile back to the trailhead, making it a 3.9-mile loop.)

4.1 Pass the Little Mountain Trail on the left. Continue straight.

5.0 Pass a sign for the Thorny Creek Trail and Lake Road. After this sign, the trail switches back to the left, descends the slope, and comes to a fence line, where it takes a sharp right.

5.4 The trail turns right, away from the fence line, and descends to a run. Cross the run, switching back to the left. Soon the trail parallels Thorny Creek for the remainder of the hike.

7.3 Arrive back at the parking lot.

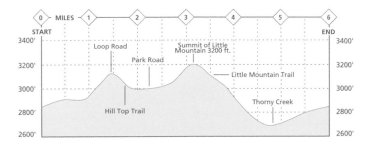

Thorny Creek Trail passes a stand of hemlocks.

HIKE INFORMATION

Local information: Pocahontas County Convention & Visitors Bureau, (800) 336-7009 or www.pocahontascountywv.com

Camping: The state forest has a 10-site campground that is open from Apr 1 to early Dec. Free overnight camping by permission of the superintendent is possible at the shelter on the Allegheny Trail/Loop Road. The forest also has pioneer cabins for rent.

Local events/attractions: The National Radio Astronomy Observatory at Green Bank is 15 miles from Seneca State Forest, www.greenbankobservatory.org/.

16 MINIE BALL TO OVERLOOK TRAIL CIRCUIT

Droop Mountain Battlefield State Park

WHY GO?

Bring the whole gang to Droop Mountain Battlefield State Park, because there really is something here for everyone: the site of one of the largest Civil War battles in West Virginia for the history buff; 4.0 miles of well-maintained footpaths for the hiker; and a playground, picnic area, and overlook tower above the Greenbrier River Valley for a family outing. Combine the park trails for an easy hike that passes by a small mountain bog, scenic overlooks, Civil War–era bunkers, a bear den, a spring, and a rock escarpment.

THE RUNDOWN

Start: Trailhead across road from park office
Distance: 2.25-mile double loop
Hiking time: About 1 hour
Difficulty: Easy
Trail surface: Dirt trail
Best seasons: Apr–May and Sept–Oct
Other trail users: Ghost hunters
Canine compatibility: Leashed dogs permitted
Land status: State park

Nearest town: Marlinton
Fees and permits: None
Schedule: Park is open year-round for day use 6 a.m. to 10 p.m.; office and museum hours are 10 a.m. to 2 p.m. and by request in the winter.
Maps: Droop Mountain Battlefield State Park map; USGS quad: Droop
Trail contact: Droop Mountain Battlefield State Park, (304) 653-4254 or www.droopmountain battlefield.com

FINDING THE TRAILHEAD

Take I-64 to exit 169 and turn north on US 219. Travel 24.5 miles and turn left onto the paved park entrance road at the park sign. Drive 0.1 mile to Park Road at a T intersection, turn right and proceed 0.4 mile to the office and parking area on the left side of the road. **GPS:** N38 06.91'/W80 16.16'

THE HIKE

Droop Mountain Battlefield State Park is situated on a high mountain plateau overlooking the beautiful and vast Greenbrier Valley. Part of the Civil War battlefield has been restored and marked for visitors. A small museum contains artifacts, and a battle reenactment is staged every other year. If you are a nineteenth-century arms aficionado, you know what the names of these trails refer to: a musket was a Civil War–era gun, while the Minie ball was the bullet.

The Minie Ball to Musket Trail Loop begins on the opposite side of the road from the park office. Follow the wide trail to the intersection with the Musket Trail and turn left. Walk about 100 yards to an intersection and turn left on the Minie Ball Trail.

View of the Greenbrier River Valley from the Droop Mountain lookout tower

The Minie Ball Trail descends to the park road. Turn right and follow the road about 50 feet to a sign for the trail, then turn right and enter the woods. Initially the descent is easy, but after a right and left switchback there is a short, steep descent. At the bottom of the descent, the trail makes a right bend and the optional moderate climb to the summit and the tower begins. During the beginning of the climb, you can hear water running under the rocks. The trail crosses a bridge, makes a short climb, and flattens out as it parallels a park road. After crossing another bridge, the trail crosses the park road and begins another short, moderate climb. The trail then crosses the park road a third time and makes a short climb to the summit.

On the summit is a tower that was built in the 1930s by the Civilian Conservation Corps, as well as a picnic area, playground, and toilets. The view to the east from the tower is spectacular. The Musket Trail enters the woods near the playground and drops to cross the park road. The trail is wide and easy to follow. After a right bend, there is a moderate descent into a small hollow dominated by tall cove hardwoods. The trail bends left on the mountain shoulder and drops gradually to the intersection with the Minie Ball Trail. Turn left and make a gradual climb back to the original trail junction.

Pick up the Cranberry Bogs Trail, which passes through a stand of second-growth hardwoods with black birch, red oak, maple, and hickory dominating the canopy. The trail is clear of brush and is easy to follow. There is little elevation gain. The trail enters a stand of tall white pine and black birch. This is the Cranberry Bog, a small wetland located in the middle of the natural area. A sign marks the location. Mountain laurel and rhododendron thrive in the understory.

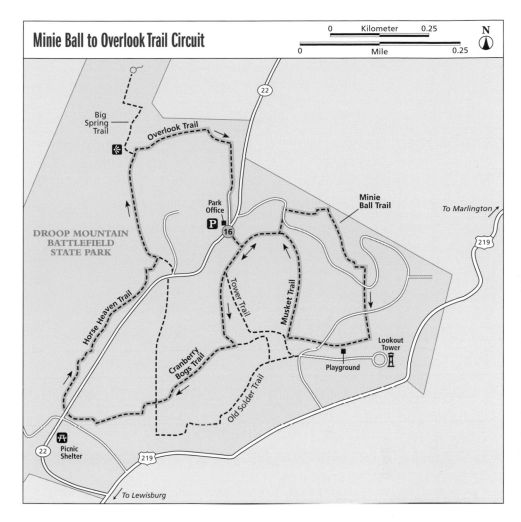

Big Spring Trail

Overlook Trail

Park Office

P

16

Minie Ball Trail

To Marlington ↗

22

219

DROOP MOUNTAIN BATTLEFIELD STATE PARK

Horse Heaven Trail

Tower Trail

Musket Trail

Lookout Tower

Playground

Cranberry Bogs Trail

Old Solder Trail

Picnic Shelter

22

219

To Lewisburg

After crossing the park road again, pick up Horse Heaven Trail, named for the cliffs where the horses killed in the 1863 Battle of Droop Mountain were disposed of. Then join the Overlook Trail, which eventually leads to another expansive view, this time to the west. Also along this trail, you pass through a rocky gap, a rhododendron thicket, an old bear den, and the remains of some Civil War trenches. Most of these features are marked with signs. After the trenches, a short, easy climb leads back to the park office.

MILES AND DIRECTIONS

0.0 START at the trailhead across the road from the park office. A sign marks the trailhead for the Cranberry Bogs, Tower, and Musket Trails. In about 200 feet, come to a junction. Take a left onto the Musket Trail.

0.1 Take a left onto the Minie Ball Trail, which is marked with a sign. In about 50 feet, come to a road. Take a left on the road and walk for another 50 feet, then pick up the trail on the other side of the road, to your right.

0.4 Cross the park road and continue directly on the trail, uphill.

0.5 Cross the park road again and continue ascending to a picnic area and a playground. (**Option:** You can walk to and climb up into the lookout tower from here.)

0.6 By the playground, look for a trailhead sign for the Musket Trail. Take the trail directly into the woods. In about 200 feet, cross the road again.

0.8 Return to the junction with the Minie Ball Trail. Take a left.

0.9 Return to the first trail junction. Continue straight, beginning the Cranberry Bogs Trail, marked with a sign.

1.1 Come to a T intersection. Take a right to stay on the Cranberry Bogs Trail, still marked with a sign.

1.3 Cross the Old Soldier Trail (an old road).

1.4 Come to a fork. The left fork leads to the picnic area. Take the right fork and continue about 150 feet to the park road. On the other side of the road is the trailhead for the Horse Heaven Trail, marked with a sign. Begin the trail.

1.75 Come to a spur on the left, which is a footbridge leading to a bench. Just past this spot, arrive back at the road. Do not cross the road; continue straight on the Horse Heaven Trail, closely paralleling the road.

1.8 Come to a junction with the Overlook Trail. Take a left.

2.0 Come to an overlook platform to your left. (**FYI:** At the overlook is the inter-section with the Big Spring Trail. This short, steep 0.3-mile side trail is an out-and-back hike that leads down the mountain to a spring.) About 100 yards past the overlook, the trail forks. Take the left fork to pass by old trenches.

2.2 At the 28th Ohio Infantry sign, take a right and follow the trail that parallels the road.

2.25 Arrive back at the park office.

HIKE INFORMATION

Local information: Pocahontas County Convention & Visitors Bureau, (800) 336-7009 or www.pocahontascountywv.com

Camping: Droop Mountain Battlefield is a day-use area only. You can camp at nearby Watoga State Park, (304) 799-4087 or www.watoga.com.

Hike tours: Contact the park in advance for a ranger-led hike tour.

17 ARROWHEAD TRAIL TO JESSE'S COVE TRAIL LOOP

Watoga State Park

WHY GO?

Watoga State Park, West Virginia's largest state park, encompasses a total of 10,100 acres. The 330-mile Allegheny Trail snakes along the eastern boundary of the park, and the scenic 80.7-mile Greenbrier River Trail borders its western end. The Arrowhead and Jesse's Cove Trails form a loop that climbs a high ridge to a wooden tower with a view to the west of the Greenbrier River Valley. A pleasant walk along a high ridge leads to a steep drop back to the Greenbrier River. There are other trails to explore in and near Watoga, so you can set up a base camp in the park at one of its two campgrounds or in a cabin if you're looking for more comfortable lodgings.

THE RUNDOWN

Start: Arrowhead Trail trailhead, across from the campground check-in building
Distance: 5.4-mile loop
Hiking time: About 2.5 hours
Difficulty: Moderate
Trail surface: Dirt trail
Best seasons: Apr–May and Sept–Oct
Other trail users: Mountain bikers on the Ann Bailey section of the trail
Canine compatibility: Leashed dogs permitted

Land status: State park
Nearest town: Marlinton
Fees and permits: None
Schedule: Open daily year-round 6 a.m. to 10 p.m. for day use
Maps: Watoga State Park trail map; USGS quads: Denmar, Hillsboro, Lake Sherwood, Marlinton
Trail contact: Watoga State Park, (304) 799-4087 or www.watoga.com
Special considerations: In high water, the last portion of this trail can be impassable.

FINDING THE TRAILHEAD

From the stoplight at the intersection of US 219 and US 39 in Marlinton, proceed south on US 219. Travel 9.4 miles to CR 27 (Seebert Road). Turn left and continue 3.0 miles to a fork in the road, where there is a state park information sign. Take the right fork and go 0.4 mile to the campground check-in. The parking area for the Arrowhead Trail is on the left, directly across the road from the check-in building. Water and restroom facilities are available here. **GPS:** N38 06.95′ / W80 10.60′

THE HIKE

Starting from the appropriately named Riverside Campground, climb the Arrowhead Trail through a forest of small hardwoods and pine. The understory is composed primarily of mountain laurel and blueberry. The grade is moderate as the trail begins climbing a

An old log cabin near the junction of Ann Bailey and Jesse's Cove Trails

finger ridge, but at the beginning of a left bend, the climb quickly changes to grueling as the trail climbs straight up the finger ridge to the Ann Bailey observation tower.

Anne (apparently spelled with or without the *e*) Bailey was a Revolutionary War–era frontierswoman who inspired the 1861 poem "Anne Bailey's Ride." She was alternately known as the White Squaw of the Kanawha Valley and the Heroine of the Kanawha Valley. (The Kanawha, of course, is the river that runs through Charleston.) The wooden observation tower sits at about 2,900 feet and offers a splendid view of the Greenbrier River and the mountains to the west. There is a picnic table in the grassy opening in front of the tower. The Arrowhead Trail ends at the tower, but the narrow, grassy Ann Bailey Trail continues past the tower and along the ridge. No blazes mark the way, but the direction is obvious. The road grade descends a short distance and then begins an easy climb to a small meadow. The forest is an old second-growth stand of upland hardwoods.

At the beginning of the meadow is the small gravestone of Forest S. Workman, who farmed this area before the land was acquired by the state. The meadow also marks the high point of the climb, slightly more than 3,000 feet. The road parallels the meadow a short distance, then drops to the junction with the yellow-blazed Jesse's Cove Trail. A sign marks the junction; turn right and descend off the ridge.

Jesse's Cove Trail follows a narrow old road and descends at a moderate rate a short distance to a left switchback. After the switchback, the trail drops down to an old log cabin located in a small clearing. There is a privy here. Past the cabin, Jesse's Cove Trail begins to parallel Rock Run. About 0.25 mile beyond the cabin, the road disappears and a footpath takes its place. Rock Run tumbles down a narrow, steep-walled ravine. Rhododendron, mountain laurel, and hemlock dominate the scenery within the narrow confines of a creek bed. The trail drops sharply down to the creek and follows the creek bed all the way to its terminus at the Greenbrier River. The trail itself crosses the creek a number of times. In these bottomlands, spring wildflowers are spectacular—expect to see trillium (including red trillium), Dutchman's-breeches, bloodroot, and other spring ephemerals.

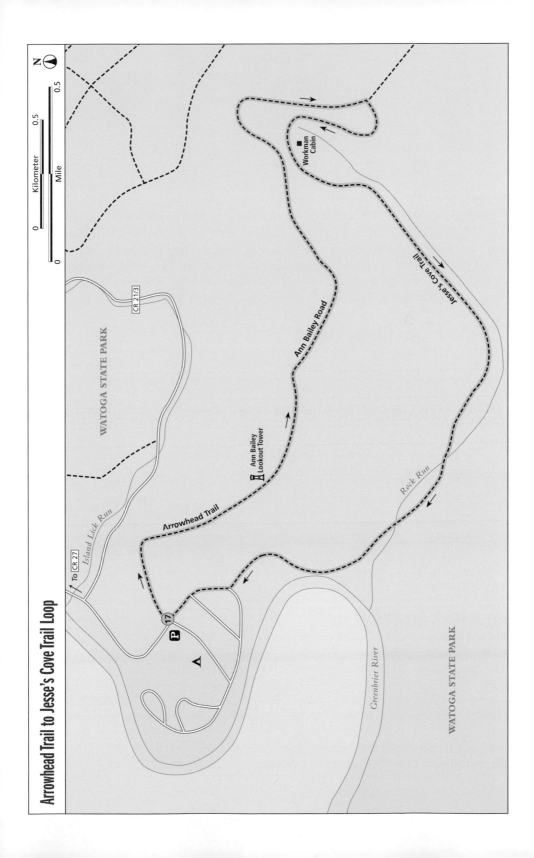

Arrowhead Trail to Jesse's Cove Trail Loop

N

Kilometer
0   0.5   0.5

Mile
0   0.5

WATOGA STATE PARK

CR 21/3

To CR 27

Island Lick Run

Arrowhead Trail

Ann Bailey
Lookout Tower

Ann Bailey Road

Workman
Cabin

Jesse's Cove Trail

Rock Run

Greenbrier River

WATOGA STATE PARK

P

17

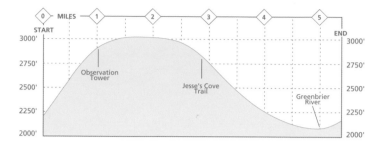

Tall hemlocks line the left side of the creek, while cove hardwoods occupy the right slope. The trail bends right and exits the Rock Run drainage, and the Greenbrier River becomes visible. The trail hugs a steep slope, then makes a steep descent to the river, turns right, and heads upstream. The trail here can be impassable when the Greenbrier is in flood stage. The grade is flat as the trail enters the Riverside Campground at site 6. Turn right on the road and follow it to the campground store.

MILES AND DIRECTIONS

0.0 START at the Arrowhead Trail trailhead, across from the campground check-in. In about 100 feet, come to a T intersection. Take a left on the Arrowhead Trail.

0.25 Come to a three-way junction with a sign marking the Arrowhead Trail. Turn right.

1.1 Arrive at the Ann Bailey Lookout Tower. After checking out the tower and the view of the Greenbrier River Valley, continue straight on the trail; it's unmarked at this point and becomes more of a road grade. It's called the Ann Bailey Trail now.

2.5 Come to the junction with Jesse's Cove Trail. Take a right. On Jesse's Cove Trail you will cross Rock Run several times before the trail curves right as it approaches the Greenbrier River.

5.3 The trail ends at the campground, near site 6. At the campground road, take a right and walk back to the trailhead.

5.4 Arrive back at the trailhead.

HIKE INFORMATION

Local information: Pocahontas County Convention & Visitors Bureau, (800) 336-7009 or www.pocahontascountywv.com

Camping: The park has two campgrounds: Riverside Campground opens Apr 1 and usually closes on the last day of Oct; Beaver Creek Campground opens the week prior to Memorial Day and closes at the end of deer rifle season, usually late Nov/early Dec.

Local events/attractions: Great Greenbrier River Race, April; www.greenbrierriver trail.com

Hike tours: A naturalist leads programs during the summer.

Organizations: Greenbrier River Trail Association, www.greenbrierrivertrail.com

18 BEARTOWN BOARDWALK

Beartown State Park

WHY GO?

Beartown State Park is just 107 acres, but it packs a punch in the scenery department. A maze of sandstone rocks and boulders are strewn about a dense forest. Wind and rain have eroded the deep walls and hallways of rock, surrounded by hemlocks, topped by moss and fern, and pocked with holes and cracks. A 0.5-mile boardwalk takes you through this gem of a park.

THE RUNDOWN

Start: Trailhead across from parking lot
Distance: 0.5-mile lollipop
Hiking time: About 0.5 hour
Difficulty: Easy
Trail surface: Boardwalk with stairs
Best season: Apr through Oct, when the park is open
Other trail users: None
Canine compatibility: Leashed dogs permitted
Land status: State park

Nearest town: Marlinton
Fees and permits: None
Schedule: Open daily year-round 6 a.m. to 10 p.m.; the gate is generally closed dusk to dawn plus in winter due to snow, but the park is still open to foot travel.
Map: USGS quad: Droop
Trail contact: Beartown State Park, (304) 653-4254 or www.beartownstatepark.com

FINDING THE TRAILHEAD

Take I-64 to exit 169 and turn north on US 219. Travel 21.5 miles and turn right at the park sign. Watch carefully for the turn; it appears quite suddenly. Continue 1.6 miles to the parking area. **GPS:** N38 03.11' / W80 16.53'

THE HIKE

Beartown's name comes from the local oral history that colonies of black bears once used pockets in these house-size stone formations as dens. The blocks of sandstone form a maze in this natural area. A boardwalk with interpretive signs explaining the ecology directs you through this unique park. A 150-foot accessible walk also allows wheelchair users to gain access to one of the major overlooks of the park.

The Beartown Boardwalk is a short interpretive hike. Begin across from the parking lot. Walk past the Beartown Boardwalk sign, and begin a gradual descent on a gravel path through a forest of tall second-growth hardwoods. The boardwalk begins about 150 feet from the trailhead. Once on the boardwalk, the trail enters an area of unique rock formations. Turn left at the loop junction and climb a set of stairs into a stand of tall, straight hemlocks (what's left of them, anyway, as many of these trees have succumbed to a pest called the hemlock woolly adelgid). The boardwalk passes over and through numerous small rock crevices. Many of the rocks are covered with elephant ear lichen, some hundreds of years old.

A view from one section of boardwalk to another in Beartown State Park

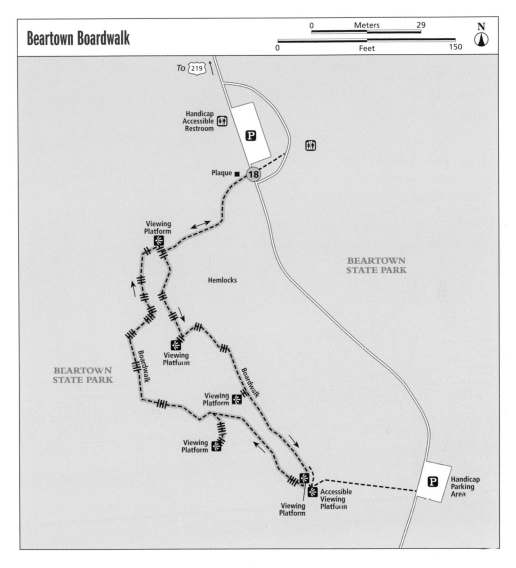

Beartown Boardwalk

0   Meters   29

0   Feet   150

N

To 219

Handicap Accessible Restroom

P

Plaque ■ 18

Viewing Platform

BEARTOWN STATE PARK

Hemlocks

Boardwalk

Viewing Platform

Boardwalk

BEARTOWN STATE PARK

Viewing Platform

Viewing Platform

P   Handicap Parking Area

Accessible Viewing Platform

Viewing Platform

After a short descent, the boardwalk bends right and begins the return trip. The boardwalk is now at the bottom of the rock face. The short cliffs are covered with many small pits, the largest of which could hold a grown person. There are a number of short spurs along the boardwalk, leading you to interpretive signs. The main boardwalk leads back to a short set of stairs and the return trail to the parking lot.

MILES AND DIRECTIONS

0.0 START at the Beartown Boardwalk trailhead across from the parking lot. The boardwalk begins about 150 feet from the trailhead. Descend the stairs and take a left at the beginning of the loop.

0.2 At a three-way junction, turn right and continue down the stairs. (Straight ahead are stairs leading up to the wheelchair-accessible boardwalk.)

0.25 Come to an intersection with a spur trail to the left that squeezes through large rocks to an overlook. Take this left to the overlook, then return to this spot and continue on.

0.4 Return to the junction where you began the loop. Take a left.

0.5 Arrive back at the trailhead.

HIKE INFORMATION

Local information: Pocahontas County Convention & Visitors Bureau, (800) 336-7009 or www.pocahontascountywv.com

Camping: Beartown State Park is day-use only; camping is available nearby at Watoga State Park, (304) 799-4087 or www.watoga.com.

Hike tours: You can request a ranger-led tour in advance.

Honorable Mentions

D BLACKWATER FALLS TRAIL, BLACKWATER FALLS STATE PARK

Your all-but-mandatory first stop in Blackwater Falls State Park is its namesake Blackwater Falls, nearly 60 feet high and even wider. One thing that gives Blackwater Falls a wild feel is the fact that you can only view it by walking to it—no waterfront parking lots, lodges, or trinket shops here. Starting from the trading post parking lot (trinkets here), take the wide, well-traveled trail down, down, and down some more 0.25 mile to a boardwalk and viewing platform. If you time it right (early morning, late evening, weekday, winter), you can even have the place to yourself. Return for a 0.5-mile round-trip hike. Don't forget your camera. For information, contact Blackwater Falls State Park at (304) 259-5216 or (800) CALL-WVA, www.blackwaterfalls.com.

To find the trailhead, start in Davis and take WV 32 to the north side of town. Turn south on CR 29 (Blackwater Falls Road). Go 1.4 miles to a sign for Blackwater Falls and turn left into the parking lot. At the east end of the parking lot you'll find the trailhead. GPS: N39 06.75'/W79 29.02'

E RICH PATCH TRAIL, SENECA STATE FOREST

Come for the camping—it's true that Seneca State Forest has above-average campsites in terms of setting, privacy, and infrastructure (reserve site 8 or 10 if you can)—and stay for the hiking. Try the 3.2-mile Rich Patch Trail loop as a day hike from the campground. (Walk from your campsite along WV 28 north about 1,000 feet to the Little Jim trailhead on the east side of the road, marked with a sign on a gate. The 1-mile Little Jim Trail leads you to the Rich Patch Trail.) If you're not car camping, begin at the Rich Patch Trail trailhead on Michael Mountain Road, which is the first right north of the park office on WV 28 (take Michael Mountain Road 0.75 mile east of WV 28 to the trailhead parking). You can even take it up a notch and do an easy backpacking trip by taking advantage of the hike-in campsite near the junction of the Rich Patch and Little Jim Trails. Look closely at the campsite and you'll find foundations of old CCC buildings from the 1930s. Stop at the park office (304-799-6213 or www.senecastateforest.com) to register and pay for the walk-in campsite if you plan to use it. GPS (Little Jim Trail): N38 18.71'/W79 54.92'

F HONEYBEE TRAIL, WATOGA STATE PARK

The Brooks Memorial Arboretum Trail System in Watoga State Park is a delight. Located near one of the cabin areas in the park, the trail system comprises three trails with signs that identify the surrounding trees. The Dragon Draft and Buckhorn Trails interconnect with the Honeybee Trail, allowing for loop hikes of various lengths. The 4.5-mile Honeybee Trail is a long loop trail around the hollow formed by Two Mile Run. This hike features great ridgetop hiking and a wonderful walk along a lush green creek bottom. Another option is to return on the Dragon Draft Trail and hike along Two Mile Run. For more information, contact Watoga State Park at (304) 799-4087 or go to www .watoga.com.

From the stoplight at the intersection of US 219 and US 39 in Marlinton, proceed south on US 219. Travel 9.4 miles to CR 27 (Seebert Road). Turn left and drive 3.1 miles to a fork in the road. Turn left and continue 1.4 miles to a parking area on the right. There is a large sign for the Brooks Memorial Arboretum. GPS: N38 7.21'/W80 9.41'

MOUNTAIN LAKES REGION

In the geographic center of West Virginia is the Mountain Lakes region. The folded ridges of the Potomac Highlands give way to the high plateau, where over eons of time, water flowing over the land has cut deep gorges into the countryside. Streams that flow out of the Highlands are harnessed and dammed to create the region's many lakes and wildlife management areas.

Even short trails in this region can be very difficult. With so much flat water, it's easy to forget that the ridges can be steep. Take care in planning your trip. Review topo maps, especially contour lines.

Riverside tent camping at Audra State Park

If the day seems too hot for hiking, the Mountain Lakes region is just the place to be. The miles of waterline offer a multitude of swimming or fishing holes.

Camping can be found in many of the region's state park campgrounds. One message of warning: During much of the fall and winter, and possibly some of the spring, wildlife management areas are frequented by hunters. Be careful in the woods, and check for local hunting seasons.

19 PARK VIEW TO FISHERMEN'S TRAIL LOOP

Cedar Creek State Park

WHY GO?

Cedar Creek State Park is named for the creek that flows lazily through its center. Located in the piedmont of West Virginia, the park offers approximately 10 miles of hiking trails. The most popular activity in the park is fishing in both Cedar Creek and the small fishing ponds located near the creek. This lightly used trail is a rugged climb to a ridge crest with a rocky overlook followed by an easy hike along a slow-moving stream.

THE RUNDOWN

Start: Park View Trail trailhead
Distance: 2.1-mile loop
Hiking time: About 1 hour
Difficulty: Moderate due to a steep ascent
Trail surface: Dirt trail
Best season: Spring
Other trail users: Hikers only
Canine compatibility: Leashed dogs permitted
Land status: State park

Nearest town: Glenville
Fees and permits: None
Schedule: Open 6 a.m. to 10 p.m. for day use
Maps: Cedar Creek State Park trail map; USGS quads: Cedarville, Glenville, Normantown, Tanner
Trail contact: Cedar Creek State Park, (304) 462-8517 or www.cedar creeksp.com

FINDING THE TRAILHEAD

From the intersection of US 33 and WV 5 in Glenville, head west on US 33. Travel 4.7 miles to CR 17 (Cedar Creek Road) and turn left. Continue 4.3 miles to the Cedar Creek State Park entrance. Take the park road to the main office on the right. Parking is available there. Walk back to CR 17, then cross the road and pass the state park sign. You will find the marked trailhead for the Park View Trail across the road to your left, past the curve. **GPS:** N38 56.46' / W80 51.40'

THE HIKE

The Park View Trail, marked with blue blazes, begins with a steep climb that has but one purpose: to reach the ridge crest. The first section of the climb leads to a small rock outcrop with a nice view to the south when the leaves are off the trees. The trail continues to climb to the crest of a high knoll, gaining 460 feet in 0.6 mile. Small pine, chestnut oak, and cedar line the trail. Some oak trees have huge round burls.

After cresting the narrow knoll, the ridge becomes wider and the trail begins following an old skid road as it starts the long descent back to Cedar Creek. At times the crest is narrow and rocky, at others it is wide and rounded. Large knurled oak trees stand as sentinels along the crest. Near the end of the trail, a series of short, steep descents leads to the road.

Walking along a fishing pond at Cedar Creek State Park

Cross the road to the small parking lot and drop down to the river. There is a mowed trail along the riverbank. Turn left on the Fishermen's Trail and begin an easy walk back to the park office. This trail is a little like the creek: It seems in no hurry to get anywhere. It weaves in and out of the sycamores that line the river, eventually passing the ponds on the left. The baseball field marks the end of the trail. You can see the park office from the baseball field.

MILES AND DIRECTIONS

0.0 START at the Park View Trail trailhead, marked with a sign. Walk up the slope.

0.2 Arrive at a rock outcropping before the very top of the ridge. Then continue to the top of the ridge and follow it.

1.3 After a series of short, steep descents from the ridge, cross the road, trending left. Pass a sign that says No Hunting and walk down stone steps to the Fishermen's Trail, which parallels the creek.

2.1 After passing by the fishing ponds, come to the end of the trail near the baseball field. You can see the park office from here. Walk across the field to the office and parking.

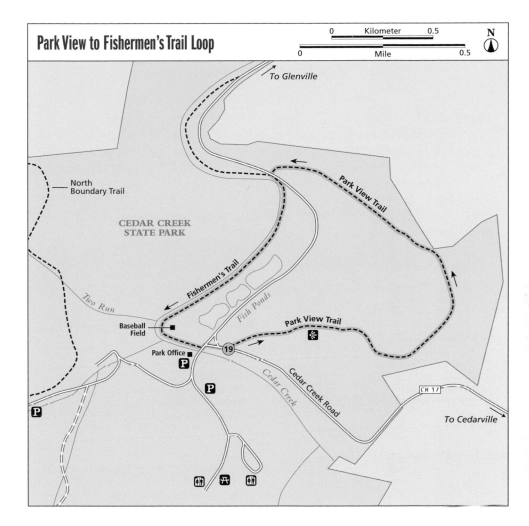

Park View to Fishermen's Trail Loop

CEDAR CREEK STATE PARK

North Boundary Trail

Park View Trail

Fishermen's Trail

Two Run

Fish Ponds

Baseball Field

Park Office

Park View Trail

Cedar Creek

Cedar Creek Road

CR 17

To Glenville

To Cedarville

HIKE INFORMATION

Local information: *Gilmer County government,* www.gilmercounty.wv.gov
Camping: Camping is available from mid-Apr to Oct. The park has 48 campsites.
Local events/attractions: The West Virginia Folk Festival in Glenville begins on the third Thurs in June, (304) 462-8900 or www.wvstatefolkfestival.com/.

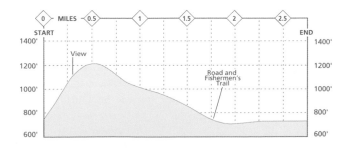

20 ALUM CAVE TRAIL

Audra State Park

WHY GO?

The ease-to-scenery ratio is in your favor at Audra State Park. This short loop hike takes you through a hemlock and rhododendron forest; parallels the swift, boulder-strewn Middle Fork River; and leads you via boardwalk under a massive recess cave. Once you've finished your hike—complete with finding your own personal swimming hole—bed down for the night at the campground along the class-IV Middle Fork.

THE RUNDOWN

Start: Trailhead from the first picnic area as you enter the park
Distance: 2.1-mile loop
Hiking time: About 1 hour
Difficulty: Easy
Trail surface: Rocky dirt trail with a section of boardwalk
Best season: Spring
Other trail users: Mountain bikers
Canine compatibility: Leashed dogs permitted

Land status: State park
Nearest town: Buckhannon
Fees and permits: None
Schedule: Open 6 a.m. to 10 p.m. for day use
Maps: Audra State Park map; USGA quad: Audra
Trail contact: Audra State Park, (304) 457-1162 or www .audrastatepark.com

FINDING THE TRAILHEAD

Take US 33 east from Buckhannon 12 miles and turn north on Talbott Road (CR 17). There is a sign for the state park here. Travel 2.0 miles and turn left at a fork on Chestnut Flats Road (CR 54). Go 3.0 miles to a T intersection and turn left onto Audra Park Road (unmarked). Continue 4.8 miles and turn right into the first picnic area. Look for the trailhead sign downhill to your right as you get to the halfway point on the picnic area loop road. **GPS:** N39 02.39' / W80 03.76'

THE HIKE

To reach the trailhead, follow the one-way loop road about halfway through the picnic area. Look for a trailhead sign to your right. The sign marks both the trail (right) and cave (left). This hike description follows the trail going right (counterclockwise), saving the best for last. The trail begins as a wide path that meanders through a forest of tall upland hardwoods. The grade is easy, and the trail is well maintained.

After approximately 0.3 mile there is a bench on the left, then the trail contours just below the summit of an unnamed knob on the right. Small hemlock and beech trees fill the understory. The trail wraps around to the west side of the ridge. On the left is a steep escarpment that drops to the Middle Fork River. The trail now begins a moderate descent to the river. Large boulders dot the steep slope. During the descent, the hardwoods are left behind and tall, straight hemlocks begin to dominate the canopy.

Under Alum Cave

Rhododendron thickets crowd the understory. Just before reaching the river, the trail passes through a narrow rock crevice and switchbacks to the right.

The trail begins to parallel the wide, swift-flowing Middle Fork River. This stretch is very scenic, and small rapids and riffles create a pleasant sound while hiking the riverside. Many moss-covered rocks and boulders are scattered about, and tree roots drape a number of the rocks along the stream. Several small side trails lead down to the river. About 0.3 mile after reaching the river, the trail begins to climb away from its bank. The climb is easy and ends in a small clearing overlooking the river. The trail splits here, with both forks leading to the same location. The lower fork is the proper trail, which descends back toward the river. Near the river, there is a set of stone steps, followed by a massive recess cave, named Alum Cave. A boardwalk leads under the overhanging cave to the opposite side.

> Audra is a Lithuanian word for "storm."

The trail bends left and makes a very short climb to a trail junction. Continue straight and make a short climb out of the hemlocks and back into the hardwood forest. Once in the hardwoods, the picnic area is only a short distance away. The trail ends at the signpost in the picnic area.

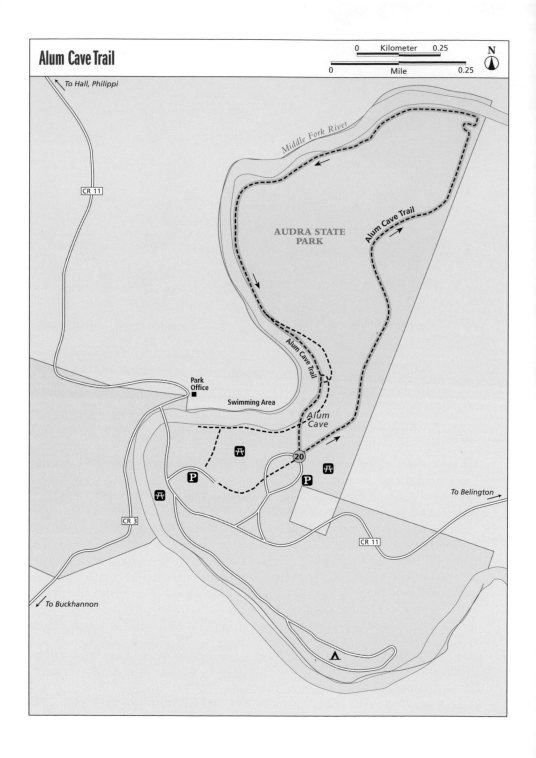

Alum Cave Trail

0 Kilometer 0.25
0 Mile 0.25

N

To Hall, Philippi

CR 11

Middle Fork River

AUDRA STATE PARK

Alum Cave Trail

Alum Cave Trail

Park Office

Swimming Area

Alum Cave

20

P

P

CR 3

CR 11

To Belington

To Buckhannon

MILES AND DIRECTIONS

0.0 START at the trailhead from the first picnic area, about halfway around the paved loop road. From the road, walk to the trailhead sign, which marks the beginning of the loop. Take a right, walking the loop in a counterclockwise direction.

1.0 At a moss-covered tulip tree, the trail takes a sharp left, passing through a gap in two rocks. The river is within earshot. After passing through the gap, the trail takes a right switchback and descends to the river. Follow the trail upstream. There are a number of side trails leading to the river.

1.7 A fork with a less-traveled trail is to the left. Stay right, nearer the river.

1.9 Come to a four-way junction. Take a right, passing a sign that reads FIRES IN FIREPLACES ONLY, and descend stone steps to the boardwalk. This takes you along the Lower Cave Trail under Alum Cave.

2.0 Exit the cave and come to another four-way junction, with the Upper Cave Trail. Continue straight, going uphill.

2.1 Return to the trailhead marker. Take a right and walk a few feet to the picnic area road.

HIKE INFORMATION

Local information: Upshur County Convention and Visitors Bureau, (304) 473–1400 or www.visitbuckhannon.org

Camping: The park's campground has 67 tent and trailer spaces, and is open from mid-Apr to mid-Oct.

Local events/attractions: The West Virginia State Wildlife Center is 12 miles south of Buckhannon; (304) 924–6211 or www.wvdnr.gov/wildlife/wildlifecenter.shtm.

21 REVERIE TO TRAMONTANE TRAIL LOOP

Holly River State Park

WHY GO?

Holly River State Park's many mountain streams create a beautiful, lush green environment. These remote, deep woods provide habitat for a wide variety of plant and animal species. Listen for deep forest birds like the black-throated green warbler, expect to see deer, and don't be surprised if you even catch sight of a black bear. The park offers an extensive 42-mile trail system with hikes for the beginner as well as trails that will challenge even the most seasoned hiker. This steep loop travels behind a small waterfall, parallels Crooked Fork as it crashes through rocks and rhododendrons, and journeys into the past as it travels by an old homestead site.

THE RUNDOWN

Start: Reverie Trail trailhead, near the campground entrance
Distance: 6.25-mile loop
Hiking time: About 4 hours
Difficulty: Difficult due to the steepness of trails
Trail surface: Dirt trail
Best seasons: Apr–May or Sept–Oct
Other trail users: Hikers only
Canine compatibility: Leashed dogs permitted

Land status: State park
Nearest town: Webster Springs
Fees and permits: None
Schedule: Open daily 6 a.m. to 10 p.m.
Maps: Holly River State Park map and trail guide; USGS quads: Goshen, Hacker Valley
Trail contact: Holly River State Park, (304) 493-6353 or www.hollyriver.com

FINDING THE TRAILHEAD

 At the intersection of WV 4 and WV 20 in Rock Cave, travel south on WV 20 about 18.5 miles to the park entrance. Turn left and proceed 0.8 mile to the campground entrance on the right. Park off the side of the campground entrance road. The trailhead for the Reverie Trail is across the park road from the campground entrance. **GPS:** N38 40.04′ / W80 21.73′

THE HIKE

The loop begins on the park entrance road just opposite the entrance to the picnic and camping area. There is a sign for the Reverie Trail, which is marked with yellow blazes and follows an old road into the woods. After 50 feet, the High Rock Trail splits off to the right. Big Run is on the left, and rhododendron crowds the trail on the right. A gradual climb leads up a narrow steep-walled hollow. The trail is rocky through this section.

After two quick creek crossings, the trail enters a small meadow called Dreamers Meadow. Two small streams come together here, and the trail climbs a short, steep ridge between them. The climb continues to the intersection with an old road. The road

The Crooked Fork

makes a switchback, but the trail continues straight. After crossing a small creek, the trail climbs a steep embankment. Stone steps have been placed into the hillside. After a left switchback, there is a moderate climb to Tecumseh Falls, which pours over a recess cave.

The trail passes under the rock overhang and behind the falls, then turns right and climbs to the top of the rock overhang. This is a short, moderate climb. Cross the creek and climb to the utility corridor. After two short, steep climbs, the Reverie Trail crests the ridge and passes to the opposite side. Contouring just below the crest, the trail passes through a hollow and around the end of the bowl before climbing back to the ridge.

There is a steep descent down the other side. Several quick switchbacks lead down the ridge to a primitive campsite. Here you'll find a fire circle, table, and a spring. Look for the damp area in the ground and a rock to find the spring. It is advisable to boil or filter the water. A sign for the Reverie Trail is on the other side of the primitive camp. Entering a narrow hollow with many small rock overhangs, the trail begins a gradual descent, which quickly changes to a very steep descent. You can hear a small creek on the left crashing down the mountainside. At the end of this steep descent is a road. A right heads back to the campground and cabins.

Cross the road and drop down to the Laurel Fork. The junction with the Wilderness Trail is just beyond the road. To shorten the loop to 3.4 miles, turn right at the trail junction and follow the blue blazes back to the park facilities. To continue the loop, turn left on the Wilderness Trail and follow the Laurel Fork upstream a short distance. Cross the stream on a footbridge and begin paralleling the trout-laden Crooked Fork along a series of small tumbling cascades. Hemlocks tower overhead and rhododendron crowds the trail and the creek bank. Cross a small feeder creek on a bridge. Many boulders are draped with tree roots and moss here. The trail begins to climb away from the creek to a large rock outcrop. Three switchbacks complete this climb.

On the crest, a spur trail leads to Tenskwatawa Falls and Potato Knob. At the junction is a sign for the park headquarters. Turn right and follow the red and blue blazes. After an easy climb, the trail drops over the ridge and into a wide hollow. Large boulders dot the landscape. The gradual descent continues to a small creek. Running cedar carpets the forest floor as far as the eye can see. After crossing the creek, the Wilderness Trail intersects the Tramontane Trail.

To continue the long loop, go straight on the Tramontane Trail, marked with yellow blazes, and climb gradually to an old homestead. The site has a small cemetery and some great stonework, the remains of an old springhouse. There is even an old holly tree, and several large stumps of old chestnut trees still survive.

Past the homestead, the trail climbs out of the hollow to the ridge crest. Cruise along the crest of the ridge to an area with several trail junctions. Follow the yellow-blazed Tramontane Trail to the U-turn and begin a steep descent into the bowl the crest has been paralleling. After several switchbacks, the trail drops to a small creek and parallels the creek a short distance before crossing it. On the left is Mystic Falls. Soon after this the trail ends, and you must follow the road back to the parking area.

MILES AND DIRECTIONS

0.0 START at the Reverie Trail trailhead, marked with a sign. There are yellow and orange blazes here. Walk into the woods, following the yellow-blazed Reverie Trail. In about 50 yards, arrive at a junction where the High Rock Trail goes right. Continue straight, paralleling the stream.

0.8 Pass through Dreamers Meadow, marked with a sign.

0.9 After a steep ascent, the trail joins a road grade. The trail and road grade split; continue straight, leaving the road grade and following the yellow blazes.

1.1 Arrive at Tecumseh Falls. The trail passes behind the falls, under the recess cave, and then climbs the ridge.

1.3 Cross an old power-line right-of-way. Continue straight.

1.9 Arrive at a primitive campsite. (**FYI:** There is a spring here; look for the damp ground and a rock. The springwater comes out near the rock. It is best to treat the water before drinking it.)

2.3 The trail descends to gravel Pickens Road. Cross the road, picking up the trail again. There is a sign here for the cabins. (**Option:** You can take a right on Pickens Road and return directly to the trailhead for a shorter 3.4-mile hike.)

2.4 Come to the junction with the Wilderness Trail, blazed blue and marked with a sign. Take a left and begin paralleling the Crooked Fork upstream. You will cross over two footbridges in the next 0.3 mile.

3.4 Come to a fork marked with a Wilderness Trail sign and a sign indicating a spur trail to the fire tower and the Railroad Grade Trail. Both trails are blazed blue. Take a right, continuing on the Wilderness Trail.

3.6 Come to a three-way junction. Take a right, toward the park headquarters. The trail is now blazed both blue and red.

Reverie to Tramontane Trail Loop

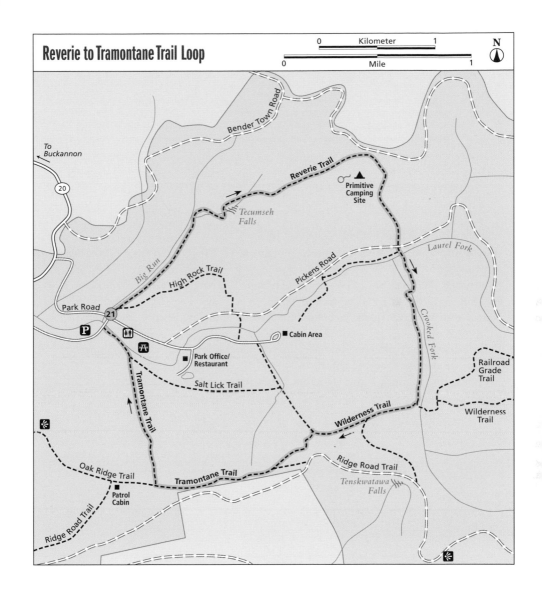

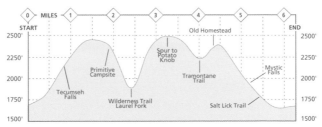

4.3 Come to another three-way junction. Cabins are to the right here, marked with a sign. Continue straight to begin the Tramontane Trail, blazed yellow. (*FYI:* Look across the drainage to your left for old stone fences/walls.)

5.2 Come to a four-way junction at the top of the mountain. Take a right, continuing on the yellow-blazed Tramontane Trail.

5.9 Descend to the junction with the Salt Lick Trail, which goes right. Continue straight, crossing a footbridge. Arrive at the Tramontane Trail trailhead, marked with a sign, at a junction with a paved footpath. Take a left onto the paved path and then another left across a footbridge over the creek.

6.0 End at the large picnic area. Walk the driveway back to the main park road and take a left.

6.25 Arrive back at the trailhead.

HIKE INFORMATION

Local information: Webster County Tourism, (304) 847-2145 or www.visitwebster wv.com

Camping: The park has an 88-site campground. Camping is available from the first week in Apr through the first week in Nov.

Local events/attractions: Webster County Woodchopping Festival, www.wood choppingfestival.org

Hike tours: The park naturalist offers programming in the summer, including an introduction to backpacking course.

Organizations: Holly River State Park Foundation; www.hollyriver.org/

Honorable Mentions

G STONE TROUGH TO TWO RUN TRAIL LOOP, CEDAR CREEK STATE PARK

Slow-moving Cedar Creek is the heart of Cedar Creek State Park. But the flat, narrow creek bottom quickly gives way to tree-covered ridges and steep narrow hollows. The rolling mountains of the park offer wonderful opportunities for backwoods hiking and solitude. This trail combination is a 4-mile loop through the backcountry of the park, complete with rugged climbs and few blazes. The Stone Trough Trail begins at site 7 in the campground. About a mile into the hike, you will come across a hand-carved stone trough, estimated to be more than a hundred years old. You can return on the Stone Trough Trail directly for a 2.25-mile loop. Alternately, at the junction with the Two Run Trail, take a left and return on this trail to complete the 4-mile loop. For more information, including a park trail map, go to www.cedarcreeksp.com or call (304) 462-7158.

To find the trailhead, at the intersection of US 33 and WV 5 in Glenville, head west on US 33. Travel 4.7 miles to CR 17 (Cedar Creek Road) and turn left. Continue 4.3 miles to the Cedar Creek State Park entrance. Take the park road to the campground gate, and park on the left near the gate. GPS: N38 52.83'/W80 51.98'

H HEVENERS ORCHARD TO CAIRNS TRAIL, STONEWALL JACKSON RESORT STATE PARK

Every hiker knows what a cairn is: a pile of rocks placed by previous hikers to help you find the trail. The idea of a cairn takes on a whole new meaning at Stonewall Jackson Resort State Park, however. The Cairns Trail is home to rock cairns—or stone walls, depending on how they look to you—whose origin is unknown. Even if they're not much to look at after all these years, other features on the trail—like pink lady's slippers and other wildflowers—are. For more information, go to www.stonewallresort.com or call (304) 269-7400.

From I-79 exit 91 in Roanoke, travel east on US 19 (State Park Road). Go 2.7 miles to the park entrance. Turn left and go to the entrance station and park there. (There is a fee to enter the park.) Walk just past the entrance station and take the first left, Heveners Orchard Road. Take this road 0.1 mile to the trailhead on the left. Begin hiking on the Heveners Orchard Trail, which is blazed with a red apple. You'll see some rock walls within the first mile. Take this trail 1.9 miles to a junction with the Cairns Trail on the left, blazed with a yellow square. Take a left onto the Cairns Trail. You'll see the old rock piles at about mile 3.3. Take the Cairns Trail to mile 4.4, where it ends at the park road. Take a right and walk south on the road 1.2 miles back to your car (or set up a car or bike shuttle). GPS: N38 56.50'/W80 30.03'

NEW RIVER / GREENBRIER VALLEY

The New River/Greenbrier Valley is often what comes to mind when out-of-staters think of West Virginia: gorge country. Southern West Virginia is characterized by high, rocky ridges and deep, whitewater-filled gorges. Kayakers flock by the thousands to run the region's rapids. Rock climbers travel from near and far to test the crags of the New River Gorge, one of the premier climbing areas in the eastern United States. Perhaps better known for whitewater rafting and rock climbing, the New River Gorge National River contains more than 70,000 acres of land bordering the waterway. This land, managed by the National Park Service, contains 80-plus miles of hiking trails.

With everything the region offers the outdoor enthusiast, it all seems to exist at two distinct speeds: fast and slow. Although there are miles of fast, world-class whitewater, the paddler can find even more miles of tranquil, slow-moving water. Rock climbers can

The famous New River Gorge Bridge

clamber and sweat their way out of a vertical gorge, while hikers follow the babbling of a trout stream as it descends into the gorge more slowly. Ridgetop hikes might meander on the high plain before diving off the ridge with the sole purpose of getting the hiker to the bottom in the least number of steps. The choice is yours. Do you want to escape from the hustle and bustle, or do you have the need for speed?

Many charming campsites can be found at each of the areas described in this region, which is also home to two of West Virginia's resort state parks: Pipestem and Twin Falls. These parks pamper you with restaurants, lodges, golf courses, and fishing lakes—everything the discriminating hiker might need, and then some.

Trips to town in the area will doubtless find you passing through Beckley and Bluefield. These small, quaint towns contain all the necessary services one might require: restaurants, hotels, stores, and so on. Fayetteville, which caters to the rafters and climbers who frequent the New River Gorge, is capable of meeting your outfitting needs. You can hire guides here if you would like some professional help with your trip.

22 ISLAND IN THE SKY TRAIL

Babcock State Park

WHY GO?

The grist mill at Babcock State Park is perhaps one of the most photographed structures in West Virginia; in fact, it's an icon of the Mountain State. Toss your camera in a bag and start on the Island in the Sky Trail, which gains elevation to an overlook of Glade Creek. Start and end at the grist mill, walking by sandstone outcroppings along the way. Spend some time exploring the working mill and taking photos before heading out on the trail.

THE RUNDOWN

Start: Island in the Sky trailhead behind the grist mill
Distance: 1.0-mile out-and-back
Hiking time: About 30 minutes
Difficulty: Easy
Trail surface: Dirt trail with a short ladder and steep sections
Best seasons: Spring and fall, or winter after snowfall
Other trail users: Hikers only
Canine compatibility: Leashed dogs permitted
Land status: State park
Nearest town: Fayetteville

Fees and permits: None
Schedule: Although the park's facilities are closed from the end of Oct through mid-Apr, park roads and trails can be used during these times. Most park roads are graded to facilitate cross-country skiing during winter months.
Maps: Babcock State Park map and trail guide; USGS quads: Danese, Fayetteville, Thurmond, Winona
Trail contact: Babcock State Park, (304) 438-3004 or www.babcocksp.com

FINDING THE TRAILHEAD

From the intersection of US 19 and US 60 north of Fayetteville, turn east on US 60; it joins with WV 41 at mile 6.9. At mile 9.6, take a right where WV 41 splits off to the south. From the split, go 3.7 miles to the state park entrance on the right. Follow the main park road downhill to the grist mill, staying to the left of two intersections along the way. The park headquarters and restaurant are located on the right side of the road at the bottom of the hill; park in this lot. Cross the bridge by foot to the grist mill. The trailhead is behind the mill. **GPS:** N37 58.77' / W80 56.81'

THE HIKE

The Glade Creek Grist Mill is a reconstructed mill made up of components of three former grist mills. The basic structure comes from the old Stoney Creek Grist Mill, which was originally constructed in 1890. Out of the 500 mills that West Virginia was once home to, only a relative few remain. The Glade Creek Grist Mill is perhaps the most beautiful and certainly the most famous of them all. The mill is the centerpiece of Babcock State Park, and a great starting point. From there, hike some of the 20-plus miles of trails in the park, go trout fishing in Glade Creek, camp or rent a cabin, and, of

The iconic grist mill at
Babcock State Park

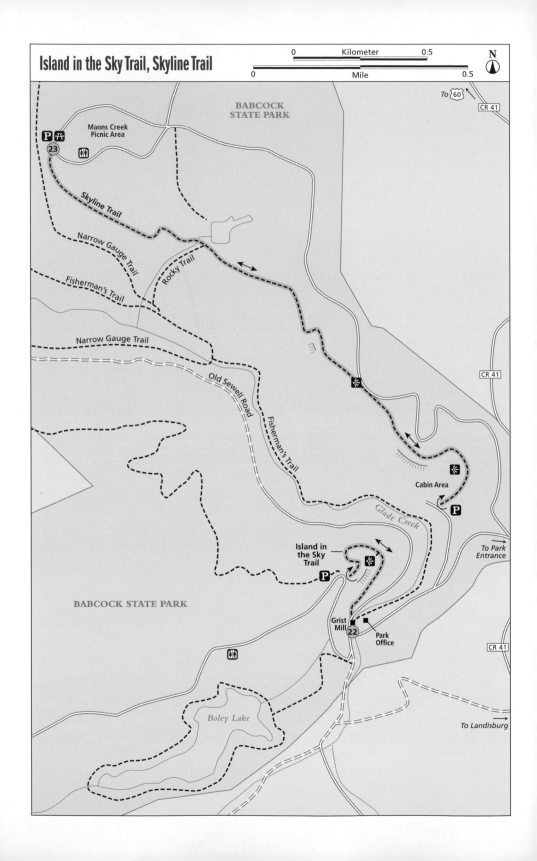

Kilometer

Mile

N

To 60

CR 41

BABCOCK
STATE PARK

P 23

Manns Creek
Picnic Area

Skyline Trail

Narrow Gauge Trail

Rocky Trail

Fisherman's Trail

Narrow Gauge Trail

Old Sewell Road

Fisherman's Trail

CR 41

Glade Creek

Cabin Area

P

To Park
Entrance

Island in
the Sky
Trail

P

BABCOCK STATE PARK

Grist
Mill

22

Park
Office

CR 41

Boley Lake

To Landisburg

course, bring your camera for photographing the mill and then the sunset from Manns Creek Picnic Area.

You can start this easy 1.0-mile hike from right behind the grist mill or from the trailhead parking area described here. Walk in a forest of hardwoods, hemlocks, and an understory of rhododendron. You will also walk atop and around sandstone rock outcroppings. There is a gazebo at the top of one rock outcropping that gives you a view of the swift-moving Glade Creek below. Plan to spend some time checking out the fully functional mill while you're here.

MILES AND DIRECTIONS

0.0 START at the Island in the Sky trailhead sign behind the grist mill. Walk steeply uphill, passing rock outcrops on your left.

0.25 Ascend to the top of the rocks and take a spur trail straight to the overlook and gazebo. Return to the main trail and go right.

0.3 Walk along the bottom of more rock outcrops and then climb up a ladder; walk between some more rocks.

0.5 The trail ends at the road. Turn around and return the way you came.

1.0 Return to the trailhead at the grist mill.

HIKE INFORMATION

Local information: New River Gorge Convention & Visitors Bureau, (800) 927-0263 or www.newrivergorgecvb.com

Camping: Babcock State Park has a 51-site campground located off WV 41, north of the main camp entrance. The campground is open from mid-Apr until the end of Oct, weather permitting.

Hike tours: The park naturalist leads hikes and provides other programming in the summer.

23 SKYLINE TRAIL

Babcock State Park

WHY GO?

Though you spend most of your time in a hardwood and rhododendron forest, this flat ridge trail follows the edge of the cliff, allowing for a number of expansive vistas over the Glade Creek valley. End your hike by returning to the Manns Creek overlook, which is a popular place to watch the sun set to the west.

THE RUNDOWN

See the map on page 108.
Start: Skyline Trail trailhead at the Manns Creek Picnic Area
Distance: 4-mile out–and-back
Hiking time: About 2 hours
Difficulty: Moderate
Trail surface: Flat dirt trail
Best season: Fall
Other trail users: Hikers only
Canine compatibility: Leashed dogs permitted
Land status: State park
Nearest town: Fayetteville
Fees and permits: None

Schedule: Although the park's facilities are closed from the end of Oct through mid-Apr, park roads and trails can be used during these times. Most park roads are graded to facilitate cross-country skiing during winter months.
Maps: Babcock State Park map and trail guide; USGS quads: Danese, Fayetteville, Thurmond, Winona
Trail contact: Babcock State Park, (304) 438-3004 or www.babcocksp.com

FINDING THE TRAILHEAD

From the intersection of US 19 and US 60 north of Fayetteville, turn east on US 60; it joins with WV 41 at mile 6.9. At mile 9.6, WV 41 splits off, heading south. Go 3.7 miles to the state park entrance on the right. There is a large sign at the entrance to the park. From the park entrance, take the first road on the right and drive 1.6 miles to a four-way intersection. Continue straight 0.3 mile to the Manns Creek Picnic Area and parking. The trailhead is on the northwest side of the parking lot, marked with a sign. **GPS:** N37 59.70' / W80 57.51'

THE HIKE

From the overlook at the Manns Creek Picnic Area parking, turn south and find the trailhead, marked with a sign and a gold blaze. Enter the woods, staying near the edge of the ridge.

The trail itself continues mostly in the forest. Walk by large sandstone boulders and occasionally come to one of the rocky overlooks, from which you can see the Glade Creek valley below. Pass the junction with the Rocky Trail and cross over a stream; continue in an oak forest with some rhododendrons and mountain laurels in the mix.

Past the halfway point, there's an overlook near the road in an open meadow area with benches. This is a good place for a rest and a snack. Continue along the ridge

The view from the
overlook on Skyline Trail

and come to some other decent overlooks. At about 1.7 miles, the trail reaches its last overlook and then turns back into the woods and begins a slow descent. The rhododendrons become denser here as you take some rock stairs down to the trailhead at the cabin area, not far above Glade Creek itself. Return the way you came. It's nice to time the hike so that you finish where you began in time to watch the sun set over Manns Creek to the west.

MILES AND DIRECTIONS

0.0 START at the Manns Creek Picnic Area trailhead, marked with a trailhead sign. Walk into the woods, paralleling the edge of the ridge.

0.5 Pass the junction with the Rocky Trail and a stream. Continue straight.

1.3 Come to an open area with benches and an overlook.

1.7 Come to the last of the overlooks; a spur trail leads to the overlook. The main trail soon begins its descent.

2.0 Reach the trailhead at the cabin area. Turn around and return the way you came.

4.0 Arrive back at the trailhead.

HIKE INFORMATION

Local information: New River Gorge Convention & Visitors Bureau, (800) 927–0263 or www.newrivergorgecvb.com

Camping: Babcock State Park has a 51-site campground located off WV 41, north of the main camp entrance. The campground is open from mid-Apr until the end of Oct, weather permitting.

Hike tours: The park naturalist leads hikes and provides other programming in the summer.

24 LONG POINT TRAIL

New River Gorge National River

WHY GO?

The beauty of the Long Point Trail is that it combines the ease of a walk in the park with a view as if you just climbed a mountain. After a flat walk through the forest, you arrive at Long Point, with a hikers-only view of the iconic New River Gorge Bridge in front of you and the whitewater-laden New River nearly 1,000 feet below—still close enough to hear the screams of delight coming from the rafters. Pack a lunch and plan to hang out here for a while.

THE RUNDOWN

Start: Long Point Trail trailhead
Distance: 3.2-mile out-and-back
Hiking time: 1.5 hours
Difficulty: Easy
Trail surface: Dirt and rock trail
Best season: Fall
Other trail users: Mountain bikers
Canine compatibility: Leashed dogs permitted
Land status: National river (National Park Service)
Nearest town: Fayetteville

Fees and permits: None
Schedule: The park is open 24/7 year-round. The Canyon Rim visitor center is open 9 a.m. to 5 p.m. daily except Thanksgiving, Christmas, and New Year's Day.
Maps: Park Service maps; USGS quad: Fayetteville
Trail contact: New River Gorge National River, (304) 465-0508 or www.nps.gov/neri

FINDING THE TRAILHEAD

From the intersection of US 19 and WV 16 in Fayetteville, turn south on WV 16 and drive 0.7 mile to Gatewood Road (CR 9). Turn left and go 1.8 miles to Newton Road on the left. Turn left onto Newton Road and at 0.1 mile turn left into the gravel parking lot. The Long Point Trail is marked with a trailhead sign. **GPS:** N38 02.50' / W81 04.63'

THE HIKE

According to geologists, the New River is quite a misnomer: It's actually one of the oldest rivers in North America—so old, in fact, that it began eroding the Appalachian Mountains while they were still rising. The New has worn rock over millennia to create a gorge up to 1,500 feet deep, exposing rock estimated to be up to one billion years old.

The human history of the gorge is, of course, not that old. Prehistoric Native Americans lived in this area, and then the Shawnee and Cherokee. The more recent history of the gorge centered around coal mining. Mother Jones, one of the nation's greatest labor leaders (1837–1930), walked from coal camp to coal camp in West Virginia to help organize miners into unions, including here. Today there is evidence of the New's mining past in the form of old coke ovens, closed-up mine entrances, old railroad tracks, and so

The hikers-only view from Long Point includes the New River Gorge Bridge and the New River below.

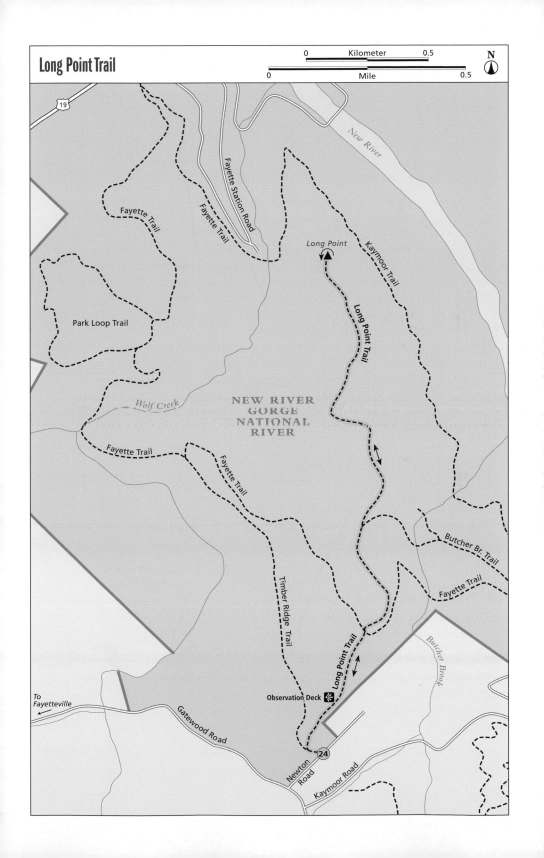

on. But the major industry today is adventure recreation: rock climbing, kayaking, rafting, mountain biking, ziplining, paddleboarding, and, of course, hiking. Some one million people per year come to the New River Gorge to get their fix of fun.

The Long Point Trail is the best starting point for a hike in the New River Gorge area. It is even wheelchair accessible to a wooden observation platform at mile 0.2. Walk past the trailhead sign and into the woods. The trail initially skirts the backyards of homes. Walk into a meadow area and then reenter the forest. This mostly flat trail goes through a mixed hardwood forest, and you will likely find mushrooms throughout the understory. As you walk, you'll notice that the ridge narrows.

Approaching Long Point, the trail becomes rockier, descending a bit through a rhododendron thicket. At the end of the trail, you emerge at Long Point, a sandstone outcropping dotted with blueberry bushes and pine trees. Straight ahead you get a rewarding view of the New River Gorge Bridge, the New River—nearly 1,000 feet below—and Wolf Creek, cutting a path to the New. After taking time for some food and photos, return the way you came.

MILES AND DIRECTIONS

0.0 START at the parking lot trailhead. Walk into the woods, behind some homes.

0.2 Come to a wheelchair-accessible observation deck on the left.

0.4 Come to the intersection with the Fayette Trail. Continue straight.

0.7 Pass the Butcher Branch Trail on the right. Continue straight.

1.6 Arrive at Long Point. (**FYI:** Plan to have lunch and spend some time here.) Turn around to return the way you came.

3.2 Arrive back at the trailhead.

HIKE INFORMATION

Local information: New River Gorge Convention & Visitors Bureau, (800) 927-0263 or www.newrivergorgecvb.com

Camping: There are 7 primitive camping areas in the park, go to www.nps.gov/neri/planyourvisit/campgrounds.htm for a list. There are also several privately owned campgrounds nearby; go to www.newrivergorgecvb.com/lodging/camping for info.

Local events/attractions: Bridge Day is held the third weekend of Oct, www.officialbridgeday.com.

Hike tours: In addition to seasonal park programming, you can take a walking tour of the New River Gorge Bridge catwalk, (304) 574-1300 or www.bridgewalk.com.

Organizations: For a list of partnership and support organizations, see www.nps.gov/neri/parkmgmt/partners.htm.

25 GLADE CREEK TRAIL

New River Gorge National River

WHY GO?

Only the world-famous New River Gorge with its bridge, whitewater, rock climbing, and many trails could make its tributary Glade Creek a relatively unknown destination in comparison. Allot a day to explore this creek upstream of the gorge, and you'll be glad you did. The flat trail parallels the swiftly flowing Glade Creek, which is trout stocked, boulder strewn, and full of cannonball-worthy swimming holes. The dense canopy of hardwoods towers over an understory of mountain laurel, rhododendron, striped maple, and witch hazel. Add a developed campground and backcountry camping where you are unlikely to see another soul, and you just may find your new favorite place to spend a summer weekend.

THE RUNDOWN

Start: Northern Glade Creek Trail trailhead
Distance: 11.2-mile out-and-back
Hiking time: About 5 to 6 hours
Difficulty: Moderate
Trail surface: Flat, wide abandoned rail bed
Best season: Apr–Oct
Other trail users: Mountain bikers
Canine compatibility: Leashed dogs permitted
Land status: National river (National Park Service)
Nearest town: Beckley
Fees and permits: None
Schedule: The park is open 24/7 year-round. The Grandview visitor center is open Memorial Day through Labor Day noon to 5 p.m. The Canyon Rim visitor center is open 9 a.m. to 5 p.m. daily year round. The Sandstone visitor center is open 9 a.m. to 5 p.m. daily April through November and 9 a.m. to 5 p.m. Friday through Monday in the winter. All visitor centers are closed Thanksgiving, Christmas, and New Year's Day.
Maps: New River Gorge National River maps; USGS quad: Beckley
Trail contact: New River Gorge National River, (304) 465-0508 or www.nps.gov/neri

FINDING THE TRAILHEAD

From I-64 east of Beckley, take exit 124 for Beckley/Eisenhower Drive. Turn north on US 19 for 1.7 miles, where you will meet up with the junction for WV 41. Follow WV 41 to the right for 5.5 miles to where it takes a right turn; continue on WV 41 to mile 9.4 at Glade Creek Road. Turn right onto gravel Glade Creek Road and drive 5.5 miles to the trailhead. **GPS:** N37 49.56' / W81 00.69'

THE HIKE

From the lower trailhead parking area, a sign indicates the Glade Creek Trail. Walk upstream along this abandoned narrow-gauge railroad bed. The 11.2-mile round-trip is leisurely, since there are no steep climbs. This streamside trail gives you constant access to the sights and sounds of the boulder-strewn creek in deep forest. The trail is wide and easy

Glade Creek in the fall

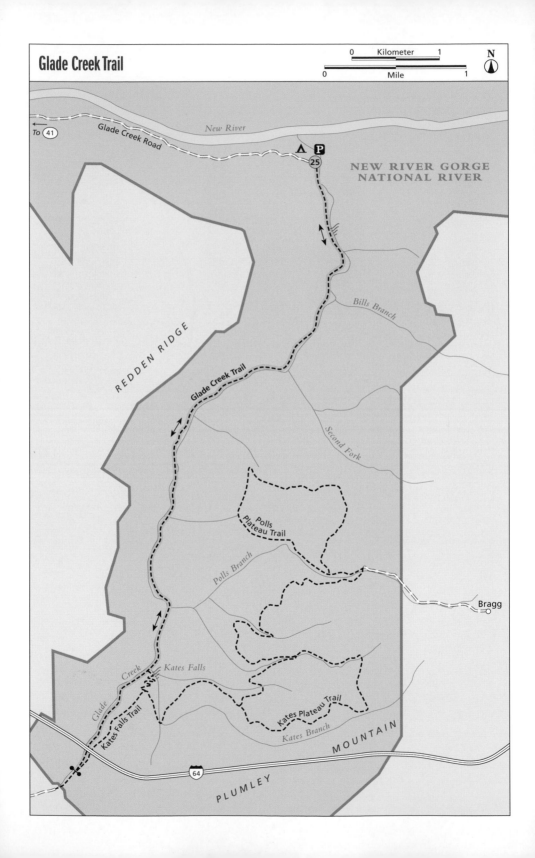

Glade Creek Trail

0   Kilometer   1

0   Mile   1

N

To 41

New River

Glade Creek Road

NEW RIVER GORGE
NATIONAL RIVER

25

Bills Branch

REDDEN RIDGE

Glade Creek Trail

Second Fork

Polls
Plateau Trail

Polls Branch

Bragg

Glade Creek

Kates Falls

Kates Falls Trail

Kates Plateau Trail

Kates Branch

MOUNTAIN

64

PLUMLEY

to follow even though the blue blazes are infrequent.

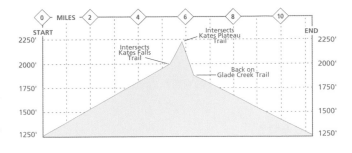

Tulip poplar, chestnut oak, and sycamore tower over the trail. Dogwood, striped maple, witch hazel, rhododendron, and mountain laurel fill the understory. You will likely see anglers casting their lines for trout. Within 0.5 mile, pass a waterfall. The trail stays to the right of the stream until reaching a footbridge at mile 3.0. This is the only stream crossing. There are a few buckeye trees in the canopy, which also contains sugar maple, beech, and hickory.

Continue on the Glade Creek Trail to the Kates Falls Trail on the left at 4.0 miles. Follow this trail a few hundred feet to check out the 15-foot waterfall and then return to the Glade Creek Trail. At about 4.5 miles, you will see I-64 high overhead. Pass a washout to the left and keep an eye out for deep swimming holes in Glade Creek. The trail ends by a gate at the southern trailhead, where you can see the partially deconstructed bridge that used to take car traffic to this southern trailhead. Return the way you came.

MILES AND DIRECTIONS

0.0 START at the Glade Creek Trail trailhead, near the parking area by the campground. It's marked with a trailhead bulletin board.

3.0 Cross Glade Creek over a footbridge.

4.0 A side trail to the left leads to Kates Falls. Take this trail a few hundred feet to explore the 15-foot waterfall before returning to the Glade Creek Trail and continuing upstream.

4.5 Look ahead as the I-64 bridge comes into view.

5.6 Reach the southern trailhead. Turn around and return the way you came.

11.2 Arrive back at the trailhead.

HIKE INFORMATION

Local information: New River Gorge Convention & Visitors Bureau, (800) 927-0263 or www.newrivergorgecvb.com

Camping: Glade Creek Camping Area has 5 tent sites. Backcountry camping is allowed, as long as you stay 100 feet away from trails, river access, and structures. No group camping allowed in the backcountry.

Local events/attractions: Bridge Day is held the third weekend of Oct, www.official bridgeday.com.

Hike tours: In addition to seasonal park programming, you can take a walking tour of the New River Gorge Bridge catwalk, (304) 574-1300 or www.bridgewalk.com.

Organizations: For a list of partnership and support organizations, see www.nps.gov/neri/parkmgmt/partners.htm.

26 GRANDVIEW RIM TRAIL TO TURKEY SPUR OVERLOOK

New River Gorge National River

WHY GO?

Grandview is the right name for this hike. The payoff comes early—walk just a few hundred feet to an expansive view to the east of a giant oxbow in the New River. This spot, Horseshoe Bend, is the deepest part of the New River Gorge, at around 1,400 feet. The trail parallels the gorge through a forest thick with rhododendrons and hardwoods. It ends at Turkey Spur Overlook, atop a rock outcropping that also provides views of the New River Gorge—this time both to the east and west, thanks to more oxbows in this snaking whitewater river.

THE RUNDOWN

Start: Grandview Rim Trail trailhead
Distance: 1.8-mile one-way or 3.6-mile out-and-back
Hiking time: 1 hour one-way or 2 hours out-and-back
Difficulty: Easy
Trail surface: Dirt and rock trail
Best season: May and June
Other trail users: Hikers only
Canine compatibility: Leashed dogs permitted
Land status: National river (National Park Service)

Nearest town: Beckley
Fees and permits: None
Schedule: The park is open 24/7 year-round. The Grandview visitor center is open Memorial Day through Labor Day noon to 5 p.m.
Maps: Park Service maps; USGS quad: Prince
Trail contact: New River Gorge National River, (304) 465-0508 or www.nps.gov/neri

FINDING THE TRAILHEAD

From I-64 east of Beckley, take exit 129B for CR 9/Grandview Road. Turn north on Grandview Road and travel 5.1 miles to the main overlook and visitor center parking lot to the right. The trailhead is directly across from the visitor center. Optional shuttle: To leave a car at the Turkey Spur Overlook parking lot, exit the visitor's center parking lot and take a right onto Grandview Road. Go 0.1 mile to a fork, take the left fork, following signs for Turkey Spur. In another 0.2 mile, turn right onto Turkey Spur Road. Go 1.2 miles to the trailhead parking at the end of the road. **GPS:** N37.831' / W81.063'

THE HIKE

While Grandview is a good name for this hike and general area, the New River isn't so much—it's actually one of the oldest rivers in North America. You can see 7 miles of the river from this spot. Look north along the ridgeline about a mile and a half to view a rock outcropping with a wooden structure on top—this is Turkey Spur Overlook, where you

The aptly named grand view of Horseshoe Bend along the New River.

will end your hike. Look down and you can watch trains travel the lines that parallel the river as well as boaters floating along the New.

After taking in the view, continue on the trail, which snakes a narrow area between the gorge and Turkey Spur Road. The forest is beautiful any time of year, with evergreen hemlocks and rhododendrons. But to see the rhododendrons in bloom, try this hike in May or June. May sees the purple Catawba rhododendrons flower, while late June to early July brings the white blooms of the great rhododendrons.

After passing the Civilian Conservation Corps-era Picnic Shelter #1, you'll come to a series of other overlooks. The final one is North Overlook, which provides perhaps a better view than the main overlook near the trailhead. The trail then becomes more tightly squeezed between the gorge to the east and Turkey Spur Road to the west, but it is still a tranquil hike except for the busiest weekends.

The hike ends at Turkey Spur Overlook, which requires a walk up steep steps to the top of the sandstone rock outcropping. Three viewing platforms offer different views of the New River, including one to the west overlooking a tight oxbow in the river.

The Grandview area has been public land since the 1930s, when it became a West Virginia state park. During this time, CCC members built roads and structures like the picnic shelter. The state transferred Grandview to the National Park Service in 1990. Since then, the National Park Service has launched programs such as the Peregrine Falcon Restoration Project, which from 2006 through 2011 introduced 122 peregrine falcons to the area.

This is a popular day trip destination for families. In addition to plenty of hiking trails, park rangers and partners occasionally offer talks and guided hikes during the summer. Check with the visitor center for programming information. A large picnic area and a playground are near the visitor center, offering a great place for a pre- or post-hike lunch.

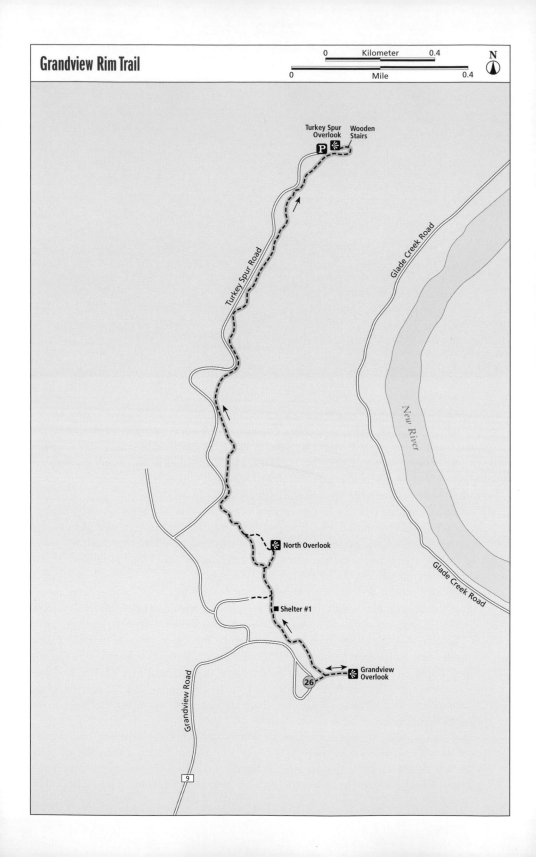

0   Kilometer   0.4

0   Mile   0.4

N

Turkey Spur
Overlook

Wooden
Stairs

P

Turkey Spur Road

Glade Creek Road

New River

North Overlook

Shelter #1

Glade Creek Road

26

Grandview
Overlook

Grandview Road

9

MILES AND DIRECTIONS

0.0 START at the trailhead kiosk with maps. The flagstone-paved trail is marked with a "Main Overlook" sign. In about 200 feet, come to a junction. Take a right to the main overlook. Retrace your steps from the main overlook to this junction (you'll pass the Tunnel Trail on the left and the Castle Rock Trail on the right). This time, go straight at the junction. Note: The Grandview Rim Trail was formerly the Canyon Rim Trail and not all Canyon Rim signs have been removed.

0.2 Come to a fork, marked with a Grandview Rim Trail sign. Take a right at the fork, stepping onto a gravel path. You will pass numbered posts corresponding with a former nature trail brochure.

0.4 Come to a T-intersection. Stay right, keeping toward the gorge. Soon you will pass informal trails on the left that lead to Shelter #1. Continue paralleling the canyon rim. Trend straight and right; there are several overlooks to the right.

0.5 Come to a post at a fork. Take the right fork to three overlooks; the final one is North Overlook with excellent views. Then return to this spot, take a hard right (the original left fork), and continue on the main trail.

0.7 Pass the Castle Rock Trail, which comes in from the right.

0.8 Approach Turkey Spur Road at a fork in the trail with a post. Do not cross the road; take the right fork and parallel the road.

1.7 Arrive at the end of the Grandview Rim Trail, at the Turkey Spur Overlook parking lot. Walk through the lot and take the stone steps next to the rock outcropping.

1.8 Take the steep wooden steps up to the top of the rocks. At the top is a landing with an option to go right and left to the three overlooks. **Option:** If you parked a car here, your hike ends.

3.6 If you select an out-and-back hike, retrace your steps to the trailhead.

HIKE INFORMATION

Local information: New River Gorge Convention & Visitors Bureau, (800) 927–0263 or www.newrivergorgecvb.com

Camping: There are 7 primitive camping areas in the park, go to www.nps.gov/neri/planyourvisit/campgrounds.htm for a list. There are also several privately owned campgrounds nearby; go to www.newrivergorgecvb.com/lodging/camping for info.

Local events/attractions: Bridge Day is held the third weekend of Oct, www.official bridgeday.com.

Hike tours: In addition to seasonal park programming, you can take a walking tour of the New River Gorge Bridge catwalk, (304) 574–1300 or www.bridgewalk.com.

Organizations: For a list of partnership and support organizations, see www.nps.gov/neri/getinvolved/partners.htm.

27 CLIFFSIDE TRAIL

Twin Falls Resort State Park

WHY GO?

Nestled in the Allegheny Plateau is Twin Falls Resort State Park, which combines a rugged mountain landscape with comfortable facilities. Comfortable yet rugged also describes the Cliffside Trail, which leaves right from the campground on a flat and easy path to two stunning overlooks of the Marsh Fork and Cabin Creek valleys below. The trail is also loaded with flora and fauna—from mountain laurel to rhododendron blooms, blueberries to wild mushrooms, songbirds to reptiles. This is an excellent camping/hiking outing for the whole family.

THE RUNDOWN

Start: Cliffside Trail trailhead, in the campground
Distance: 3.0-mile lollipop
Hiking time: About 1.5 hours
Difficulty: Easy
Trail surface: Dirt trail with rock outcroppings
Best seasons: Dogwoods bloom in Apr, mountain laurel and rhododendron bloom in May and June
Other trail users: Mountain bikers
Canine compatibility: Leashed dogs permitted

Land status: State park
Nearest towns: Saulsville and Pineville
Fees and permits: None
Schedule: Open 6 a.m. to 10 p.m. for day use
Maps: Twin Falls Resort State Park map and trail guide; USGS quads: McGraws, Mullins
Trail contact: Twin Falls Resort State Park, (304) 294-4000 or www.twinfallsresort.com

---

FINDING THE TRAILHEAD

From I-64/I-77 in Beckley, take exit 42. The entire way to the state park is marked with brown signs. Turn south onto WV 16/97 and continue 3.3 miles to WV 54. Exit right onto WV 54/97. Follow this road 13.7 miles to the town of Maben and turn right onto WV 97 west, where it splits from WV 54. Follow WV 97 another 5.3 miles to a stop sign and turn left onto Bear Hole Road (Park Road 803). Take the park road 0.7 mile to the park entrance and follow signs for the campground. Continue 3.4 miles to the junction with the campground road; turn right and go 1.8 miles to the campground. As you enter the campground, turn right just past the registration booth at a sign that reads Dogwood Flats Sites 16 through 46. Pass the sign and park across from the restroom facility. The trailhead is at a gate near the restrooms and parking, and is signed with a red blaze. **GPS:** N37 37.15' / W81 25.79'

THE HIKE

The Cliffside Trail leaves the camp road past a wooden gate. The trail is wide and appears to be an old fire road. Mountain biking is allowed on this trail. The red-blazed trail travels

Cliffside Trail, Falls Trail

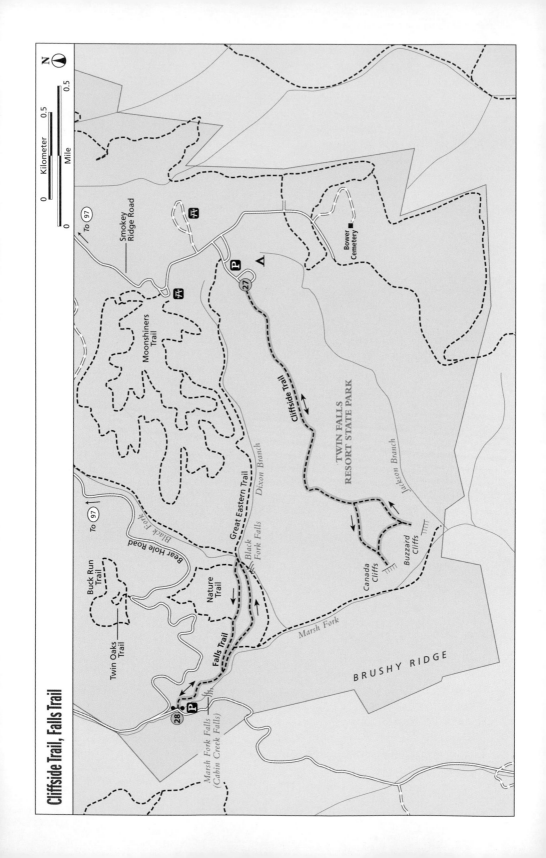

N

Kilometer 0.5

Mile 0.5

To 97

Smokey Ridge Road

Moonshiners Trail

P

27

Cliffside Trail

TWIN FALLS
RESORT STATE PARK

Bower Cemetery

Jackson Branch

Canada Cliffs

Buzzard Cliffs

Great Eastern Trail

Dixon Branch

Black Fork Falls

Black Fork

Bear Hole Road

To 97

Buck Run Trail

Twin Oaks Trail

Nature Trail

Falls Trail

Marsh Fork

BRUSHY RIDGE

28

P

Marsh Fork Falls
(Cabin Creek Falls)

west through an oak, hickory, maple, and hemlock forest. The trail is relatively flat and easy. The forest here has little understory, which belies the jungles to come.

At an opening in the forest canopy, red blazes go off in either direction as the trail forks. This is the beginning of a triangular loop with overlooks at two of the points. Turn right at this intersection. The trail travels down slightly to a drainage and then back up before beginning an abrupt descent. Rhododendron and mountain laurel fill the understory. Reach another fork; a right leads 30 yards to Canada Cliffs and seasonal views of Marsh Fork (also known as Cabin Creek) below—in the summer, the forest is so dense that you can see the river valley but not the river itself.

After soaking in the view, continue on the loop toward the second vista. The trail makes a right switchback around a large boulder, then bends left and contours across the ridge to an intersection with the third side of the triangle. Turn right and enjoy the views from Buzzard Cliffs. You might see snakes here, since this is a good sunning spot for them. Do not disturb the snakes or any other wildlife. The large stone slabs offer beautiful views to the south, and the roar of the state park's twin falls can sometimes be heard far below. Look for a few snags in the canopy where you might see birdlife.

From Buzzard Cliffs, follow the trail back up the ridge to the apex of the triangle. The climb from the cliffs is steep but short. After closing the loop, it's a leisurely walk back to the parking area.

MILES AND DIRECTIONS

0.0 START at the Cliffside Trail trailhead, located in the campground, across from the restrooms. A sign marks the trailhead. Walk past the gate into the woods.

1.1 Come to an opening in the forest canopy and a fork. Red blazes mark a trail in each direction. Take the right trail to complete a counterclockwise loop.

1.3 Come to another fork in the trail, with red blazes marking each trail. Take the right fork to Canada Cliffs. Return here and continue on the trail.

1.6 Come to a T intersection. Take a right to Buzzard Cliffs. When you return to this junction, continue straight to complete the loop.

1.9 Return to the junction where you began the loop. Walk straight, retracing your steps to the trailhead.

3.0 Arrive back at the trailhead.

HIKE INFORMATION

Local information: Southern West Virginia Convention and Visitors Bureau, (304) 294-5151 or www.visitwv.com

Camping: A 50-site campground is open year-round; from late fall through early spring, you have to check in at the lodge.

Local events/attractions: Twin Falls is home to a pioneer farm, nature center, golf course, horseshoe pits, basketball courts, tennis courts, and other amenities. Contact the park for up-to-date programming information at (304) 294-4000 or www.twinfalls resort.com or www.facebook.com/WVSPTwinFalls.

Hike tours: The nature center has year-round programming, (304) 294-4000 or www .twinfallsresort.com.

Organizations: West Virginia Scenic Trails Association, www.wvscenictrails.org; Twin Falls Foundation, Hillbilly Bike Club, and Tire on the Mountain bike club all support or partner with Twin Falls State Park. If you'd like to get involved, contact the park for more information.

28 FALLS TRAIL

Twin Falls Resort State Park

WHY GO?

When a park has more than 25 miles of developed trails, it can be difficult to choose where to begin. Not so with Twin Falls Resort State Park. The Falls Trail is a no-brainer: This short, flat path takes you to the park's namesake twin falls, Marsh Fork Falls and Black Fork Falls. Shoulder the tripod and head out with your camera. These crashing falls embody the definition of picturesque, nestled in steep mountain slopes and framed by rhododendrons and hardwoods.

THE RUNDOWN

See the map on page 128.
Start: Falls Trail trailhead
Distance: 1.2-mile lollipop
Hiking time: About 45 minutes
Difficulty: Easy
Trail surface: Asphalt and dirt trail
Best season: Spring, when the falls are running high
Other trail users: Mountain bikers
Canine compatibility: Leashed dogs permitted
Land status: State park

Nearest town: Beckley
Fees and permits: None
Schedule: Open 6 a.m. to 10 p.m. for day use
Maps: Twin Falls Resort State Park map and trail guide; USGS quads: McGraws, Mullins
Trail contact: Twin Falls Resort State Park, (304) 294-4000, www.twinfallsresort.com or www.facebook.com/WVSPTwinFalls

FINDING THE TRAILHEAD

From I-64/I-77 in Beckley, take exit 42. The entire way to the state park is marked with brown signs. Turn south onto WV 16/97 and continue 3.3 miles to WV 54. Exit right onto WV 54/97. Follow this road 13.7 miles to the town of Maben and turn right onto WV 97 west, where it splits from WV 54. Follow WV 97 another 5.3 miles to a stop sign and turn left onto Bear Hole Road (Park Road 803). Go 1.0 mile to a fork and a sign for the Falls Trail to the right. Take this right fork and travel 0.1 mile to another fork. Take a left and go another 0.2 mile to the trailhead parking. **GPS:** N37 37.26' / W81 27.41'

THE HIKE

The Falls Trail is quite popular, and for a reason: Marsh Fork and Black Fork Falls are high-volume cascades surrounded entirely by densely forested mountains. If you can plan it, try to hike this trail after a rain, when the falls will be running high and fewer people will be on the trail.

From the parking area, hike past the metal gate and onto the blacktop. There are two blazes here; the yellow blazes mark the Falls Trail, while the blue blazes mark the Great Eastern Trail. The trail begins traveling east, with Marsh Fork down to the right. There are mountain laurel and rhododendron in the understory and maple and hemlock in the canopy. The roar of the falls becomes louder with each step. At a fork, the pavement

Marsh Fork Falls

stops. Turn to the right and walk over to the creek bank. You can see Marsh Fork Falls (also known as Cabin Creek Falls) cascading some 15 feet from a large rock slab. Look for an old wall for the mill constructed by Marion Foley in 1882. Some still know the waterfall as Foley Falls.

To continue the hike, return to the intersection and take the right fork, which follows more closely to the creek bank. The trail angle is nearly flat, and the hiking is very easy. This section of trail travels over a century-old logging road, which is the old entrance into the park. Occasionally the remnants of cross-ties from the old logging operation can be seen. The trail follows Marsh Fork and then bends to the left to follow Black Fork. At mile 0.6, the trail reaches Black Fork Falls, taller and narrower than Marsh Fork Falls. The rock overhangs a recess cave, and Black Fork Falls crashes noisily into a pool below.

The trail continues past Black Fork Falls and soon reaches a trail junction. Take a switchback to the left to continue on the Falls Trail. A sign points out all trails at this junction. After the switchback, the Falls Trail will be traveling west. Almost immediately the Nature Trail goes to the right.

At just under 1.0 mile, the Falls Trail reaches another intersection as the Nature Trail comes in from the right. Continue straight to follow the Falls Trail. Shortly the trail crosses a small meadow and reaches the paved pathway from the beginning of the hike. Enjoy another look at Marsh Fork Falls and then follow the paved pathway back to the parking area.

MILES AND DIRECTIONS

0.0   START from the parking area; hike past the metal gate and onto the black-top. The trail begins traveling east. Within 200 feet, you'll see the first of two spur trails to the right, taking you down to Marsh Fork Falls, formerly known as Cabin Creek Falls. (**FYI:** These are not formal trails down to the falls; exercise caution, as they are steep and often wet.)

0.1   After returning to the trail from the falls, continue to the end of the asphalt path. Here the trail forks and is marked with a sign for the Falls Trail Loop. Take the right fork and begin the loop in a counterclockwise direction.

0.3   Come to a fork. Take the left fork, walking away from the creek. Look for the yellow blaze for the Falls Trail and the blue blaze for the Great Eastern Trail.

0.6   Come to a spur trail to the right that takes you down to Black Fork Falls, visible from the trail. After checking out the falls, return to the trail and continue. (**FYI:** This is also an informal trail down to the falls; exercise caution, as it is very steep and often wet.)

0.7	Come to a trail junction. The Falls Trail turns left here, marked with a sign and yellow blazes. To the right is the creek; do not cross it. In about 50 feet, pass the Nature Trail on the right, continuing straight.
0.9	Pass the second junction with the Nature Trail; continue straight.
1.1	End the falls loop where you began. Take a right and follow the asphalt trail back to the trailhead.
1.2	Arrive back at the trailhead.

HIKE INFORMATION

Local information: Southern West Virginia Convention and Visitors Bureau, (304) 294-5151 or www.visitwv.com

Camping: A 50-site campground is open year-round; from late fall through early spring, you have to check in at the lodge.

Local events/attractions: Twin Falls is home to a pioneer farm, nature center, golf course, and other amenities. Contact the park for up-to-date programming information at (304) 294-4000, www.twinfallsresort.com, or www.facebook.com/WVSPTwinFalls.

Hike tours: The nature center has year-round programming, (304) 294-4000 or www.twinfallsresort.com.

Organizations: West Virginia Scenic Trails Association, www.wvscenictrails.org; Twin Falls Foundation, Hillbilly Bike Club, and Tire on the Mountain bike club all support or partner with Twin Falls State Park. If you'd like to get involved, contact the park for more information.

29 FARLEY RIDGE TO MASH FORK FALLS TRAIL LOOP

Camp Creek State Park

WHY GO?

Mash Fork Falls is impressive enough to be included in a West Virginia waterfalls picture book for sale at the park office. If you're a photographer, you can do a "drive-by shooting" of the falls, since they are accessible by road. Instead, opt to walk up and down Farley Ridge to the falls, allowing yourself the pleasant experience of hearing them before seeing them.

THE RUNDOWN

Start: Farley Ridge Trail trailhead, across from the playground parking area

Distance: 2.1-mile loop

Hiking time: About 1 hour

Difficulty: Moderate due to a steep ascent

Trail surface: Dirt trail, gravel road, paved road

Best season: Spring, when the falls are running high

Other trail users: Mountain bikers; horseback riders on the Farley Ridge Trail; hunters during hunting season

Canine compatibility: Leashed dogs permitted

Land status: State park

Nearest town: Princeton

Fees and permits: None

Schedule: The state park and campground are open year-round; day use hours are 6 a.m. to 10 p.m.

Maps: Camp Creek State Park map; USGS quads: Odd, Flattop

Trail contact: Camp Creek State Park, (304) 425-9481 or www .campcreekstatepark.com

FINDING THE TRAILHEAD

From I-77 take exit 20 (US 19) for Camp Creek. Follow US 19 south, then turn right at the first intersection onto Camp Creek Road (CR 19-5) and go 1.7 miles to the park entrance. Once at the park, go 0.4 mile, cross a bridge over the creek, and turn left at the sign for Mash Fork Campground. Park in the gravel lot by the playground. The trailhead is across the road; into the woods up the trail is an official trail marker. **GPS:** N37 30.29' / W81 8.12'

THE HIKE

Camp Creek was a popular camping area long before it ever became a state park (hence the name). Native Americans, settlers, and later Civil War soldiers set up camp here, as did others during the early part of the twentieth century: namely, moonshiners. Both of the park's main waterfalls—Campbell Falls and Mash Fork Falls—had grist mills. As for Mash Fork Falls, well, the name says it all. "Liquor" Charlie Mills ran stills here from the early 1900s through the Depression. He is buried in Camp Creek State Forest.

The state purchased land in 1947 to create Camp Creek State Forest. Camp Creek State Park is made up of 550 acres that were carved out of the forest in 1987. What the park lacks in size it makes up for in location. First, the proximity to the interstate makes

Mash Fork Falls

Camp Creek State Park extremely accessible as a destination or as a place to set up camp when passing through. Second, the park borders the 5,400-acre Camp Creek State Forest, increasing the "elbow room" almost tenfold. Two trails traverse the park proper; both are relatively short and easy to hike. Chances are good that you will see anglers during fair weather because Camp Creek is one of the better-stocked trout streams in the area. The area is also a favorite among hunters; blaze orange is a must during hunting seasons.

Starting from the playground near the amphitheater, walk up the ridge. All the trails are marked at intersections with trail markers; look for the first trail sign in the woods, not right at the road. The forest here has magnolia in the canopy and fern covering the floor. The trail begins with a moderate uphill climb. Initially traveling north, the trail bends to the left and starts heading west up a steep valley.

At a fork, the Farley Ridge Trail continues up the ridge to the right. Take the Mash Fork Falls Trail to the left. The trail starts a moderate descent and enters the first in a series of switchbacks. Mash Fork Campground can be seen down the ridge to the left. After the last switchback, which is a left-hand turn, a rock stairway leads down to Mash Creek. Mash Fork Falls can be seen from here. The trail leads down to a gravel road, a parking area, and a small bridge that crosses Mash Creek. A gate blocks the bridge. The land across the creek is Camp Creek State Forest.

To return to the parking area, follow the gravel road away from the bridge. This road will lead you past Mash Fork Campground. The paved park road is reached within 0.25

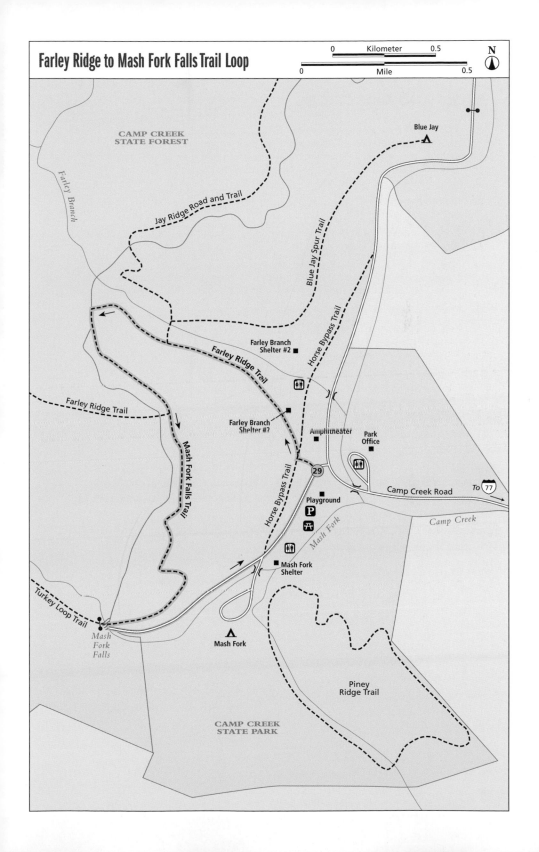

Farley Ridge to Mash Fork Falls Trail Loop

0   Kilometer   0.5

0   Mile   0.5

N

CAMP CREEK
STATE FOREST

Farley Branch

Blue Jay

Jay Ridge Road and Trail

Blue Jay Spur Trail

Horse Bypass Trail

Farley Branch
Shelter #2

Farley Ridge Trail

Farley Ridge Trail

Farley Branch
Shelter #?

Amphitheater

Park
Office

Mash Fork Falls Trail

Horse Bypass Trail

29

Camp Creek Road

To 77

Playground

P

Camp Creek

Mash Fork

Mash Fork
Shelter

Turkey Loop Trail

Mash
Fork
Falls

Mash Fork

Piney
Ridge Trail

CAMP CREEK
STATE PARK

mile. Continue straight and to the left, and follow the paved road another 0.25 mile back to the parking area.

MILES AND DIRECTIONS

0.0 START at the trailhead across from the gravel parking area for the playground. A wooden post is located where the trail meets the road. Hike up and into the woods; you will soon see a trail sign that marks the Farley Ridge Trail. In about 100 feet, cross the Horse Bypass Trail, which is also marked. Continue straight, up the ridge.

0.4 Pass the junction with the Blue Jay Spur Trail on the right. Continue straight, still ascending the ridge.

0.8 Come to a fork. The Farley Ridge Trail continues up to the right. Take the left fork and begin the Mash Fork Falls Trail, which goes down the slope.

1.5 The trail makes a left switchback at the top of stone steps. You can take these steps to the top of Mash Fork Falls and return to the trail here. Continue on the trail toward the bottom of the falls.

1.6 The Mash Fork Falls Trail ends at a gravel road. Take a left and follow the road.

1.9 Come to the paved park road. Continue straight on the pavement, back to the gravel parking lot.

2.1 Arrive back at the parking lot and trailhead.

HIKE INFORMATION

Local information: Mercer County Convention and Visitors Bureau, (800) 221-3206 or www.visitmercercounty.com

Camping: There are 52 campsites at the state park's four campgrounds.

Local events/attractions: Camp Creek State Park hosts the Timbersports Competition & Ramp Feast in April and a Fall Festival in September; contact the park for details.

Organizations: Camp Creek State Forest and Park Foundation; contact the park for information about getting involved.

30 RIVER TO FARLEY LOOP TRAIL

Pipestem Resort State Park

WHY GO?

Pipestem Resort State Park, encompassing the plateau and valley of the Bluestone River Gorge, is ruggedly beautiful. This hike has some quality high points: crossing the Bluestone National Scenic River, walking through a lovely mountain meadow past an old log cabin, taking in the view from atop Raven Rocks overlook. And they come hard earned—you hike down, up, down, and back up the steep mountain slopes . . . unless, of course, you decide to take the seasonal tram ride to whittle down the 9.75-mile hike to 6.5 or 3.4 miles.

THE RUNDOWN

Start: Canyon Rim Trail trailhead, at the Canyon Rim Center
Distance: 9.75-mile lollipop, with 6.5- and 3.4-mile options
Hiking time: About 5 hours for the full length
Difficulty: Difficult due to very steep and sometimes poor trail conditions
Trail surface: Dirt trail with a river crossing
Best season: May through Oct when the tram is running
Other trail users: Horseback riders, mountain bikers
Canine compatibility: Leashed dogs permitted
Land status: State park
Nearest town: Hinton
Fees and permits: Fee required to ride the tram
Schedule: Pipestem Resort State Park is a four-season resort. The tram operates daily May through Oct

(exact dates vary) 8 a.m.–midnight (subject to change; tickets are sold until 10 p.m.). On Tues and Thurs the tram closes 1–4 p.m. for maintenance. It also closes for one 24-hour period per month. In short, call ahead for hours. A tram schedule may be obtained by calling the park or (800) CALL-WVA.
Maps: Pipestem Resort State Park map and trail guide; USGS quads: Flattop, Pipestem
Trail contact: Pipestem Resort State Park, (304) 466-1800 or www .pipestemresort.com
Special considerations: The Bluestone River is not always crossable by foot. The Army Corps of Engineers operates a gauge on the river that measures water level. A recorded message of the Pipestem gauge reading is at (304) 466-0156.

FINDING THE TRAILHEAD

From I-77, take exit 14 and travel north on WV 20 for 11.2 miles to the entrance to Pipestem Resort. From I-64, take exit 139 and travel south on WV 20 for 22 miles. The entrance to Pipestem is on the west side of the road, marked with a large sign. After turning into Pipestem Resort State Park, follow the paved road past the camping area and horse stable for 2.1 miles to a fork in the road. Take a left at the fork and follow this road to the Canyon Rim Center parking lot. The trailhead for Canyon Rim Trail is located just north of the Canyon Rim Center. **GPS:** N37 33.47' / W81 6.87'

THE HIKE

This modified loop is a strenuous traverse of the Bluestone River Gorge. The River Trail travels down the eastern ridge, crosses then follows the river, and then the Farley Loop Trail climbs the western ridge. The Farley Loop Trail brings you back down to the river in a hurry. From the river, you can take the tram back to the trailhead or you can return the way you came on the River Trail. The River to Farley Loop Trail begins on the Canyon Rim Trail, which is a short spur leading to the River Trail near the Canyon Rim Center.

At the Canyon Rim Center, pass by the northern corner of the structure to reach the Canyon Rim Trail trailhead. A sign marks the trailhead where the lawn meets the woods, and blue blazes mark the trail. The Canyon Rim Trail is wide and lined with tulip poplar, hickory, and dogwood. The trail drops to the intersection with the River Trail. At the trail junction, turn left and follow the River Trail downhill. This section of the River Trail is an old fire road. The ridges of the gorge are extremely steep, and the trail is sometimes quite steep and eroded as well. Mountain bikes are allowed on the River Trail, but there is little evidence of their use. Evidence of horses, on the other hand, is everywhere. There is a good chance you will see a group of horseback riders on the trail. Yield to horses when you encounter them.

The log cabin along the Farley Loop Trail

At 1.0 mile, the trail passes to the right of what looks like a rock slide and bends to the north. Shortly after this spot, reach the County Line Trail. At this intersection, continue to hike downhill, passing a small meadow where locust trees are filling the gap in the canopy. The trail makes two switchbacks and then bends right through a drainage area. It continues an easy descent as the ridge drops off steeply to the right. The drainage is populated with large hemlock and beech trees.

When the trail reaches the river's floodplain, a right switchback points the trail north. Reach the river at mile 2.3. Now it's time to take off the boots and ford the Bluestone. At the west bank of the river there is a trail sign as well as a picnic table. Pass by the sign, hike across a small meadow, and turn right on the gravel road. The gravel road is not particularly scenic (it was actually a county road at one time), but it gets you to the Mountain Creek Lodge in less than a mile. The lodge has a restaurant, gift shop, and the lower tram station. Passing the lodge, the River Trail reenters the woods. The trail follows the river at an easy grade. Sycamore, maple, and beech dominate the canopy.

Another 1.0 mile from the lodge, a double orange blaze marks a trail junction. The Bluestone Turnpike Trail travels straight and follows the river another 7.5 miles to Bluestone State Park (see hike 31). The Farley Loop trail begins here, taking a left and ascending the ridge steeply. After a brief section of trail along the ridge, pass a cabin that's situated in a wildflower-strewn meadow with views of the tram on the ridge where you began.

The next portion of the Farley Loop Trail begins near a sign at the eastern edge of the meadow that reads FARLEY RIDGE (the old trail name). A word of warning: This section of trail is steep. You will need to use both hands and feet along some sections of this trail. Look for the white blazes to stay on the trail. After hopping down some boulders, there is a sign and a 20-yard spur to Raven Rock overlook. The views to the south are outstanding. After resting at the rocky outcrop, continue following the trail downhill. After a right switchback, the trail travels past the rocky base of the overlook then switches back to the left. The lodge and tram station are now visible.

From the lodge, backtrack and hike the River Trail and Canyon Rim Trail back to the parking area. If you're not interested in finishing the hike with yet another mountain ascent, you can ride the tram back to the Canyon Rim Center. The views from the tram are magnificent, and you don't have to "earn" them.

MILES AND DIRECTIONS

0.0 START at the Canyon Rim Trail trailhead on the north side of the Canyon Rim Center. There is a trailhead sign, and the trail is blazed blue. Hike into the woods. (**FYI:** You can take the tram down to the lodge and hike the 3.4-mile loop that starts and ends at the Mountain Creek Lodge.)

0.3 Come to the junction with the River Trail. Take a left onto the River Trail, blazed orange.

1.2 Pass the junction with the County Line Trail, marked with a sign. Continue straight on the River Trail.

2.0 An unmarked trail joins from the right. Continue straight, following the sign and blazes for the River Trail.

2.2 At river level, the trail forks. Take the right fork.

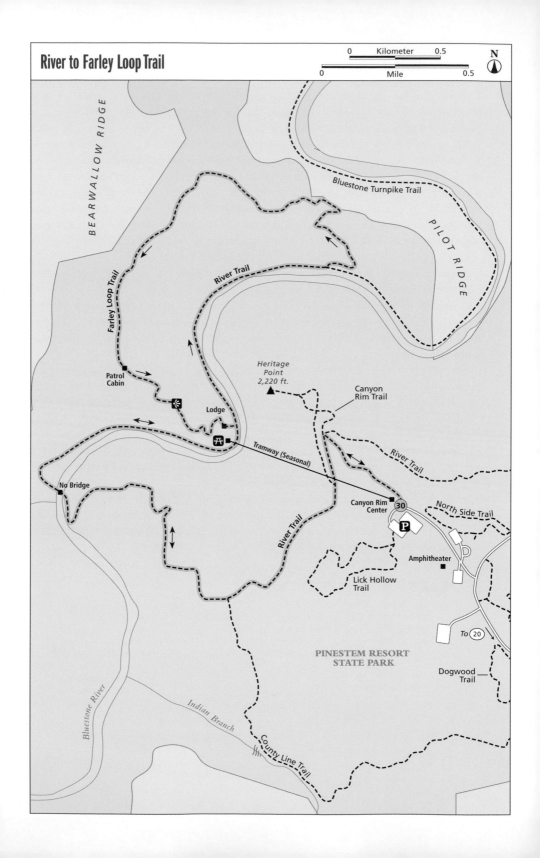

River to Farley Loop Trail

0 Kilometer 0.5
0 Mile 0.5

N

BEARWALLOW RIDGE

PILOT RIDGE

Bluestone Turnpike Trail

River Trail

Farley Loop Trail

Patrol Cabin

Lodge

Heritage Point 2,220 ft.

Canyon Rim Trail

River Trail

Tramway (Seasonal)

No Bridge

River Trail

Canyon Rim Center

30

P

North Side Trail

Amphitheater

Lick Hollow Trail

To 20

PINESTEM RESORT STATE PARK

Dogwood Trail

Bluestone River

Indian Branch

County Line Trail

2.3 The River Trail crosses the Bluestone River here. After crossing the river, the trail parallels the river, heading downstream, on a road. (**FYI:** Be prepared for this wet river crossing. The river is too dangerous to cross by foot when the water is running high and swift. Call for the river level before beginning your hike.)

3.1 Reach the lodge. Walk on the grass between the lodge and the river, continuing downstream. You will see a River Trail sign on the downstream side of the lodge. Follow the orange blazes.

4.1 Come to a junction marked with a sign for the Bluestone Turnpike Trail (straight) and the Farley Loop Trail (left). Take a left and begin the Farley Loop, ascending the mountainside. This section of trail is blazed white.

5.1 Come to a trail sign by a massive oak tree. The trail curves sharply left at this point. Continue following the white blazes.

5.9 The trail intersects with a doubletrack road. Take a left toward the log cabin and the Farley Loop Trail, marked with a sign. In about 100 feet, the road grade goes off to the right. Continue straight here, crossing the meadow to the left of the cabin.

6.1 A sign marks the Farley Ridge Trail and warns of a steep descent. This warning is accurate; you will need both hands and feet for a section of trail to come.

6.3 Arrive at the Raven Rock overlook spur, marked with a sign. Here the trail curves left and down.

6.5 The Farley Loop Trail ends behind the lodge. You can return to the Canyon Rim Center by tram or on the River Trail the way you came.

9.75 If you hiked the River Trail back, arrive at the Canyon Rim Center

HIKE INFORMATION

Local information: Southern West Virginia Convention and Visitors Bureau, (304) 294-5151 or www.visitwv.com

Camping: Pipestem Resort State Park has 50 deluxe campsites with water and electric hookups, and 32 basic campsites. A minimum stay of two nights is required when making a reservation.

Local events/attractions: Pipestem Resort has horseback riding, golf, a nature center, cross-country skiing, and special programming, including participation in the Audubon Christmas Bird Count. Contact the park's nature center at (304) 466-1800 for programming information.

Hike tours: The nature center has programming, including naturalist-led hikes, year-round.

BLUESTONE TURNPIKE TRAIL

Bluestone National Scenic River

WHY GO?

The Bluestone National Scenic River is wonderfully wild, and the ridges of the gorge are so steep that when you sit by the river, it appears that there are only two ways out: upstream or downstream. Luckily, both directions lead to top-notch state parks: Pipestem Resort State Park to the south and Bluestone State Park to the north. The Bluestone Turnpike Trail travels the distance between these parks. Birch and sycamore crowd the riverbank and produce shade during the heat of summer. If the shade isn't enough to cool you off, there is a constant supply of swimming holes just a few steps away.

THE RUNDOWN

Start: Mountain Creek Lodge, accessible from the Canyon Rim Center by tram
Distance: 8.5 miles one way
Hiking time: About 3.5 to 5 hours
Difficulty: Moderate due to distance
Trail surface: Flat dirt trail
Best season: Summer through fall
Other trail users: Mountain bikers, horseback riders
Canine compatibility: Leashed dogs permitted
Land status: National scenic river, state parks, state wildlife management area
Nearest town: Princeton
Fees and permits: Fee required to ride tram
Schedule: The Bluestone National Scenic River is open year-round, as are Pipestem Resort State Park and Bluestone State Park. The tram operates daily May through Oct (exact dates vary) 8 a.m.–midnight (subject to change; tickets are sold until 10 p.m.). On Tues and

Thurs the tram closes 1–4 p.m. for maintenance. It also closes for one 24-hour period per month. In short, call ahead for hours. A tram schedule may be obtained by calling the park or (800) CALL-WVA.
Maps: National Park Service map; USGS quads: Flattop, Pipestem
Trail contacts: Bluestone National Scenic River, (304) 465-0508 or www.nps.gov/blue; Bluestone State Park, (304) 466-2805 or www .bluestonesp.com; Pipestem Resort State Park, (304) 466-1800 or www .pipestemresort.com
Special considerations: Access to the southern end of the trail depends on either taking the tram from Pipestem Resort State Park, which is open only seasonally, or fording the Bluestone River, which is not possible during high water. Check on both before starting at the southern trailhead. Also, check on hunting seasons, which occur between fall and spring.

FINDING THE TRAILHEAD

Southern trailhead: To access the trail from the south at Pipestem Resort State Park, take exit 14 off I-77 and travel north on WV 20 for 11.2 miles to the entrance to Pipestem Resort State Park. To reach Pipestem from I-64, take exit 139 and travel south on WV 20 for 22 miles. The entrance to Pipestem is on the west side of the road. After turning into Pipestem Resort State Park, follow the paved road past the camping area and riding stable for 2.1 miles to a fork in the road. Take a left at this intersection and follow this road to the Canyon Rim Center (**GPS:** N37 33.47'/W81 6.87'). Park here and take the tram to the bottom of the gorge. The trail description begins from the lodge.

Northern trailhead: From the junction of WV 3 and WV 20 in Hinton, take WV 20 south 4.2 miles to the entrance of Bluestone State Park. Turn right (west) and drive 2.2 miles to the park office. Just past the park office, the road forks. Take the left fork and continue toward the campgrounds. Go another 1.3 miles to the entrance of the Old Mill Campground. Go straight (do not enter the campground) and drive another 0.4 mile to a gate and the trailhead, marked with a sign. **GPS:** N37 36.13'/W80 56.79'

THE HIKE

The Bluestone Turnpike Trail follows the banks of the swift-moving Bluestone River from Pipestem Resort State Park to Bluestone State Park. Managed by the National Park Service, the national scenic river designation protects the unspoiled nature of the river and the surrounding land. The Bluestone earned its status in 1988 with the passage of the Wild and Scenic Rivers Act. The Park Service has done its job well protecting this special place—you will only rarely see signs of civilization along the river. The ridges that rise above the Bluestone are steep, and the sound of this rushing river is your companion almost the entire length of the trail.

More than 1,000 plant species live within the boundaries of the Bluestone National Scenic River. Sycamore, maple, and river birch make up much of the canopy near the river; they give way to oak and hickory toward the ridgetops. Wildflowers carpet the forest floor throughout the year; look for showy spring wildflowers like trillium, phlox, and wild geranium. In the summer look for coreopsis, rhododendron, butterfly weed, and purple flowering raspberry, and in the fall expect to see goldenrod, ironweed, and joe-pye weed. The park is also home to some 200 bird species. You have a good chance of sighting a great blue heron, kingfisher, wild turkey, or ruffed grouse along your hike. You will likely see common animals like deer and eastern box turtles as well. There are enough aquatic species here to make it worth your while to turn over a few rocks. The Bluestone is a warm-water fishery, and sport fish include bass and catfish.

The hike itself is shady and easy. The trail is relatively flat throughout, making it accessible for hikers, mountain bikers, and horseback riders alike (be sure to grant right-of-way to horses). The trail hugs the northwest bank of the river, and there are no stream crossings. This is lucky for you because many pools in the river are deeper than the average hiker is tall. Once you arrive at the riverside trail, it's pretty much impossible to get lost. When all else fails, just keep walking downstream, near the river. The river starts to widen toward the end of this trail, as it nears Bluestone Dam, which has created Bluestone Lake.

MILES AND DIRECTIONS

0.0 START from the Mountain Creek Lodge. At the lodge, pick up the River Trail and hike it downstream. The River Trail is marked with a trailhead sign on the downstream side of the lodge, between the buildings and river.

1.0 Come to a trail junction with the Farley Loop Trail, marked with a sign. Continue straight on the River Trail.

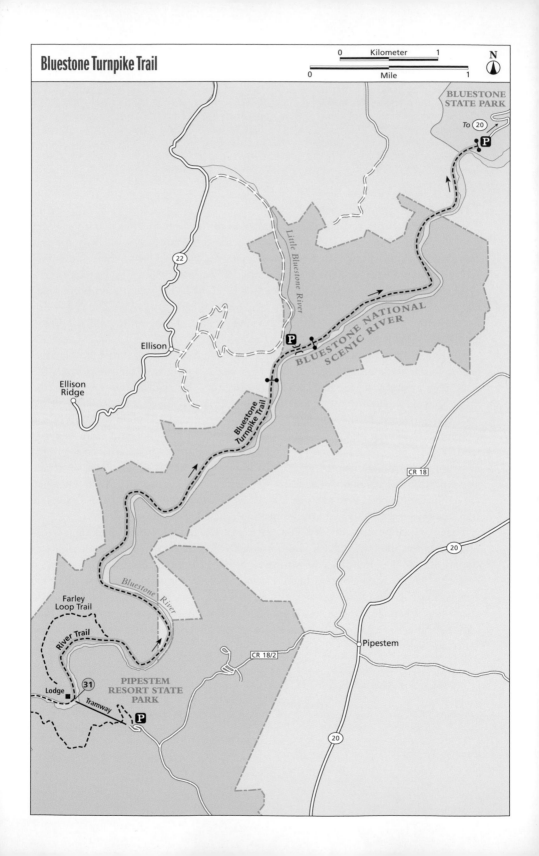

0   Kilometer   1

0   Mile   1

N

BLUESTONE
STATE PARK

To 20

P

22

Little Bluestone River

Ellison

BLUESTONE NATIONAL
SCENIC RIVER

Ellison
Ridge

P

Bluestone
Turnpike Trail

CR 18

20

Bluestone River

Farley
Loop Trail

River Trail

CR 18/2

Pipestem

Lodge

31

PIPESTEM
RESORT STATE
PARK

Tramway

P

20

Rock hopping on the Bluestone National Scenic River

1.4 The Bluestone Turnpike Trail begins at a National Park Service sign, which announces the boundary of the Bluestone National Scenic River.

6.0 Come to a stream crossing and a gate. Continue straight, passing the gate.

6.3 Pass a parking area on the left. Continue straight, trending right. In about 150 feet, cross a footbridge over a tributary to the Bluestone.

6.4 Pass another gate.

8.5 After an ascent, come to the northern trailhead at a gate. A paved road and parking area are on the other side of the gate.

HIKE INFORMATION

Local information: Visit Southern West Virginia, 800-847-4898 or www.visitwv.com/

Camping: Although camping is not allowed along the Bluestone National Scenic River, there are campgrounds at both Bluestone (304-466-2805 or www.bluestonesp.com) and Pipestem (304-466-1800 or www.pipestemresort.com) State Parks.

Local events/attractions: The John Henry Days Festival is held annually in Talcott, at John Henry Memorial Park, (800) 636-1460 or www.visitwv.com.

Hike tours: Rangers lead 2- and 9.5-mile hikes along the Bluestone Turnpike Trail on weekends May through Oct; to register, call (304) 466-0417.

32 KATES MOUNTAIN LOOP
Greenbrier State Forest

WHY GO?
If you're looking for an easy-access destination where you can get some miles under your feet in a day, try Greenbrier State Forest. Just minutes from I-64 and the famous Greenbrier Resort, the Kates Mountain Loop combines several forest trails and takes you from Harts Run to the top of 3,200-foot Kates Mountain, the region's dominant geographical feature. You then head back down again, through hollows filled with cove hardwoods, wildflowers, and flowering azaleas in the understory.

THE RUNDOWN

Start: Old Roads Trail trailhead, behind the office and gift shop
Distance: 9.5-mile loop
Hiking time: About 5 hours
Difficulty: Difficult due to both length and steepness
Trail surface: Dirt trail and gravel road
Best season: Fall
Other trail users: Horseback riders, mountain bikers, hunters during hunting season
Canine compatibility: Leashed dogs permitted

Land status: State forest
Nearest towns: Lewisburg and White Sulphur Springs
Fees and permits: None
Schedule: Open 6 a.m. to 10 p.m. for day use
Maps: Greenbrier State Forest map; USGS quads: Glace, White Sulphur Springs, Ronceverte
Trail contact: Greenbrier State Forest, (304) 536-1944 or www.greenbriersf.com

FINDING THE TRAILHEAD

Take I-64 to exit 175, turn south on CR 60/14, and go 1.2 miles to the state forest office and gift shop. Take a left just past the office/gift shop and park in the small parking area near the office (additional parking is across the road). Walk on the gravel road about 50 yards to the Old Roads Trail, by a gate and marked with a trailhead kiosk. **GPS:** N38 31.34' / W80 16.13'

THE HIKE
The Kates Mountain Loop is a combination of the Old Roads Trail, Rocky Ridge Trail, Holsapple Trail, Young's Nature Trail, and Black Bear Trail. From the park office, follow the gravel road past the park buildings. The trailhead is located at the base of the mountain at an elevation of 1,825 feet. Begin by following the Old Roads Trail into Dynamite Hollow. In about 0.25 mile, turn left on the Rocky Ridge Trail.

The Rocky Ridge Trail climbs from the junction with the Old Roads Trail to the summit of Kates Mountain. This short but demanding trail is well marked with yellow diamonds and is well maintained. The forest here is a mix of hardwoods with azaleas in

Azaleas blooming in Greenbrier State Forest

the understory. An even greater mix of flora dots the forest floor, including mayapple, a variety of ferns, wild yam, and wild geranium.

At the tree-covered summit of Kates Mountain (elevation 3,200 feet), the trail bends left and descends to CR 60/32. At the road, a left leads to an overlook (that is becoming overgrown as trees mature) with a view to the northwest in 0.3 mile, and then the Holsapple Trail on the right, which is an old logging road—or perhaps not so old. There are some Weyerhaeuser-sponsored views from this trail. There is also a very strong spring coming out of the mountainside along this trail; you won't miss it.

The Holsapple Trail ends at the road. Turn left on the road. A former picnic area (it burned down but the chimney is still standing) is on the right about 100 yards from the junction. Past the old picnic area, turn right on Young's Nature Trail, which makes a rapid descent from the crest of Kates Mountain to the Black Bear Trail. The Black Bear Trail follows a creek for a short distance, makes a left bend, and begins a moderate climb to the crest of a finger ridge. It crosses the crest and passes through two scenic hollows on an easy grade. After passing through the second hollow, the trail makes a moderate descent on a finger ridge to the junction with the Old Roads Trail.

The Old Roads Trail goes along an old logging road. The soundscape of your hike here may well be that of gunfire—a muzzle-loader firing range is nearby. Take the Old Roads Trail back to the starting point.

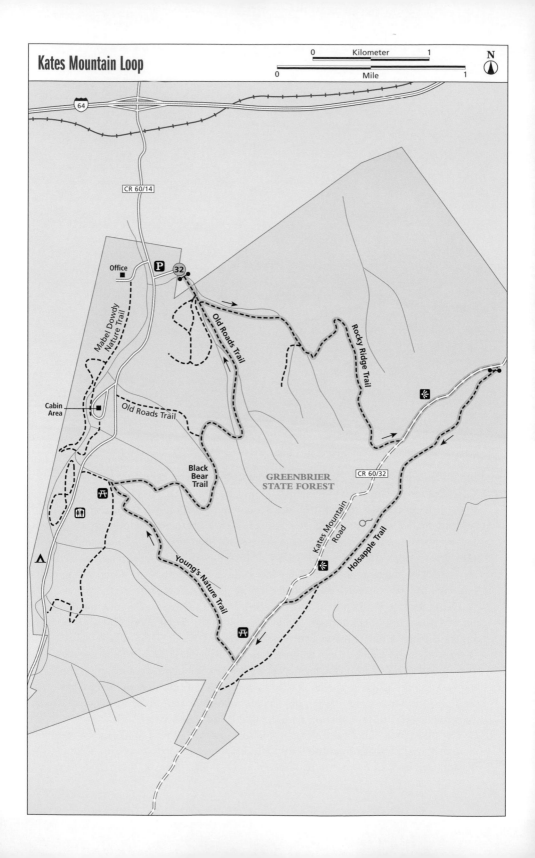

Kates Mountain Loop

0   Kilometer   1

0   Mile   1

N

64

CR 60/14

Office

P

32

Mabel Dowdy Nature Trail

Old Roads Trail

Rocky Ridge Trail

Cabin Area

Old Roads Trail

Black Bear Trail

GREENBRIER STATE FOREST

CR 60/32

Kates Mountain Road

Holsapple Trail

Young's Nature Trail

MILES AND DIRECTIONS

0.0 START at the Old Roads Trail trailhead, behind the office and gift shop. Pass the gate and walk along a gravel road, heading south.

0.1 At the fork at a sign for the muzzle-loader and archery range, take the left fork and cross a stream by footbridge. Come immediately to another fork with a sign for the Rocky Ridge Trail. Take a left and begin the Rocky Ridge Trail, blazed yellow.

0.7 Come to a junction where the Rocky Ridge Trail leaves the road to the left. Take this left and begin the footpath, which ascends the mountain. Soon you will cross the stream.

0.8 Come to the gravel road again at a five-way junction. Go straight, crossing the road and hiking up a steep section of trail. (**FYI:** The official trail goes right and follows the gravel road down about 150 yards, then takes a left onto a footpath, up the ridge, and joins again in just a few yards from this point.)

2.2 Reach Kates Mountain Road, a gravel road at the top of the mountain. Take a left and follow the road to a grassy overlook area lined with boulders at mile 2.5.

3.0 Take a right off Kates Mountain Road onto a doubletrack gravel road. Pass an orange gate. At the gate, there is a trailhead sign marking the Holsapple Trail.

3.5 The road forks. Take the right fork, staying close to the mountaintop.

3.6 The road forks again. Take the right fork; the Holsapple Trail is marked here. Continue along the road grade. If you see red "blazes" in this area, they are not trail markers. Stay on the road grade. (**FYI:** At mile 4.0, a strongly flowing spring comes out of the ground on your right.)

4.3 Come to another fork. Take another right.

4.6 Come to a fork marked with a sign for the Kates Mountain Picnic Area. Take a right, toward the picnic area.

5.0 Arrive back at Kates Mountain Road. Take a left and walk along the road. In about 100 yards, you'll pass the remains of the picnic area on the right.

5.4 Still on the road, come to a pullout on the left and the trailhead for Young's Nature Trail on the right, marked with a trailhead sign. Take this right and begin Young's Nature Trail, which descends the mountain.

6.7 Come to the junction with the Black Bear Trail. A sign at this junction also marks the Kates Mountain Loop, Young's Nature Trail, and Harts Run Road. Take a hard right and begin the Black Bear Trail.

8.0 The trail curves left at the Black Bear Trail sign. Follow the sign and go left.

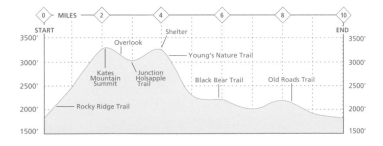

8.1 Come to a three-way intersection with the Old Roads Trail and an access trail to the cabins. Take a right on the Old Roads Trail.

8.6 Before reaching a sign for the forest office, the trail turns left at a junction. Take this left, paralleling the creek.

9.3 Come to the junction with the Rocky Ridge Trail. Go straight and cross the creek to return to the trailhead, retracing your steps from the beginning of the hike. You will again pass the side trail to the archery and muzzle-loader range.

9.5 Arrive back at the trailhead.

HIKE INFORMATION

Local information: Greenbrier County Convention & Visitors Bureau, (800) 833-2068 or (304) 645-1000, www.greenbrierwv.com

Camping: The state forest has a 16-unit campground, open from Apr 15 through the first week of Dec, along with 13 rustic cabins.

Local events/attractions: The Greenbrier Resort, (855) 453-4858 or www.greenbrier.com

Hike tours: Naturalist-led hikes are conducted between Memorial Day and Labor Day; contact the forest for more info.

Arthur Frommer's Budget Travel named nearby Lewisburg "America's Coolest Small Town" in 2011.

33 GREENBRIER RIVER TRAIL

WHY GO?

The Greenbrier River Trail has the combined raw beauty plus infrastructure to make for an idyllic West Virginia outing. The flat 80.7-mile rail trail hugs the riffling Greenbrier River, the longest undammed river in the East. Mountains rise steeply 1,000 feet above the river valley, revealing new vistas with every step. You can travel for miles without any intrusion by civilization, yet primitive trailside campsites are augmented by the occasional small town or bed-and-breakfast for resupply and creature comforts.

THE RUNDOWN

Start: Cass trailhead, at milepost 80.1
Distance: 24.1-mile shuttle (of 80.7 miles total)
Hiking time: About 3 miles per hour
Difficulty: Easy
Trail surface: Flat, mostly crushed limestone; some paved sections
Best season: Spring through fall
Other trail users: Bicyclists, horseback riders, hunters during hunting season
Canine compatibility: Leashed dogs permitted
Land status: State park
Nearest towns: Cass and Marlinton
Fees and permits: None

Schedule: Open 6 a.m. to 10 p.m. for day use; open 24/7 for overnight use
Maps: Greenbrier River Trail map and trail guide; a downloadable map at http://wordpress.greenbrierrivertrail.com/trail-map/; USGS quads: Cass, Cloverlick, Edray, Marlinton
Trail contact: Greenbrier River Rail Trail State Park, (304) 799-7416 or www.greenbrierrailtrailstatepark.com
Special considerations: You can hire a shuttle for your hike with enough advance notice; try Appalachian Sport in Marlinton, (304) 799-4050 or www.appsport.com.

FINDING THE TRAILHEAD

This is a point-to-point trail; transportation is needed at each end. Remember to make sure to bring your car keys. For the Cass trailhead, take US 219 to WV 66. Travel east on WV 66 for 10.7 miles to the trailhead parking, marked with a large sign. Take a right and drive to the parking lot. **GPS:** N38 23.52' / W79 55.32'

For the Marlinton trailhead, at the intersection of US 219 and WV 39, turn east on WV 39. Proceed 0.2 mile to the train depot located on the left. **GPS:** N38 13.38' / W80 05.54'

THE HIKE

The Greenbrier River is a constant companion for the entire length of the Greenbrier River Trail. The 1 percent grade from start to finish makes you want to hike the whole thing, and why not? The combined ease and beauty of the trail make the 24.1 miles described here doable in a (very long) day with a shuttle. But trailside camping—including shelters along this stretch of the trail—make an overnighter a simple proposition.

Start just south of Cass at milepost 80.1 (the actual length of the trail is more like 78 miles, as it begins at milepost 3 at the southern terminus). At some point before or after your hike, take in the Cass Scenic Railroad. Walk downstream and enjoy the clear

The riffling Greenbrier River from the trail

bass- and trout-laden river. Spring through fall, you'll encounter seasonal wildflowers, from phlox, Dutchman's-breeches, and trillium (spring) to joe-pye weed, ironweed, and goldenrod (fall). The forest canopy includes water-loving trees like sycamore and river birch near the river, with maple and mountain ash close by as well. You'll surely encounter birds and other wildlife. If you put in enough miles, you might see a bald eagle or a black bear.

Altogether the trail crosses over thirty-five bridges and passes through two tunnels, traveling through small, not-quite-forgotten railroad towns. For example, at mile 71, Clover Lick, the C&O depot that was originally built near the turn of the twentieth century has been restored. At mile 56, visit the Marlinton Depot, originally built in 1901, and restored after a 2008 fire. Mile 65 is home to an old railroad tunnel, Sharp's Tunnel, which is 511 feet long, followed by the 229-foot-long Sharp's Bridge crossing the river.

The Greenbrier River's history dates back to long before the old railroad. The Seneca Trail was used by Seneca Indians and their ancestors long before Europeans settled in what is today West Virginia. The footpath extended from what is now New York into West Virginia. Today's US 219 roughly traces the route of the old Seneca Trail. Nowadays, you're lucky to share this trail with other hikers, anglers, cyclists, and equestrians—but no cars!

Hike any section or length of the trail. If you choose to do the 24.1 miles described here in a day or two, set up a shuttle or hire one to return to the trailhead.

MILES AND DIRECTIONS

0.0   START at milepost 80.1 at the parking area south of Cass. Walk south/downstream.

1.6   Come to a campsite at milepost 78.5.

8.9   Arrive at milepost 71.2 and the small community of Clover Lick, with its old railroad depot.

10.5 A campsite and Adirondack shelter at milepost 69.6 has a privy and clean water supply.

13.0 Reach a waterfall and pool where Big Run drains into the Greenbrier. A picnic shelter is here, too (milepost 67.1).

14.9 Come to the 511-feet-long Sharp's Tunnel and 229-feet-long bridge (milepost 65.2).

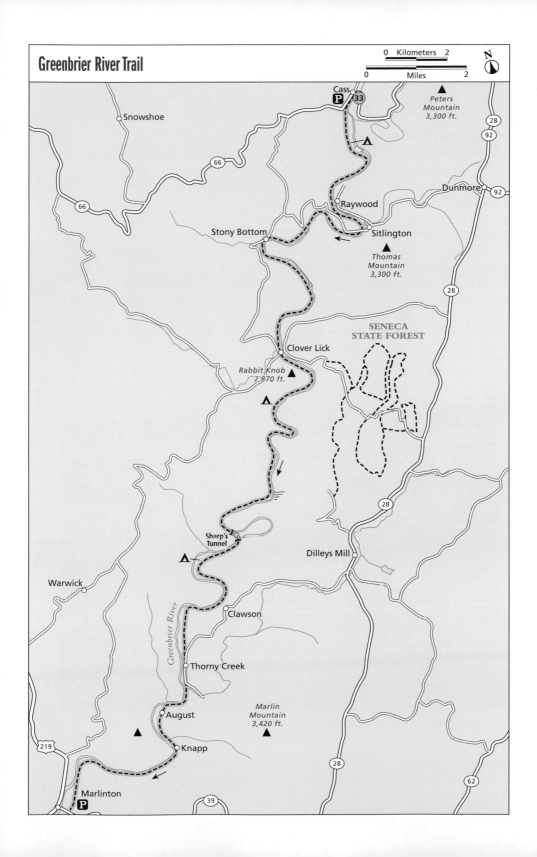

Greenbrier River Trail

0 Kilometers 2

0 Miles 2

N

Snowshoe

Cass
P
33

Peters
Mountain
3,300 ft.

28

92

66

Raywood

Dunmore

92

Stony Bottom

Sitlington

Thomas
Mountain
3,300 ft.

28

SENECA
STATE FOREST

Clover Lick

Rabbit Knob
2,870 ft.

28

Sharp's
Tunnel

Dilleys Mill

Warwick

Greenbrier River

Clawson

Thorny Creek

August

Marlin
Mountain
3,420 ft.

219

Knapp

28

62

Marlinton
P

39

16.3 Arrive at another Adirondack shelter, campsite, and water at milepost 63.8.

24.1 At milepost 56, the trail enters the town of Marlinton. This section of the hike ends at the Marlinton depot, a yellow single-story building located near US 39.

HIKE INFORMATION

Local information: Pocahontas County Convention & Visitors Bureau, (800) 336-7009 or www.pocahontascountywv.com; Greenbrier County Convention & Visitors Bureau, (800) 833-2068 or (304) 645-1000, www.greenbrierwv.com

Camping: There are 15 primitive campsites along the trail (free; first come, first served), including Adirondack shelters at mileposts 69.6 and 63.8. Camping is also available at Seneca State Forest and Watoga State Park, which border the trail. There are also cabin and bed-and-breakfast options along the trail; go to www.greenbrierrailtrail statepark.com/milepostdescriptions.pdf for a listing.

Local events/attractions: Cass Scenic Railroad State Park offers rides on steam-driven locomotives plus lodging options in cabooses and a wilderness cabin accessible by the train, (304) 456-4300 or www.cassrailroad.com.

Organizations: Greenbrier River Trail Association, www.greenbrierrivertrail.com; West Virginia Rails-to-Trails Council, www.wvrtc.org

The Greenbrier River Trail is paved through Marlinton.

Honorable Mentions

| ENDLESS WALL TRAIL, NEW RIVER GORGE NATIONAL RIVER

The Endless Wall Trail proves that you can have just as much fun above the New River as you can in it. The name refers to the seemingly endless crag of Nuttall sandstone that averages about 100 feet in height and goes on for miles on end. This section of trail takes you across the babbling Fern Creek, to a couple of climbing access ladders that allow you to explore the rock face, and to a number of rocky overlooks, including Diamond Point with views of the Endless Wall and the New River upstream as well as the New River Gorge Bridge downstream. The trail is 2.4 miles one way (4.8 miles round-trip); a popular option is to return on the road for a 2.8-mile loop. Exercise caution near the edge of the rocks; keep children and pets away from the edge, where they might knock down rocks or debris that could injure climbers. For more information, stop at the visitor center north of the New River Gorge Bridge, call (304) 465-0508, or go to www.nps.gov/neri.

To find the trailhead from the intersection of US 19 and WV 16 in Fayetteville, drive north on US 19 for 2.3 miles, crossing the New River Gorge Bridge. The second road past the bridge on the east side is Lansing-Edmond Road. Turn east and go 1.3 miles to the Fern Creek parking lot, clearly marked. GPS: N38 03.79'/W81 03.43'

Exploring Honeymoon Ladders along the Endless Wall Trail

J HOMESTEAD TO TURKEY ROCK TRAIL LOOP, PINNACLE ROCK STATE PARK

Pinnacle Rock is a unique geologic feature and, quite literally, a roadside attraction. The park was formed in 1938 when the first 26 acres were purchased in order to preserve this special feature. Today, the park is made up of nearly 400 acres and is home to 7 miles of hiking and biking trails. Hit a concentration of scenic features in the park by making a 4-mile loop out of several trails. Start on the Homestead Trail to the Acorn Trail, where you can get a view of the natural "windows" (holes) through Pinnacle Rock. Continue to Jimmy Lewis Lake and take a right to cross over the lake on CR 52/6 (about 100 feet on the road). Take a right onto the Beaver Pond Trail where you will see—you guessed it—a beaver pond and also a log cabin from the 1800s. Then take a left on the Turkey Rock Trail and walk along the base of Turkey Rock, which is like a smaller version of Pinnacle Rock. Return to the Homestead Trail and retrace your steps to the trailhead. Request a trail map from the park at (304) 248-8565 or download one from www.pinnaclerockstatepark.com.

To reach the trailhead from the intersection of US 52 and WV 71 in Bluewell, drive 1.8 miles to Pinnacle Rock parking on the left. The homestead trail leaves from the parking area. GPS: N37 19.25'/W81 17.55'

METRO VALLEY

Encompassing the most populated region of West Virginia, the Metro Valley contains the economic corridor between Charleston and Huntington and the land to the southwest. All the creature comforts can be found in the two major cities: hotels, restaurants, universities, college sports, nightlife. Even with nearly one-third of the entire population of West Virginia living in the Metro Valley, the region is surprisingly rural. The majority of the residents make the two urban areas and the I-64 corridor their home.

The land in this region is characterized by flat-topped hills and short, sometimes steep ridges. Hikes here will often climb quickly out of the valley, but steep climbs are not sustained. Streams may topple noisily to a shallow valley, flowing lazily once they reach it. On the ridge crests, the hiking is easy. Many hiking destinations are located minutes away from the region's urban centers. On particularly nice spring and fall days, expect to see other hikers. To disperse use, try to hike areas near the cities during the week or during off-peak seasons.

Undoubtedly the most curious hike in the region, and possibly in the entire state, is the Kanawha Trace Trail. This linear trail travels 31.8 miles and almost entirely across private property. The trail is well managed by Boy Scouts, who will even guide you on your trip. You won't find this kind of treatment on any other hike in the state.

Adams Hollow, Kanawha Trace Trail

34 KANAWHA TRACE TRAIL

WHY GO?

Backpacking without the backpack? This is a dream come true on the 31.8-mile Kanawha Trace Trail. Perhaps nowhere else in West Virginia can you tackle a fully supported long-distance trail with only a day pack, complete with overnight shelters, potable water, stream crossings via footbridges, and even a 238-foot tunnel routing you underneath the highway. Members of the Tri-State Area Council of Boy Scouts of America will shuttle you to and from the trail and even stash your provisions in shelters along the way. This diverse path takes you along roadways and past homes, but for the most part it winds its way along lush stream bottoms, over 300-foot-tall ridges, and through dense forest.

THE RUNDOWN

Start: At mile 0 at the junction of WV 193 and Mud River Road.
Distance: 31.8-mile shuttle
Hiking time: About 2 to 4 days
Difficulty: Difficult due to length and hilly terrain
Trail surface: Dirt trail with some sections on road
Best season: Apr through Oct
Other trail users: Mountain bikers; hunters during hunting season
Canine compatibility: Leashed dogs permitted, but be aware there may be unleashed dogs on private property along the way.
Land status: Right-of-way through private land

Nearest town: Barboursville
Fees and permits: None; suggested donation for gas and time
Schedule: The trail is open 24/7 for backpacking; dawn to dusk for day hiking.
Maps: USGS quads: Barboursville, Glenwood, Mount Olive, Milton, Winfield
Trail contact: Tri-State Area Council of Boy Scouts of America, (304) 523-3408 or www.tsacbsa.org
Special considerations: You will have to negotiate barbed wire fences and livestock. The trail is actively maintained and long, so check online for updates.

FINDING THE TRAILHEAD

To mile 0: Take I-64 to exit 18 (WV 193) and turn south. Take an immediate left onto Mud River Road. Mile 0 is at the junction of WV 193 and Mud River Road. There is a pullout across from the bank that's large enough for one or two cars. **GPS:** N38 25.04' / W82 17.37'

To Camp Arrowhead: Take I-64 to exit 20A (West Mall Road). At the stoplight, turn south and proceed 0.2 mile to US 60. Turn left on US 60, travel 1.3 miles to the stoplight for Blue Sulphur Road, turn left, and proceed 1.5 miles to CR 17/4 (Scout Camp Road). Turn right and continue 0.5 mile to Camp Arrowhead. At the fork where the road becomes gravel, take a right and park in the gravel lot by the pond. Transportation to the trailhead is available from the Boy Scout camp. **GPS:** N38 26.14' / W82 14.16'

To mile 31.8: From I-64 and US 35 in Teas Valley, take US 35 north 10.9 miles to Stave Branch Road (CR 24) and exit right. Follow Stave Branch 1.3 miles to the junction with Old US 35. There is a parking pullout on the left side of Stave Branch just before you reach Old US 35.

THE HIKE

Once a dream of ambitious Boy Scouts, the 31.8-mile Kanawha Trace Trail is now a testing ground for outdoor adventure athletes, from backpackers to ultra-marathoners. Originally built in 1962 by Boy Scouts from the Tri-State Area Council, the Kanawha Trace celebrated its fiftieth anniversary in 2012. The trail runs entirely through private land, but is legally open to the public. That said, stay on the trail and know that not every landowner is pleased with the trail running through their property. The state of West Virginia has supported trail building and maintenance to the tune of hundreds of thousands of dollars in grant funding for infrastructure (some are federal grants), including the 238-foot-long pedestrian tunnel under US 35 at mile 30.1.

Popular with backpackers and day hikers alike, the Kanawha Trace has more recently gained favor with long-distance runners and mountain bikers. It has hosted several 50-kilometer races in recent years. Perhaps the best feature of the trail is how easy it is to do a supported multiday hike. If you plan ahead, someone from the council will ferry gear to the three shelters, and provide a ride to the trailhead and a ride back at the end of the hike. It would be good form to make a donation to cover time and fuel. For a through hike, you can break up the mileage in a leisurely fashion by covering 5.6 miles on day one to Williams Shelter, continuing on to mile 9.7 on day two to Eagle's Nest Shelter, then to mile 19.8 on day three to Blackjack School, and finishing up at mile 31.8 on day four.

Williams Shelter on the Kanawha Trace

For a day trip, try the section of trail between miles 1.4 (where the trail leaves the road) and 9.5 (near the Eagle's Nest Shelter). You will travel along bottomlands filled with fresh water, a dense green understory, and wildflowers like phlox, fire pink, miterwort, larkspur, rue anemone, and bloodroot. Listen for the abundant birdlife, and if you're lucky (though it's more likely if you're spending nights on the trail), you could possibly encounter a coyote, bobcat, or black bear.

The Kanawha Trace begins near the junction of Merritts Creek and the Mud River. For the first 1.4 miles, the trail follows a paved road. The eastbound route is marked by a yellow blaze with a white rectangle above and below it. The westbound blaze is white with yellow rectangles. Once you enter the woods, the trail is a natural roller coaster of sorts: Hike over ridgetops, down into hollows, and back up and down again. You will walk behind houses and trailers and along roads occasionally, but expect to spend most of your time in the woods, whether on an old road grade or singletrack trail. Stream crossings are often aided with footbridges (some are Eagle Scout projects), and you will come across three overnight shelters, all with water available. The water should be potable, but Blackjack School water comes from a cistern, so it might be a good idea to treat it.

The Kanawha Trace is long and actively maintained, so be sure to check for up-to-date trail information. The trail conditions are quite good, and it is clearly and regularly blazed. As long as you're paying attention, you have little chance of getting lost.

MILES AND DIRECTIONS

Because this is a 30-plus-mile trail, only the major directions are given below; for example, the trail takes more turns than noted here, but the turns are obvious and blazed, and it is an ever-changing/upgraded trail.

0.0 START at the south end of the trail at mile marker 0 at the junction of WV 193 and Mud River Road. Walk along the road, heading east. (**FYI:** If you can get a ride to the trail where it leaves the road at mile 1.4, do so.)

0.3 Take a left on Wildcat Road (unmarked) and go under the overpass.

1.4 The trail leaves the road and enters the woods to the right.

4.1 Pass the sign for Teas Valley and continue straight. If the blazes and the mowed path diverge, follow the blazes. Then take a left into the woods, entering Tag Hollow. Again, look for the blazes.

4.6 Come to Blue Sulphur Road and take a left. In about 150 yards, take a right into the woods.

5.4 After crossing over Little Cabell Creek on a footbridge, come to a trail junction at Laurel Branch. There is an old latrine here. Take a left.

5.6 Arrive at Williams Shelter and a junction. Kanawha Trace continues straight, passing the shelter. The trail then turns left, heading uphill, after the water pump. (**FYI:** Water is available here, and you will learn why it's called Blue Sulphur Road.)

6.25 Come to a doubletrack road and turn left, then right, continuing uphill. Pass a sign for Old Baldy Trail. The trail forks several times in the next half mile; keep an eye out for blazes.

6.8 At the bottom of the hill, come to a T intersection. Take a left and then a right into Adams Hollow.

7.3 Veer left after the log barn.

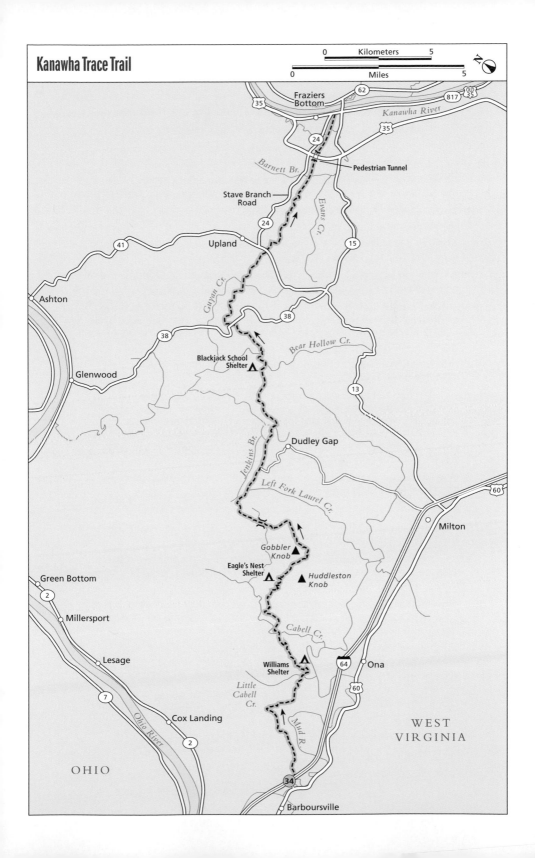

Kanawha Trace Trail

Kilometers 0 — 5

Miles 0 — 5

N

Fraziers Bottom

62

35

817

OLD 35

Kanawha River

35

24

Pedestrian Tunnel

Barnett Br.

Stave Branch Road

Evans Cr.

24

15

41

Upland

Ashton

Guyan Cr.

38

38

Bear Hollow Cr.

Glenwood

Blackjack School Shelter

13

Dudley Gap

Jenkins Br.

Left Fork Laurel Cr.

60

Milton

Gobbler Knob

Eagle's Nest Shelter

Huddleston Knob

Green Bottom

2

Millersport

Cabell Cr.

Lesage

Williams Shelter

64

Ona

60

7

Little Cabell Cr.

Ohio River

Cox Landing

2

Mud R.

WEST VIRGINIA

OHIO

34

Barboursville

7.7 After crossing Big Cabell Creek on a high footbridge, come to a gravel road. Take a left onto Big Cabell Creek Road. Keep an eye out for blazes.

8.0 Pass a red metal gate and continue straight onto an old road grade with large gravel.

8.3 Veer right off the old road grade onto an ORV doubletrack, heading uphill.

8.5 Veer right again, this time off the doubletrack onto a singletrack trail.

9.3 Take a right on Howells Mill Road. In another 0.1 mile, take a left off the road, up a grassy hill. Look for a blaze on a pine tree.

9.7 Come to a junction at the Eagle's Nest Shelter. Take a right. (**FYI:** Camping and city water are available at the shelter.)

10.2 Take a left onto Jericho Road, which is paved. When the road forks, take the right fork.

10.5 After the pavement turns into gravel, the trail takes a left into the woods on a doubletrack.

11.25 The trail comes to a paved road. Take a left and in about 50 feet take a right onto a gravel road, which turns to pavement again.

12.6 The trail turns left off the paved road. Pass a double-wide trailer and then come to a pasture with a barbed wire fence and a sign that says BULL IN THE FIELD. Crawl under the barbed wire and walk down into a grassy bowl, trending left toward the woods.

13.1 After crossing a stream, climb up a steep embankment and cross a gravel road. The blaze is not visible here.

14.0 Walk through a chain-link gate. Veer left into a pasture. Woods are on the right, a ridgetop on the left. Walk toward four buildings where you will find a gate near the right-most building. Go through the gate and take a right on a paved road. Then take a left onto Left Fork Barkers Ridge Road. From this road, the trail goes right, under a fence into a cow pasture and toward the woods.

14.9 Veer right at a huge tulip tree. Parallel Jenkins Branch. This section of trail has a number of fences and stiles.

17.3 Reach a paved road (Barkers Ridge Road, unmarked) and take a right.

17.6 Come to a junction with another unmarked road (Trace Fork Road). Take a left. The trail goes right off of this road and into the woods.

19.3 Come to Dry Ridge Road and take a left on the road. The trail then takes a right, off the road, past a red gate, and by a sign that reads BLACKJACK SCHOOL ¼ MI.

19.8 Arrive at Blackjack School. (**FYI:** You can bed down here for the night. There is water in a cistern, but you should filter or boil it.) After the building, the trail takes an immediate left.

22.1 The trail follows a series of roads: left on Mount Olive Glenwood Road (paved), two rights on Meadows Hollow Road (gravel; second right turn is unmarked), right on Uplands Mason Road (paved), left on Mount Zion Road (43/2; paved).

26.7 Take a left at a fork in Mount Zion Road. The trail then enters the woods on the left side of the road.

27.8 Cross under power lines and walk downhill to Stave Branch Road. Cross the road. This section of trail has several junctions and forks. Watch for the blazes to stay on the trail.

30.1 Walk through a pedestrian tunnel under US 35. After the tunnel and some hiking in the woods, the trail comes out at Stave Branch Road. Take a right.

31.8 The trail ends at the junction of Stave Branch and old US 35. There is a mile marker in front of the antiques shop across old US 35.

HIKE INFORMATION

Local information: Cabell Huntington Convention and Visitors Bureau, (800) 635-6329 or (304) 525-7333, www.wvvisit.org

Camping: Backcountry shelters along the Kanawha Trace are free and on a first-come, first-served basis. Camp Arrowhead rents cabins and primitive campsites seasonally and when they are not in use by Boy Scouts.

Local events/attractions: Whether you like trains, scenery, or just something different, take a ride on the New River Train from Huntington to other points in West Virginia and beyond, (866) NEW-RIVR or www.newrivertrain.com.

Hike tours: If you make arrangements ahead of time, you can get Boy Scouts to lead you on a Kanawha Trace hike.

Organizations: West Virginia Scenic Trails Association, www.wvscenictrails.org

35 SENSORY TO TULIP TREE TRAIL LOOP

Huntington Museum of Art

WHY GO?

No other hike in the state combines nature and art like the nature trails at the Huntington Museum of Art. This easy stroll takes you through a butterfly garden, along a "sensory trail," and through woods dotted with rock carvings. This destination stands in contrast to a wilderness hike—it's not only urban, it's urbane.

THE RUNDOWN

Start: Steelman Butterfly Garden, near where McCoy Road and the parking lot intersect
Distance: 0.8-mile loop
Hiking time: About 30 minutes
Difficulty: Easy
Trail surface: Concrete and dirt trail with rock steps
Best seasons: Spring for wildflowers, summer for butterflies in the butterfly garden
Other trail users: None
Canine compatibility: Leashed dogs permitted
Land status: Private land
Nearest town: Huntington

Fees and permits: None for trail access; admission charge for museum
Schedule: Trails are open dawn to dusk daily. Museum hours are 10 a.m. to 9 p.m. Tues, 10 a.m. to 5 p.m. Wed through Sat, noon to 5 p.m. Sun; closed Mon and holidays.
Maps: Huntington Museum of Arts trail map, available at www.hmoa.org/nature/hiking-trails/; USGS quad: Huntington
Trail contact: Huntington Museum of Art, (304) 529-2701 or www.hmoa.org

FINDING THE TRAILHEAD

Take I-64 to exit 8 and turn north on WV 527. At 0.2 mile, take the first right onto Miller Road and proceed 1.4 miles to a T intersection. Turn left onto McCullough Road and drive to the top of the hill. Take a left onto McCoy Road and then an immediate left to enter the parking lot for the Huntington Museum of Art. The Sensory Trail is on the right, just as you enter the parking lot. **GPS:** N38 23.63' / W82 25.97'

THE HIKE

Art is expanded beyond the four walls of the Huntington Museum of Art and into 40 acres of nature's gallery here. Although the length of this trail is just 0.8 mile, plan enough time to stop and enjoy the extras, which include rock art and a sensory trail.

Find the trailhead near the intersection of the parking lot and McCoy Road. The Teubert Foundation for the Blind Sensory Trail is paved and begins by passing through a butterfly garden. Expect to find butterflies during summer months. Stations allow you to stop and explore your non-sight senses, including smell and hearing (though one sound you'll hear is the nearby interstate). At the end of the paved path, join the

Rock art along the Tulip Tree Trail

dirt path, which begins the Tulip Tree Trail. Take in views (using your sight sense, of course) of the ravine created by Fitzpatrick's Branch. You'll find mature hardwoods here, white-tailed deer, and something you won't see on many trails: artwork carved into the existing rocks along the trail. There are a handful of these carvings along the trail; begin to look for them after the first set of footbridges. All the carvings were done by artist Earl Gray.

The trail is wide and level for the most part, though it does include stairs for a descent to an amphitheater and wooden overlook near the halfway point of the trail. Continue past the overlook to the junction with the Spicebush Loop, a short trail that descends to the creek and then climbs back up the hill to rejoin the Tulip Tree Trail. You can easily tack this onto your hike.

The second junction with the Spicebush Loop is about 100 yards beyond the first, and if you look to the right, you'll see one of the rock carvings next to the trail. The Tulip Tree Trail contours along the hillside just below a rocky bluff; look for

Huntington is where British celebrity chef Jamie Oliver brought his Food Revolution to America. The onetime Jamie's Kitchen is now Huntington's Kitchen, www.huntingtons-kitchen.org. While the aim of the Food Revolution is to help people eat healthier, don't forget the other part of the equation: exercise. Now hit the trail!

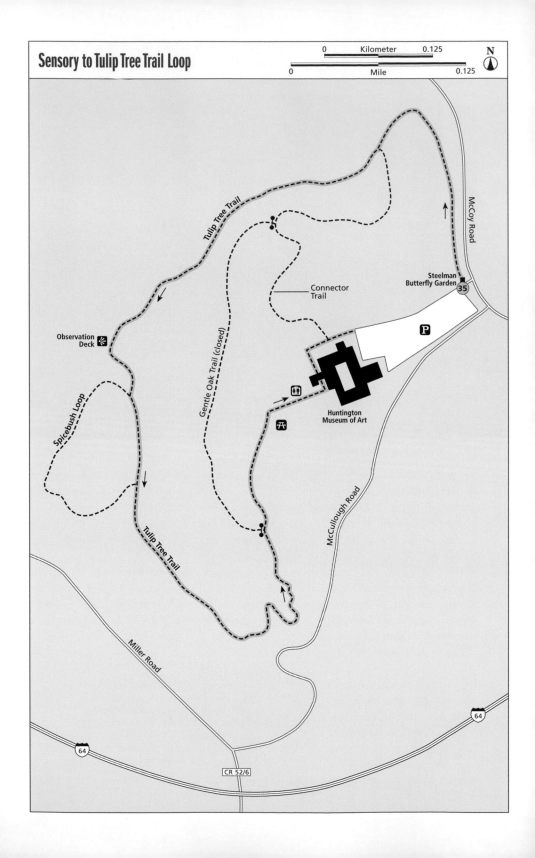

Sensory to Tulip Tree Trail Loop

0   Kilometer   0.125

0   Mile   0.125

N

McCoy Road

Tulip Tree Trail

Connector Trail

Steelman Butterfly Garden

35

P

Observation Deck

Gentle Oak Trail (closed)

Huntington Museum of Art

Spicebush Loop

Tulip Tree Trail

McCullough Road

Miller Road

64

64

CR 52/6

another rock carving along this section. Just before the gate, the trail turns left and begins a short, moderate climb. There is one switchback during the climb. The trail begins to angle toward the rocky bluff and climbs through a narrow rocky crevice where you will find another rock carving. At the top of the bluff, the grade is easy all the way to your return to the museum complex.

MILES AND DIRECTIONS

0.0 START at the butterfly garden and Sensory Trail trailhead. This is a paved path near the intersection of the parking lot and McCoy Road. Walk into the woods, paralleling McCoy Road.

0.1 The Sensory Trail and paved portion of the path end. Continue straight onto the dirt trail. This is the beginning of the Tulip Tree Trail.

0.2 Come to a fork. Take the right fork and take the stairs down to continue on the Tulip Tree Trail.

0.4 Come to a three-way junction. Take a right for the Tulip Tree Trail, which is marked. Pass an observation platform on your right and come to another three-way junction. Take a left to continue on the Tulip Tree Trail. (**FYI:** The Spicebush Loop begins here to the right. You can take this trail as an option.)

0.5 Come to the second junction with the Spicebush Loop. Continue straight. (**FYI:** There is a rock carving at this junction.)

0.7 Come to a junction with the Gentle Oak Trail on the left. Continue straight.

0.8 The trail ends behind the museum complex. Take a left and follow the road back to the parking lot.

HIKE INFORMATION

Local information: Cabell Huntington Convention and Visitors Bureau, (800) 635-6329 or (304) 525-7333, www.wvvisit.org

Camping: There is no campground in Huntington. Beech Fork State Park is about 30 minutes away and has a campground, www.beechforksp.com or (304) 528-5794.

Local events/attractions: The C. Fred Edwards Conservancy, accessed through the museum, features orchids and tropical plants. Museum admission includes the conservatory.

Hike tours: Contact the museum two weeks in advance to request a volunteer nature docent to lead you or your group on a guided hike.

36 SLEEPY HOLLOW TRAIL

Cabwaylingo State Forest

WHY GO?

The name may be strange, but this hike in Cabwaylingo State Forest is classic West Virginia: Follow a hemlock-framed mountain stream that has a hidden waterfall and an amphitheater of sandstone cliffs. Enjoy the sights of mountain laurel and orchids like rattlesnake plantain, and listen for wild turkey and ruffed grouse.

THE RUNDOWN

Start: Across from Cabin 1, near the Sweetwater Picnic Area
Distance: 2.2-mile out-and-back
Hiking time: About 1 hour
Difficulty: Easy
Trail surface: Dirt trail with stream crossings
Best season: Spring
Other trail users: Hunters during hunting season; deer rifle season is late Nov to early Dec.
Canine compatibility: Leashed dogs permitted

Land status: State forest
Nearest town: Wayne
Fees and permits: None
Schedule: Open 6 a.m. to 10 p.m. for day use
Maps: Cabwaylingo State Forest map and trail guide; USGS quads: Naugatuck, Kiahsville, Radnor, Webb, Wilsondale
Trail contact: Cabwaylingo State Forest, (304) 385-4255 or www.cabwaylingo.com

FINDING THE TRAILHEAD

From the south side of Huntington, follow US 152 south about 40 miles (pass Dunlow) and turn left onto CR 35. Follow CR 35 for 3.9 miles and turn left at an unmarked intersection where CR 35 turns into the Sweetwater Picnic Area (if you cross the bridge, you've gone too far; you can see the picnic area sign only once you've turned left). The trailhead is across the road from Cabin 1. Park at the Sweetwater Picnic Area and walk up the road to the trailhead. **GPS:** N37 59.37' / W82 21.44'

THE HIKE

Cabwaylingo State Forest is home to deep hollows and thickly forested ridgetops that combine to make trails worth a visit. Springtime in the forest brings anglers to the trout-stocked waters of Twelvepole Creek, while hopeful hunters pack the cabins during the various hunting seasons. The Civilian Conservation Corps originally built up the 8,123-acre forest in the 1930s. Many of the structures that the CCC built still exist today.

From the Sweetwater Picnic Area, walk the road toward two cabins. Across the road from the cabins, you will come across the Sleepy Hollow Trail trailhead, marked with a sign that's set back from the roadside. The trail begins with an easy to moderate ascent in a stand of beech and hemlock. Downed timber and boulders are covered with moss, and the stream drops away to the right. The valley is shady, with steep ridges on both

A hidden waterfall along the
Sleepy Hollow Trail

sides. To your right, look down to the stream and, if the water is running, you will likely see and hear a small waterfall, especially in the winter when the leaves are off the trees.

The trail bends through a couple of drainages, then drops down to the stream, crosses it, and continues up. Before climbing, however, take a short detour by turning right and hiking downstream about 100 yards. A short but sketchy bushwhack reaches this hidden waterfall that drops a total of about 10 feet. The seclusion of the falls makes it seem as though no one else in the world knows of their existence.

> Cabwaylingo State Forest is named for the four nearby counties— Cabell, Wayne, Lincoln, and Mingo.

Travel back upstream to the trail and follow it uphill. The forest is filled with mature hemlocks. About 0.7 mile from the stream crossing, stay to the right as the Sleepy Hollow Trail passes by an old trail that travels down and to the left. The Sleepy Hollow Trail soon levels off, and a gorge of sandstone cliffs comes into view to the left. Cliffs drop off 20 to 30 feet as the stream snakes through boulders. The shady mini-gorge is green with moss. Although the streambed is inaccessible from above, if you're adventurous, you can reach the bottom of this canyon by bushwhacking the aforementioned side trail. The side trail is littered with downed timber, so be prepared to crawl on your belly and scramble over logs. Because the view from the bottom may be better than that from above, the reward is well worth the effort.

The Sleepy Hollow Trail continues past the cliffs by crossing the stream, where it climbs out of the bowl and then crosses to the opposite ridge, providing a 180-degree view of this area. On the opposite ridge, the trail starts up again, traveling west. The trail bends right and is wide and well marked. There is mountain laurel in the understory. Upon reaching the top of the ridge, you will come to the end of the Sleepy Hollow Trail and see a sign for the Martin Ridge Trail. At this point, the best part of the hike is complete. It's most scenic to simply turn around and return the way you came.

MILES AND DIRECTIONS

0.0 START at the Sleepy Hollow Trail trailhead near the Sweetwater Picnic Area; the trailhead is across the road from Cabin 1. Hike north, paralleling the stream.

0.4 The trail drops down to the stream, crosses it, and continues up. (**Option:** Before climbing the hillside, take a short detour by turning right and hiking downstream to a "hidden" waterfall.)

0.9 The Sleepy Hollow Trail crosses back over the stream.

1.0 Near the top of the ridge, come to a T intersection with an old fire road. Take a left, following the pink blazes.

1.1 A sign for the Martin Ridge Trail points left. This is the end of Sleepy Hollow Trail. Turn around at this point and return to the trailhead the way you came. (**Option:** You can make a 3.9-mile loop out of it by following the pink blazes and gas pipeline markers to the Martin Ridge Trail. Take the Martin Ridge Trail to CR 35, where you turn left to walk back to your car.)

2.2 Arrive back at the trailhead.

Sleepy Hollow Trail

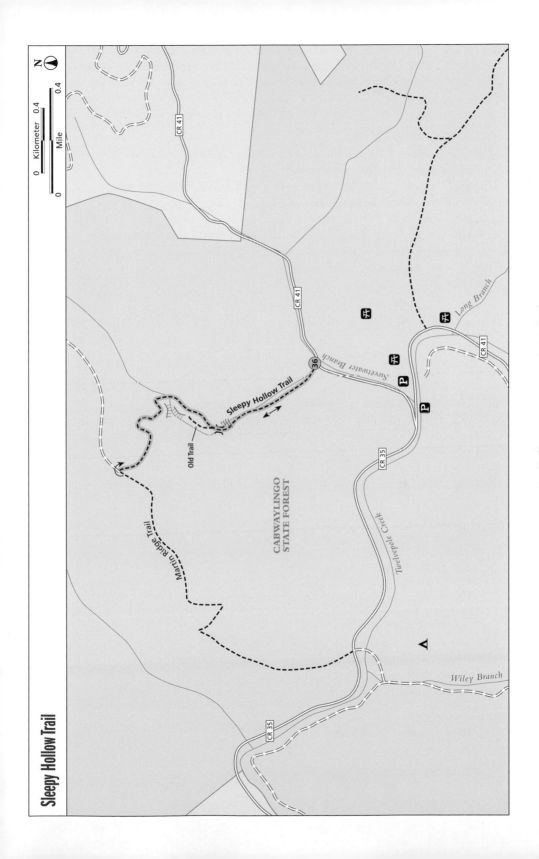

Option: You can follow the pink blazes and the gas pipeline markers 0.9 mile to the Martin Ridge Trail. (It's a muddy dirt and gravel road.) You can then follow the Martin Ridge Trail down to CR 35 and walk along the road back to your car. The loop is 3.9 miles in length.

HIKE INFORMATION

Local information: Cabell Huntington Convention and Visitors Bureau, (800) 635-6329 or (304) 525-7333, www.wvvisit.org

Camping: Cabwaylingo has 19 campsites, each with a fireplace and firewood for sale, electricity, water, a picnic table, and access to a shower house. Campsites are on a first-come, first-served basis. There are also 15 log cabins and a 100-person group camp area, which consists of a dining hall, two buildings that sleep 50 each, and a shower house. The group camp area is open May through Oct, the cabins Apr through Oct, and the 19-site campground Apr through Nov.

37 OVERLOOK ROCK TRAIL

Kanawha State Forest

WHY GO?
Located just minutes from Charleston, Kanawha State Forest is busy with outdoor activity. The 9,300-acre forest has more than 25 miles of trails for hikers, mountain bikers, and horseback riders. Trails travel from rocky ridges to wooded coves. The Overlook Trail is one of the most popular, as it affords a bird's-eye view of the forest from a rock outcropping.

THE RUNDOWN

Start: Northern Overlook Rock trailhead
Distance: 1.5-mile loop
Hiking time: About 45 minutes
Difficulty: Moderate due to a fairly steep climb and descent
Trail surface: Dirt and rock trail
Best season: Spring through fall
Other trail users: Hunters during hunting season; deer rifle season is usually late Nov to early Dec.
Canine compatibility: Leashed dogs permitted; leash must be 10 feet or shorter

Land status: State forest
Nearest town: Charleston
Fees and permits: None
Schedule: Open 6 a.m. to 10 p.m. for day use
Maps: Kanawha State Forest map and trail guide (free); Kanawha State Forest hiking/biking guide and topo map (fee); USGS quads: Belle, Charleston East, Charleston West, Racine
Trail contact: Kanawha State Forest, (304) 558-3500 or www .kanawhastateforest.com

FINDING THE TRAILHEAD
From I-64 in Charleston, take exit 58A and turn south on US 119, following it for 0.8 mile. Take a left onto Oakwood Road and continue for 1.0 mile (watch for a left turn in the road), then take a right onto Bridge Road, which eventually turns into Loudon Heights Road. Take a right onto Connell Road and follow it for 2.0 miles before turning left onto Kanawha Forest Drive. It's 2.4 miles to the park entrance. Follow the park road past the main picnic and swimming area. The trailhead is located 1.6 miles from the park entrance on the right side of the road near a small sign just past the main picnic area. There is limited parking on the opposite side of the road. **GPS:** N39 13.45′ / W81 57.51′

THE HIKE
The Overlook Rock Trail leaves the trailhead across from the small parking area and enters the forest. The trail, marked by infrequent gold blazes, heads uphill at a moderate angle. The path parallels a small drainage that is free of water most of the year and continues steeply uphill, passing some boulders. It crosses through the drainage and then bends to the left. Another difficult climb leads to the top of the shoulder. At the crest of the shoulder, the trail reaches a junction and a short side trail leads to a scenic outcropping of rocks, the trail's namesake, where there are views to the south.

Overlook Rock

The next portion of the hike is along the top of this small ridge. The trail continues up at a light angle as it makes its way across the ridge crest. There are limited views in winter along this section of the trail. Turn to the northwest (left) and continue along the crest through a forest of chestnut oaks with briars in the understory. The trail heads downhill to the south-southeast, making its way at easy and moderate angles toward the bottom of the valley below. There is one short, difficult section as the trail passes by moss-covered boulders.

The trail then drops into the western side of the ridge. This valley is shaded and cool in the morning hours. The trail makes a few switchbacks and finally reaches the drainage at the valley floor. The switchbacks in this section of trail are badly eroded by "cutters," hikers who don't follow a switchback all the way through its turn but instead travel steeply downhill several feet before the switchback. The trail suffers greatly, as this steep-cut section becomes badly eroded by surface-water runoff during heavy rains. Following switchbacks completely helps preserve the very ground we hike on. Please respect the trail.

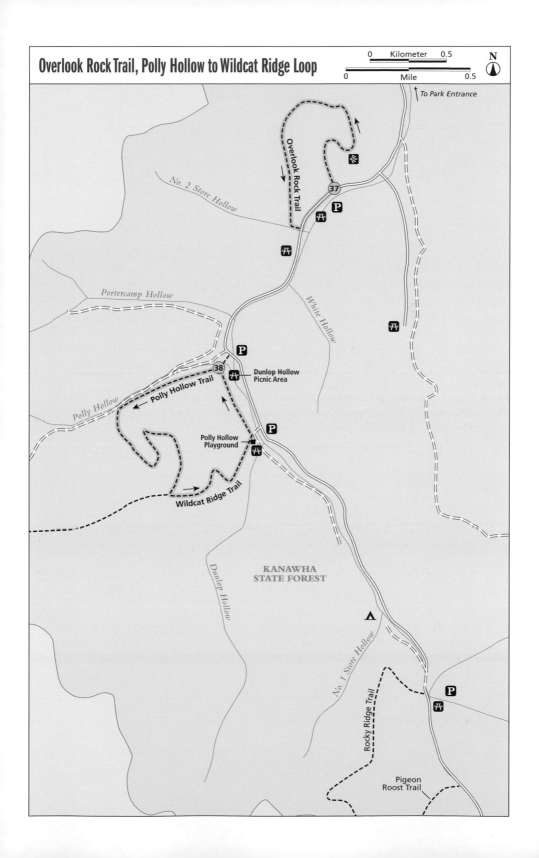

Overlook Rock Trail, Polly Hollow to Wildcat Ridge Loop

0   Kilometer   0.5

0   Mile   0.5

N

↑ To Park Entrance

Overlook Rock Trail

No. 2 Store Hollow

37

P

Portercamp Hollow

White Hollow

P

Polly Hollow

38

Dunlop Hollow Picnic Area

← Polly Hollow Trail

Polly Hollow Playground

P

Wildcat Ridge Trail →

→

KANAWHA STATE FOREST

Dunlop Hollow

No. 1 Store Hollow

Rocky Ridge Trail

P

Pigeon Roost Trail

MILES AND DIRECTIONS

0.0 START at the northern Overlook Rock trailhead, 1.6 miles from the main park entrance. Walk into the forest, paralleling a small drainage then crossing over it.

0.5 At the top of the ridge, a side trail leads to the overlook rocks. It is visible from the main trail.

0.9 The trail reaches a junction, marked with a sign. Take a left and start heading downhill.

1.2 The trail ends at the road. Take a left here and walk north toward the trailhead.

1.5 Arrive back at the trailhead.

HIKE INFORMATION

Local information: Charleston, WV Convention and Visitors Bureau, (800) 733-5469 or (304) 344-5075, www.charlestonwv.com

Local events/attractions: Mountain Stage, (304) 556-4900 or (888) 596-9729, www.mountainstage.org

Camping: The state forest has 46 campsites, 23 of which may be reserved. The campground is open from mid–Apr to the end of deer rifle season, usually around late Nov or early Dec.

Hike tours: Naturalist-led hikes occur from mid-May through Labor Day.

Organizations: Kanawha State Forest Foundation, www.ksff.org; www.facebook.com/Kanawhatrailclub/

38 POLLY HOLLOW TRAIL TO WILDCAT RIDGE TRAIL LOOP

Kanawha State Forest

WHY GO?

Located in the figurative "backyard" of the state capital is the 9,300-acre Kanawha State Forest. Included in the 25 miles of trails in the forest is the Polly Hollow to Wildcat Ridge loop that takes you along a swiftly flowing stream, up to a ridgetop with rock outcroppings, and through a forest of mixed hardwoods and hemlocks.

THE RUNDOWN

See the map on page 177.
Start: Polly Hollow trailhead, in the Dunlop Hollow Picnic Area
Distance: 2.5-mile loop
Hiking time: About 1.5 hours
Difficulty: Moderate due to ascents and descents
Trail surface: Dirt trail
Best season: May and June for rhododendron and mountain laurel bloom
Other trail users: Mountain bikers on Wildcat Ridge Trail; hunters in hunting season; deer rifle season is usually late Nov to early Dec.

Canine compatibility: Leashed dogs permitted
Land status: State forest
Nearest town: Charleston
Fees and permits: None
Schedule: The state forest is open year-round.
Maps: Kanawha State Forest map and trail guide (free); Kanawha State Forest hiking/biking guide and topo map (fee); USGS quads: Belle, Charleston East, Charleston West (location of hike), Racine
Trail contact: Kanawha State Forest, (304) 558-3500 or www.kanawhastateforest.com

FINDING THE TRAILHEAD

From I-64 in Charleston, take exit 58A and turn south on US 119, following it for 0.8 mile. Take a left onto Oakwood Road and continue for 1.0 mile (watch for a left turn in the road), then take a right onto Bridge Road, which eventually turns into Loudon Heights Road. Take a right onto Connell Road and follow it for 2.0 miles before turning left onto Kanawha Forest Drive. It's 2.4 miles to the park entrance. From the park entrance, travel 2.5 miles to the Dunlop Hollow Picnic Area on the right. Pull in here and park; across from the swings, you will find the trailhead.
GPS: N38 15.56' / W81 40.14'

THE HIKE

This hike travels up Polly Hollow past several rock outcrops to the top of Wildcat Ridge, then down to Davis Creek before looping back around the ridge to the starting point. From the picnic and playground area, look west toward the woods and you will see two trailheads, one for Wildcat Ridge on the left and one for Polly Hollow on the right. Take the Polly Hollow Trail and enter the woods; red blazes mark the trail as it starts up.

The forest along Polly Hollow Creek with maple, beech, and hemlock

The climb is light to moderate, leading around the ridge where it parallels the creek in Polly Hollow. The swiftly flowing creek is surrounded by a dense forest of hemlock, maple, and beech. Hike to the top of the ridge, where you will walk by a recess cave and rock outcroppings. The forest now is dominated by oaks and hickories. Atop the ridge you have some views, and this is a great place to see mountain laurels and rhododendrons in bloom during May and June. The last portion of the trail joins Wildcat Ridge and descends the opposite side of the ridge, switching back under a canopy of hemlocks. The trail ends at the Dunlop Hollow Picnic Area, near where the Polly Hollow Trail begins.

MILES AND DIRECTIONS

0.0　START at the Polly Hollow trailhead. Enter the woods and start ascending the ridge.

0.5　Pass the Polly Hollow spur trail to the Polly Hollow parking area on the right.

1.0　After paralleling the stream, the trail turns left and heads up to the top of the ridge.

1.5　Walk past a recess cave and take a right switchback through rock outcroppings to the ridgetop.

1.6　Come to the intersection with the Wildcat Ridge Trail and turn left.

2.0 Watch for double blue blazes as the trail switches back down this steep section.

2.5 Arrive at the Wildcat Ridge trailhead, only about 30 feet from the Polly Hollow trailhead where you started.

HIKE INFORMATION

Local information: Charleston, WV Convention and Visitors Bureau, (800) 733-5469 or (304) 344-5075, www.charlestonwv.com

Camping: The forest has 46 campsites; 23 may be reserved. The campground is open from mid-Apr to the end of deer firearms season, usually around late Nov/early Dec.

Local events/attractions: Mountain Stage, (304) 556-4900 or (888) 596-9729, http://mountainstage.org

Hike tours: Naturalist-led hikes occur from mid-May through Labor Day

Organizations: Kanawha State Forest Foundation, www.ksff.org; www.facebook.com/Kanawhatrailclub/

Honorable Mentions

K LOST TRAIL, BEECH FORK STATE PARK

The Lost Trail is popular among mountain bikers, who keep the trail clear for hikers as well. The 3-mile Lost Trail travels the banks of Beech Fork Lake. In addition to hiking, the park is good for bird watching, lake views, and fishing. There are eighty waterfront campsites. In 2012 the park used grant funding to make improvements to the Lost Trail and the Mary Davis Trail. Learn more when you contact the park office (304) 438-3004 or visit www.beechforksp.com.

From I-64, take exit 11 for WV 10 and downtown Huntington. At the bottom of the exit ramp, turn south onto WV 10. After 3.7 miles, turn right onto CR 43 (Hughes Branch Road). Go 3.8 miles to a stop sign and a Beech Fork State Park sign at this intersection. Turn left and continue 1.9 miles, turn right, and enter the park near the park headquarters. Pass by the headquarters and the Old Orchard camping area. Turn left onto Moxley Branch and cross a small bridge, then take the first right and park at the campground restroom. The trailhead is near Moxley Branch camping sites 34 and 35. Limited parking can be found near the trailhead. There is plenty of parking at the park headquarters, which adds approximately 0.2 mile to the hike, round-trip. GPS: N30 20.09'/W82 05.49'

L ROCKY RIDGE TO PIGEON ROOST TRAIL LOOP, KANAWHA STATE FOREST

Another nice Kanawha State Forest trail is the 2.75-mile loop linking the Rocky Ridge and Pigeon Roost Trails. Start on the accurately named Rocky Ridge Trail in a beech-maple forest and almost immediately hike to the top of a, well, rocky ridge. From here, enjoy the rock outcroppings and the dense upland oak-hickory forest. The well-blazed and marked trail leads you to the Pigeon Roost Trail (take a left), shared by mountain bikers. Shortly after starting on the Pigeon Roost Trail, the trail forks and then comes back together. Take the right fork to avoid a huge washout on the left. Slowly descend again, paralleling Pigeon Roost Hollow. Return to the trailhead by walking less than a mile along the park road. For more information, contact Kanawha State Forest at (304) 558-3500 or go to www.kanawhastateforest.com.

From I-64 in Charleston, take exit 58A and turn south on US 119, following it for 0.8 mile. Take a left onto Oakwood Road and continue for 1.0 mile (watch for a left turn in the road), then take a right onto Bridge Road, which eventually turns into Loudon Heights Road. Take a right onto Connell Road and follow it for 2.0 miles before turning left onto Kanawha Forest Drive. It's 2.4 miles to the park entrance. From the park entrance, drive 4.1 miles to the Rocky Ridge trailhead on the right. Parking is across the road on the left. GPS: N38 14.50'/W81 39.26'

MID-OHIO VALLEY

Like the slow-moving Ohio River for which this region is named, the Mid-Ohio Valley is a laid-back, slow-moving, rural delight. In this region, rolling hills and shallow hollows give way to the mighty river to the west.

Hikes here are leisurely, with minimal elevation gains and losses. On the North Bend Rail Trail, it is often difficult to discern whether you are traveling uphill or down. The Island Road hike even includes a ride on a stern-wheeler—now that's easy on the feet! Wildlife management areas provide prime wildlife viewing, and some hiking routes can make you feel miles from civilization.

Many hikes in the area incorporate the flavor of the people into the hiking experience. The North Bend Rail Trail passes through charming small towns. Likewise, Blennerhassett Island incorporates a mansion and wagon rides into its "heritage" experience.

Red trillium grow in moist soil.

In the Mid-Ohio Valley, all roads lead to Parkersburg, the metro center of the region. The city sits on the banks of the Ohio River and offers most services one might need. Victorian architecture dots the city, and coal barges as well as stern-wheelers travel the river. A joy to visit in its own right, Parkersburg can serve as a base camp for hikes in the Mid-Ohio Valley.

39 ISLAND ROAD

Blennerhassett Island Historical State Park

WHY GO?

A walk on Blennerhassett Island feels like less a hike and more like a Sunday constitutional. Your first step is aboard a stern-wheeler for a short trip on the Ohio River. Landing on Blennerhassett Island feels like stepping back in time, with reconstructed eighteenth-century buildings, carriage rides, and old-growth trees. The 500-acre island is located near the confluence of the Ohio River and the Little Kanawha River. Blennerhassett Island is privately owned but is held in a long-term lease by the state. The fifth-largest island on the Ohio River, it is less than 0.25 mile wide, but is 3.8 miles long. The state of West Virginia has developed the eastern end of the island as a historical site.

THE RUNDOWN

Start: Ticket booth on Blennerhassett Island
Distance: 1.5-mile loop
Hiking time: About 45 minutes
Difficulty: Easy
Trail surface: Gravel road
Best season: May through Oct, when the island is open to visitors
Other trail users: Bicyclists, horse-drawn carriages
Canine compatibility: You must sign a form to take your dog on the stern-wheeler and onto Blennerhassett Island; you can get this form at the museum when you purchase your ticket. Dogs are not allowed in any of the buildings on the island.
Land status: State park

Nearest town: Parkersburg, WV
Fees and permits: Fee charged to ride the stern-wheeler to Blennerhassett Island
Schedule: The island is open to visitors May 10–Oct 30; closed Mon and holidays. Stern-wheeler departure times vary according to season and day of the week; call ahead when planning your trip.
Maps: Blennerhassett Island Historical State Park map; USGS quad: Parkersburg
Trail contact: Blennerhassett Island Historical State Park, (304) 420-4800 or www.blenner hassettislandstatepark.com

FINDING THE TRAILHEAD

Take I-77 to exit 176 and travel west on US 50 for 3.0 miles to WV 14. Take a right, cross the bridge, and get into the left lane. Take a left on Market Street and go 3 blocks to Second Street. Take a right and go 1 block to the corner of Juliana Street. The Blennerhassett Museum is the brick building on the corner. Take a left and park in the lot behind the museum. You must purchase your stern-wheeler tickets at the museum. This is where you will take the stern-wheeler to the island.
Museum GPS: N39 15.89' / W81 33.88'

The black walnut grove
on Blennerhassett Island

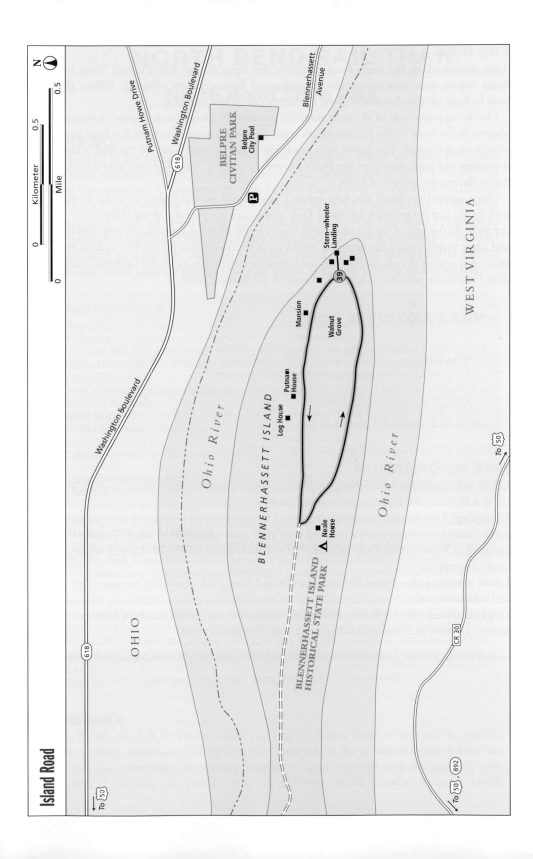

> The Silver Run Tunnel (#19) on the North Bend Trail is supposedly haunted. If you find yourself hiking through the tunnel at, say, midnight and see a very pale woman wearing a thin white dress, start running.

Bend's Quest program, which offers outdoor adventure programming of all kinds. You can arrange a shuttle through Quest; contact the park to do so. Otherwise, all hikes on the rail trail are out-and-back. Thus, a 4-mile one-way is already an 8-mile day. The flat, easy-hiking nature of this rail trail, however, will allow you to hike a longer, faster day than just about anywhere else in West Virginia.

To hike west from North Bend State Park, turn left at the intersection of the rail trail and the Extra Mile Trail, and immediately cross a bridge over the Hughes River. The trail crosses the Hughes several more times and passes through the crossroads of Cornwallis during the 3.0 rail trail miles to Cairo. Have lunch in Cairo and then take a leisurely walk back to the state park. Another option is to rent a bike in Cairo at Country Trails Bikes & The Cairo Supply Co. (304-628-3100).

MILES AND DIRECTIONS

0.0 START at the trailhead for the Access Trail. It's a gravel road by the picnic shelter.

0.6 Come to the junction with the North Bend Rail Trail. Turn left to hike west toward Cairo, crossing over Bonds Creek on a bridge. (**FYI:** First explore the Bonds Creek Tunnel, just to your right.)

1.7 Enter Cornwallis and then cross CR 8 (Bonds Creek Road).

3.6 Enter the town of Cairo. After checking out Cairo, turn around and retrace your steps the way you came.

7.2 Arrive back at the trailhead.

Option: From the parking area at North Bend State Park, follow the Access Trail from the picnic shelter to where it intersects with the North Bend Rail Trail. To travel the trail east, turn right and immediately hike through a tunnel. The trail travels through several tunnels before crossing under US 50 just before reaching Ellenboro, about 4.0 miles from the park.

Continuing east, the rail trail travels through rural America on its way to Pennsboro, about 10.0 miles from the state park. The trail passes over creeks and streams and through another tunnel on its way. Be sure to see the Old Stone House in Pennsboro, an old stagecoach inn that is now a museum.

HIKE INFORMATION

Local information: Ritchie County Tourism and Visitors Bureau, (304) 869-4070 or www.visitritchiecounty.com

Camping: Primitive camping (free) is permitted along the trail. North Bend State Park has a lodge, cabins, and a campground; go to www.northbendsp.com or call (304) 643-2931 for reservations.

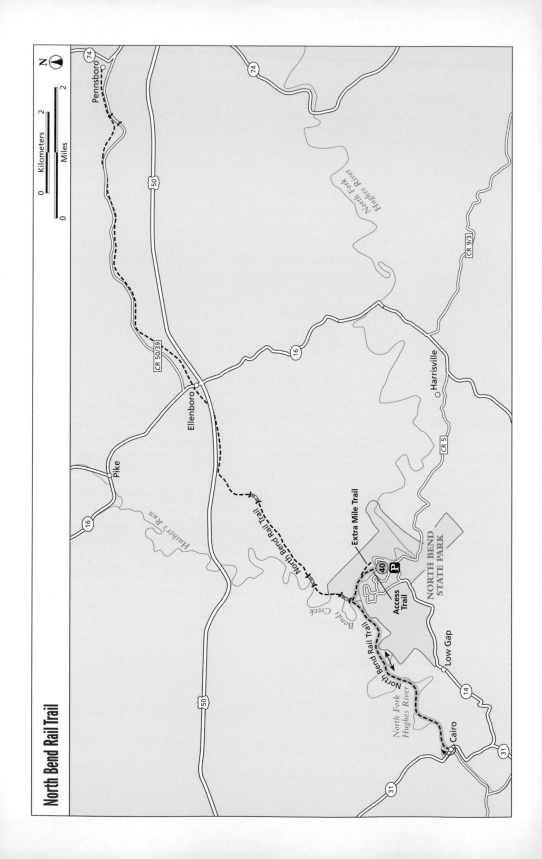

North Bend Rail Trail

Local events/attractions: North Bend State Park and the town of Cairo host a number of events throughout the year, including an annual bluegrass festival in May; contact the park for a calendar.

Hike tours: The Quest program at North Bend offers guided outdoor adventures and can coordinate a shuttle for a point-to-point hike; the park periodically offers naturalist-led nature walks; contact the park for information about both.

Organizations: North Bend Rails to Trails Foundation, (304) 628-3777 or www.northbendrailtrail.net

Honorable Mentions

M OVERHANGING ROCK TRAIL, NORTH BEND STATE PARK

Hiking the 0.5-mile Overhanging Rock Trail is one of the best things you can do with twenty or thirty minutes in North Bend State Park. Start at the trailhead near the stop sign at the bridge over the North Fork of the Hughes River between the camping area and the amphitheater area. Follow the white blazes as the trail makes its way up the ridge, past rock outcroppings, and through a dense hemlock forest. Come to a set of stairs that takes you down to a small stream that has eroded nature's half-pipe into the hillside. Vines and ferns dangle over the rock edges. Enjoy this spot and then take a footbridge over the stream and descend the other side of the narrow hollow to join with the Extra Mile Trail. For more information, call (304) 643-2931 or go to www.northbendsp.com.

To reach the park, travel first to Cairo, located on WV 31 south of US 50, approximately 50 miles west of Clarksburg and 20 miles east of Parkersburg. From WV 31, turn south and travel 5.1 miles to CR 14 (Low Gap Run Road). Take a left and follow CR 14 for 3.3 miles to the park entrance. Continue straight into the park and follow the signs for the campground and rail trail. At the campground, turn left and cross a bridge over the Hughes River. Take another left and pass the playground and amphitheater to park in a gravel lot near picnic shelter #3. After parking, walk back past the amphitheater to the bridge over the North Fork of the Hughes River. At the stop sign by the bridge, you will see the trailhead sign across the road. GPS: N39 13.52' /W81 06.29'

N MCDONOUGH TRAIL LOOP, MCDONOUGH WILDLIFE REFUGE

The McDonough Wildlife Refuge is a 277-acre area managed for wildlife and used largely by people who live in or near Vienna. If you're in the region, it's worth a visit for you, too, especially in the spring for wildflowers or in the fall when the trails are carpeted with fallen maple leaves. All of the trails are easy to follow and are well maintained. Try the 2.1-mile McDonough Trail, which loops from the parking area, passing by a couple of duck ponds and ascending to the top of the hill before skirting by some homes and returning to the trailhead parking. True to its name as a wildlife refuge, you have a good chance at encountering white-tailed deer and waterfowl. If you're quiet (and lucky), you may glimpse a coyote or fox. For information, call (304) 295-4473 or 4541 or go to www .vienna-wv.com/portal/departments-2/vienna-life.

To find the trailhead, take I-77 to exit 179. Turn south on WV 68 (Emerson Avenue) and proceed 3.0 miles to a stoplight at Rosemar Avenue. Turn right on Rosemar and continue 2.1 miles to the refuge entrance on the right. Proceed 0.1 mile straight to the parking area. The trailhead is located at the end of the parking area. GPS: N39 19.48' /W81 31 38'

○ TECUMSEH TO LAKE TRAIL, MOUNTWOOD PARK

This county park is popular among mountain bikers, who built much of the trail system here. Primitive and developed campgrounds are at the park, and fishing or special programming can round out your visit. Try hiking the Tecumseh Trail to the forested ridgetop and back down to the lake for views. Take a left at the lake on the Lake Trail and return to the trailhead for a 3-mile counterclockwise loop. If you want something a little longer, take a right at the lake and continue to the next loop, Medicine Man, for a 6-miler. You'll be able to scout out the primitive lakeside campsites while you're out here. For more information, go to www.mountwoodpark.org.

From US 50 12 miles east of Parkersburg, turn south into the entrance for Mountwood Park, marked with a sign. At 0.1 mile, take the first right (follow the signs for primitive camping and the shooting range). Drive another 0.3 mile, past a hairpin turn and the shooting range. Park in the lot by the beach house. Pass the gate and follow a gravel road to the Tecumseh Trail trailhead on the right. GPS: N39 14.81'/W81 18.48'

MONONGAHELA NATIONAL FOREST

Since 1915, when the first 7,200 acres were purchased, the Monongahela National Forest has grown to more than 919,000 acres. This land is a dream for the outdoor enthusiast. Trout streams cascade off ridges, rock climbers cling to the lofty crags of Tuscarora sandstone, and the whoop of whitewater rafters can be heard in the valleys. More than 800 miles of hiking trails traverse the land. So many miles, so little time.

Hikes in the Monongahela are rugged. Elevations in the forest range from 900 to 4,800 feet. Hikes to ridge crests are steep and sustained, and creek bottoms are deep and shadowed. Five federally designated wilderness areas provide the promise of solitude, bringing with it added personal responsibility. When hiking in the Mon, take special care to ensure self-sufficiency. Bring extra clothes, food, and a map and compass (see the essential gear list in the introduction). If you become lost or hurt in the Monongahela, it could

Bluebells in the Laurel Fork campground

be quite some time before you are found. Don't count on another hiker happening by in your time of need.

Camping possibilities are limitless in the Mon. Although campgrounds dot the land, this is the place to don the backpack and camp in the backcountry, where beautiful streamside or ridgetop campsites can be found. The sheer joy of being utterly alone and looking out your tent into a star-filled sky cannot be underestimated.

The area surrounding the Mon is, in a word, rural. Enjoy the small towns that line the county routes, but be sure you are well equipped before leaving for your trip. Finding an outfitter to replace a worn-out hip belt on your backpack will not be an option.

Finally, exercise caution during hunting seasons, which generally, but not exclusively, occur during the fall and early winter. Before heading out on your hike, please review local hunting regulations and be aware of any season that is open. If you choose to hike during a hunting season, wear blaze orange and stick to well-marked, well-traveled trails.

41 OTTER CREEK TRAIL

Otter Creek Wilderness

WHY GO?

Otter Creek is classic Mon wilderness. The namesake creek is the heart of this 20,000-acre area. It's all about the creek, which is a perfect destination on a hot summer day. Nearly 50 miles of trails travel this area, making it possible to create day hikes and backpacking trips of various lengths. Stellar backcountry campsites dot the main trail along Otter Creek, which features waterfalls, chutes, and swimming holes galore. The creek is surrounded by mountains, spruce forests, high plateau bogs, laurel and rhododendron thickets, black bears and other wildlife, and quite a few creek crossings. Otter Creek is not for the faint of heart, but is for the adventurous water lover.

THE RUNDOWN

Start: Southern Otter Creek Trail trailhead, off FR 303
Distance: 10.5 miles one way
Hiking time: About 5 to 6 hours
Difficulty: Difficult due to length and creek crossings
Trail surface: Dirt trail with several stream crossings
Best season: Summer
Other trail users: Horseback riders
Canine compatibility: Controlled dogs permitted
Land status: National forest
Nearest town: Elkins
Fees and permits: None
Schedule: The wilderness is accessible 24/7 year-round.

Maps: Otter Creek Wilderness map, available from the Potomac office of the Cheat-Potomac Ranger District; USGS quads: Bath Alum, Green Valley, Montrose, Parsons
Trail contact: Potomac office of the Cheat-Potomac Ranger District, Monongahela National Forest, (304) 257-4488 or www.fs.usda.gov/mnf
Special considerations: Otter Creek is designated wilderness, so maximum group size is 10 people. Snow may make access impossible during winter, and spring (or any recent) rainfall may make stream crossings impossible. Be prepared to make camp or turn back if the water is too high.

FINDING THE TRAILHEAD

From the junction of US 219/US 33 in Elkins, take US 33 east 10.9 miles to the top of Shavers Mountain. Turn left onto FR 91 (it's easy to miss; if you start descending the other side of Shavers Mountain, you've gone too far). On FR 91, go 1.3 miles to a fork. Take the right fork on FR 303 and continue 0.5 mile to the parking area. **GPS:** N38 56.48' / W79 40.14'

To shuttle, leave one car at the northern trailhead. From the stoplight in downtown Parsons, take US 219 0.2 mile across the Shavers Fork bridge, then take a right followed by an immediate left. Brown Otter Creek signs are here where the road becomes Billings Avenue. Parallel the Allegheny Trail bike path and Dry Fork upstream. At mile 2.6, the road forks; there is a sign for the gravel FR 701 here. Take the right fork. At mile 5.3, the road forks again (unmarked). Take a left and head uphill. At mile 5.9, come to the Otter Creek Trail trailhead on the left. There is a

Waterfall along Otter Creek

bulletin board here (though signs may be ripped down) and a wooden sign for the Zero Grade Trail. If you arrive at the Turkey Run trailhead, you've gone too far. **GPS:** N39 02.63' / W79 39.79'

THE HIKE

If you're ambitious, set up a shuttle and hike most of the 11.8-mile length of the Otter Creek Trail (TR 131) in the beautiful and remote Otter Creek Wilderness in a day. If you're ambitious in a different way altogether, take a week off to do the same trip. Take your time walking along Otter Creek and checking out the many campsites, ranging from intimate to large, that line this rushing mountain stream. Alternately, make a base camp at your favorite site and head out on a series of day hikes along the nearly 50 miles of trails in this backcountry.

Like most of West Virginia, this area was logged in the past—in this case, during the late nineteenth and early twentieth centuries. The federal government acquired what is today the Otter Creek Wilderness in 1917, but the area only gained wilderness protection in 1975, eleven years after passage of the Wilderness Act. With the passage of the Wild Monongahela Act in 2009, Otter Creek gained another 698 acres of protected wilderness, bringing the total acreage above 20,000. The area is large enough to support a breeding population of black bears, which makes proper food storage a must.

Because this is a wilderness area, make sure your topo map–reading skills are up to par. Most trail junctions are not marked. The Otter Creek Trail itself is relatively easy to stay on, as it parallels its namesake creek through the wilderness area. You also need to be prepared to cross the creek a number of times. Because of this, take note of the weather conditions and forecast: Flash floods have left more than one hiker stranded, unable to cross the swollen creek.

The southern trailhead is easily accessible from Elkins. Starting there, you can hike north (downstream) to the Big Springs Gap Trail (TR 151) and uphill away from the creek to the Big Springs Gap Trailhead. (The Otter Creek Trail continues past Big Springs Gap another 1.3 miles to the Dry Fork Trailhead.) Along the way, you'll pass the Yellow Creek Trail (TR 135), Mylius Trail (TR 128), Moore Run Trail (TR 138), Possession Camp Trail (TR 158), and finally the Green Mountain Trail (TR 130). A good out-and-back day hike would be the walk to the largest set of waterfalls on Otter Creek and back, totaling 9.2 miles.

MILES AND DIRECTIONS

0.0 START at the southern Otter Creek Trail trailhead, marked with a sign for Condon Run at the end of FR 303. Walk past the gate onto the gravel road. In about 75 yards, pass the Hedrick Camp Trail on the right and cross the creek over a footbridge. After the bridge, take a right and parallel the creek downstream on a combination of trail and gravel road.

0.25 The trail leaves the road to the left. A sign marks the trail. Take this left.

1.2 Make your first side-creek crossing, then pass the Yellow Creek Trail on the left. You will cross Otter Creek or a tributary four times over the next 2.5 miles. Stay close to the creek.

4.1 The unmarked Mylius Trail comes in from the right. Continue straight.

4.7 The trail forks. Take the right fork, continuing along the edge of the creek.

5.3 Just past where Devil's Gulch pours into Otter Creek from the west, come to a junction with the Possession Camp Trail on the right, marked with a rock cairn. Continue straight, following the Otter Creek Trail. (The Moore Run Trail begins across Otter Creek, not quite visible from this spot.)

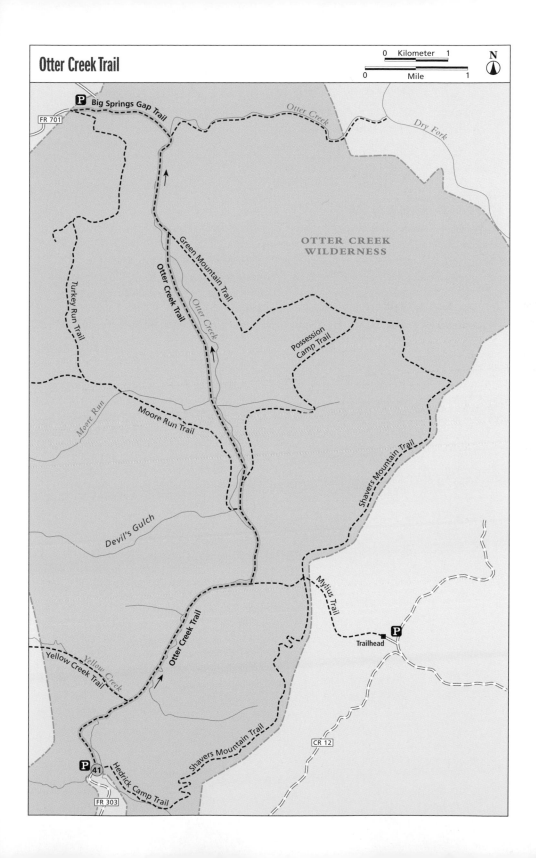

Otter Creek Trail

0 Kilometer 1

0 Mile 1

N

FR 701

Big Springs Gap Trail

Otter Creek

Dry Fork

OTTER CREEK WILDERNESS

Green Mountain Trail

Otter Creek Trail

Otter Creek

Turkey Run Trail

Possession Camp Trail

Moore Run

Moore Run Trail

Shavers Mountain Trail

Devil's Gulch

Mylius Trail

P

Trailhead

Otter Creek Trail

Yellow Creek

Yellow Creek Trail

CR 12

Shavers Mountain Trail

P 41

Hedrick Camp Trail

FR 303

5.5	About 50 yards past a campsite situated right along the trail, the Otter Creek Trail crosses the creek. The crossing is marked with cairns.
6.6	Pass a campsite and then cross over a tributary of Otter Creek, then pass more campsites.
8.3	Cross Otter Creek to the east.
8.5	Pass the Green Mountain Trail on the right, marked with a rock cairn.
9.75	Make the last Otter Creek crossing, to the west, then follow the trail uphill.
10.5	End at the Big Springs Gap trailhead.

HIKE INFORMATION

Local information: Randolph County Convention and Visitors Bureau, (304) 636-2780 or (800) 422-3304, www.randolphcountywv.com/

Camping: Because this hike is in designated wilderness, backcountry camping is permitted throughout the area. There are no developed campsites. As in all designated wilderness, camp in sites that have been used before in high-use areas; in low-use parts of the wilderness, dispersed camping is recommended.

Organizations: West Virginia Highlands Conservancy, www.wvhighlands.org

42

DOLLY SODS NORTH CIRCUIT

Dolly Sods Wilderness

WHY GO?

In truth, the trails in Dolly Sods North can be eroded and muddy, and the seemingly relentless wind can just about knock you off your feet. But it won't be able to knock the smile off your face. This is because of the vistapalooza that is Dolly Sods North, from the sweeping views as far as the distant Shenandoah Mountains to the east to the nearby Canaan Valley to the west, and everything you'll encounter in between, including A-list wildlife such as black bears and bald eagles. August is a great time for blueberry picking.

THE RUNDOWN

Start: Bear Rocks Trail trailhead, off FR 75

Distance: 10.8-mile lollipop

Hiking time: About 6 hours

Difficulty: Difficult due to distance and trail surface, including stream crossings

Trail surface: Dirt and rock trail

Best season: Spring through fall; access in winter can be impossible due to snow

Other trail users: Horseback riders

Canine compatibility: Controlled pets permitted

Land status: National forest

Nearest town: Davis

Fees and permits: None

Schedule: The wilderness is accessible 24/7 year-round, but access roads are often not passable in the winter.

Maps: Dolly Sods and Roaring Plains hiking guide map (available from Forest Service); USGS quads: Blackbird Knob, Blackwater Falls, Hopeville, Laneville

Trail contact: Monongahela National Forest, Potomac office of the Cheat-Potomac Ranger District, (304) 257-4488 or www.fs.usda.gov/goto/DollySods

Special considerations: Groups larger than 10 are not allowed in the Dolly Sods Wilderness.

FINDING THE TRAILHEAD

From either Petersburg or Seneca Rocks, take WV 55/WV 28 to Hopeville. Turn north on CR 28-7 and go 12.4 miles to FR 75 (there is a sign for Dolly Sods). Turn left and drive up the mountain 5.1 miles to the Bear Rocks trailhead. **GPS:** N39 03.85'/W079 18.16'

THE HIKE

With the passage of the Wild Monongahela Act in 2009, the wilderness designation of Dolly Sods expanded to include Dolly Sods North, creating a 17,000–acre playground for day hikers and backpackers alike. Tackle this circuit hike in a day or break it into two with a night of camping. The trails on this circuit are planned so that there are no strenuous ascents, but this is not an easy hike. Come prepared for stream crossings. Wear waterproof footwear or plan to cross barefoot or in a pair of sandals.

Take some time to explore Bear Rocks before setting out on the trail. These are the rock outcroppings with easterly views at the top of the ridge where the road takes a

hairpin turn before the trailhead parking—note that the trailhead parking is not at the turn; it's 0.1 mile south on FR 75. The trailhead is well marked with a Bear Rocks Trail (TR 522) sign. All the trails are easy to follow, and all junctions are marked with signs that indicate trail names and numbers. Begin by hiking west along a wide dirt road/trail through blueberry heaths and red spruce stands.

Cross Red Creek and continue through blueberry-laden sods and stands of red spruce (note the flagged spruce from the relentless wind coming from the west). You'll see the next ridge a mile away as well as distant ridges dozens of miles away. Reach the edge of the wilderness boundary to the west. When you reach the Rocky Ridge Trail, walk south, now along the eastern rim of the Canaan Valley. You'll walk past, through, and over quartzite boulders. Find a nice spot to lunch here.

Turn eastward again at the Dobbin Grade Trail. Cross the Left Fork of Red Creek and walk through more wooded sections of trail. Descend to Red Creek, where the water is flowing, blueberries are nearby for the picking, and there's a mix of open sods, red spruce, and deciduous trees. Nice backcountry sites have easy access to water here. Cross Red Creek, then parallel Red Creek upstream to the Bear Rocks Trail where you began.

MILES AND DIRECTIONS

0.0 START at the Bear Rocks Trail (TR 522) trailhead and hike west, away from the road.

Dolly Sods North Circuit

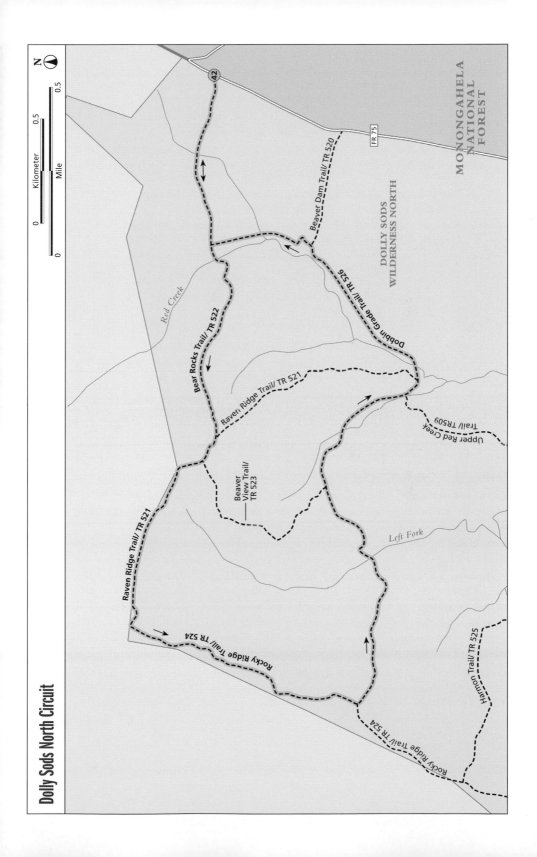

1.0 Pass straight through the intersection with the Dobbin Grade Trail (TR 526).

1.1 Cross Red Creek.

2.4 The Bear Rocks Trail ends at the junction with the Raven Ridge Trail (TR 521). Continue straight/slightly right at this three-way intersection.

2.6 Pass the Beaver View Trail (TR 523) on the left. Continue on the Raven Ridge trail to its end at the western edge of the wilderness area.

3.8 Arrive at the intersection with the Rocky Ridge Trail (TR 524). Turn left (south) and soon you'll come to views of the Canaan Valley to the west. (***FYI:*** Find some nice rock outcroppings along this stretch of trail for lunch.)

5.5 Arrive at the junction of the Dobbin Grade Trail (TR 526). Turn left (east) and walk until you cross the Left Fork of Red Creek.

6.2 Cross the Left Fork of Red Creek and come to a T intersection, although this is not an official junction. Turn right. Soon you will join an old railroad bed.

7.0 Come to the junction with the Beaver View Trail (TR 523) on the left. Continue straight. (***FYI:*** If the trail has been wet up until this point, do not continue straight—it only gets wetter. In wet conditions, turn left on the Beaver View Trail and take it back to the Raven Ridge Trail, where you can retrace your steps to the trailhead.)

7.9 Pass the Upper Red Creek Trail (TR 509) on the right. Continue straight.

8.0 Pass the Raven Ridge Trail (TR 521) on the left. Continue straight.

8.1 Cross Red Creek. The trail curves north and parallels Red Creek. (***FYI:*** Find backcountry campsites along this stretch with easy access to water.)

9.1 Pass the Beaver Dam Trail (TR 520) on the right. Continue straight.

9.8 Come to a T intersection with the Bear Rocks Trail. Take a right.

10.8 Arrive back at the trailhead.

HIKE INFORMATION

Local information: Tucker County Convention and Visitors Bureau, (800) 782-2775 or http://canaanvalley.org; Randolph County Convention and Visitors Bureau, (304) 636-2780 or (800) 422-3304, www.randolphcountywv.com/

Camping: Free backcountry camping is permitted throughout the Dolly Sods Wilderness. Red Creek Campground is located on FR 75, just outside the boundary of the wilderness. The campground has 12 fee campsites that are filled on a first-come, first-served basis.

Organizations: The Nature Conservancy, www.nature.org; West Virginia Highlands Conservancy, www.wvhighlands.org

43 SODS CIRCUIT

Dolly Sods Wilderness

WHY GO?

Dolly Sods is practically an official requirement for the West Virginia backpacker. It's not an exaggeration to say there's no place like this. Just the main highlights include a forest rich in biodiversity, backcountry waterfalls along Red Creek, perfect backcountry campsites, and, of course, what Dolly Sods is best known for: sweeping vistas in the upland sods area among acres of rock outcroppings, wind-flagged red spruce trees, and blueberry thickets. You will wonder if you're still in West Virginia.

THE RUNDOWN

Start: Red Creek trailhead, off FR 19
Distance: 16.2-mile lollipop, with a 9.4-mile option
Hiking time: About 8 to 10 hours for the full length, over 1 or 2 days
Difficulty: Difficult due to distance, trail surface, and elevation gain
Trail surface: Dirt and rock trail
Best season: Spring through fall; access in winter can be impossible due to snow
Other trail users: Horseback riders
Canine compatibility: Controlled pets are permitted
Land status: National forest
Nearest town: Davis
Fees and permits: None

Schedule: The wilderness is accessible 24/7 year-round, but access roads are often not passable in winter.
Maps: Dolly Sods and Roaring Plains hiking guide map (available from Forest Service); USGS quads: Blackbird Knob, Blackwater Falls, Hopeville, Laneville
Trail contact: Monongahela National Forest, Potomac office of the Cheat-Potomac Ranger District, (304) 257-4488 or www.fs.usda.gov/goto/DollySods
Special considerations: Groups larger than 10 are not allowed in the Dolly Sods Wilderness.

FINDING THE TRAILHEAD

From the junction of US 33/WV 55 and WV 32 in Harman, drive north on WV 32 for 3.8 miles to Bonner Mountain Road (CR 32-3). Turn right (east) and go 4.9 miles to the junction with Laneville Road (CR 45-4). (Here Bonner Mountain Road is marked CR 45-1.) Take a right onto Laneville Road and drive 1.3 miles to the bridge, where FR 19 begins. Cross the bridge and the trailhead is on the left, just past the Laneville wildlife cabin. **GPS:** N38 58.35'/W79 23.87'

THE HIKE

Truly one of the most unique ecosystems in West Virginia is that contained in Dolly Sods. Northern hardwood forests characterize the lower elevations, while open heath barrens and wide-open sods occupy higher elevations. The beauty of the area is stunning.

While the landscape may be beautiful to behold, it is the unnatural history of Dolly Sods that has created this ecosystem. When settlers arrived in the area, the red spruces averaged 4 feet in diameter and the forest floor consisted of a humus layer more than 5

Red Creek

feet thick. During the late nineteenth century, most of the eastern forests were cut; the Dolly Sods area was not spared. The years after the logging saw forest fires rage through the leftover slash timber, burning the humus layer to bedrock. The extreme environment that was left was barely hospitable for the red spruce to regenerate and was subsequently used for grazing livestock. It is a family of sheep farmers, the Dahle family, for which the area is named. The Civilian Conservation Corps reclaimed the area by planting red spruce in the 1930s, but it was not until 1975 that Congress officially protected the 10,215-acre wilderness. In 2009 Congress passed the Wild Monongahela Act, which expanded the wilderness area to 17,371 acres.

> The US military used the Dolly Sods area for various exercises during WWII. Some remnants of these exercises still remain. Live mortars are sometimes found in the area, albeit rarely. If you find a mortar, do not touch it. Note the location and alert the Forest Service by calling (304) 257-4488, or (888) 283-0303 after hours.

Begin the hike by paralleling Red Creek, following it upstream. As for footwear, be prepared for a number of stream crossings, the first of which comes in a half mile. This lowlands section of trail is through dense, rich forest. The understory is full of rhododendron, and look for wildflowers throughout the season. In the spring you may see species hard to find elsewhere, like pink lady's slippers.

The hiking gets a little more difficult as the angle of the trail becomes steeper. You can shorten the hike by going directly to Rocky Point on the Rocky Point Trail, off the Red Creek Trail. This trail section up to Rocky Point—a must-do—is a rocky ankle-twister, so exercise caution.

Continuing on the Red Creek Trail, soon you'll come to some side trails that take you to cascading waterfalls along the creek. Just past the junction of the Red Creek and Breathed Mountain Trails, you can take a side jaunt to The Forks, at the confluence of Red Creek and the Left Fork, where the most sought-after campsites are. The trail soon emerges into the upland sods area. In late summer, gorge yourself on blueberries here while admiring less common wildflowers such as gentian. The Breathed Mountain Trail takes you west along the high sods with some of the vistas Dolly Sods is known for. Join the Big Stonecoal Trail and parallel this smaller stream, which is clear and swift. Descend back into the forest and return to the Red Creek Trail.

Along the way, take the Rocky Point Trail to Rocky Point, where you take in a 270-degree view of practically nothing but miles of the Red Creek Valley and tree-covered mountains in every direction. Plan to spend some time at Rocky Point. The southern tip of this massive rock outcropping has a feature called the Lion's Head, which does look somewhat like a lion's head in profile.

MILES AND DIRECTIONS

0.0 START at the trailhead for the Red Creek Trail (TR 514). There is a bulletin board here with trail and conditions information. Hike upstream along an old forest road.

0.5 Cross a small stream that feeds into Red Creek. Continue paralleling Red Creek.

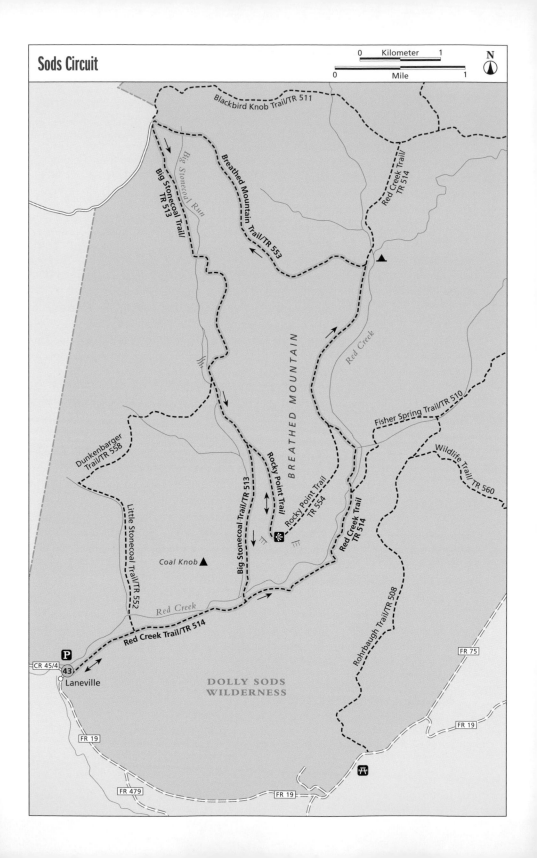

Sods Circuit

Kilometer
0   1
0   1
Mile

N

Blackbird Knob Trail/TR 511

Big Stonecoal Run

Breathed Mountain Trail/TR 553

Big Stonecoal Trail/ TR 513

Red Creek Trail/ TR 514

B R E A T H E D   M O U N T A I N

Red Creek

Fisher Spring Trail/TR 510

Dunkenbarger Trail/TR 558

Rocky Point Trail

Rocky Point Trail/ TR 554

Wildlife Trail/ TR 560

Big Stonecoal Trail/TR 513

Little Stonecoal Trail/TR 552

Red Creek Trail TR 514

Coal Knob ▲

Red Creek

Rohrbaugh Trail/TR 508

Red Creek Trail/TR 514

FR 75

P

CR 45/4

43

Laneville

DOLLY SODS
WILDERNESS

FR 19

FR 19

FR 479

FR 19

0.7 Pass the Little Stonecoal Trail on the left. The Red Creek Trail bends right and hikes moderately up the eastern ridge, moving out of the creek valley.

1.5 Come to an intersection with a rock cairn. The Red Creek Trail moves over to the creek bank and intersects with the Big Stonecoal Trail (TR 513), which crosses Red Creek and hikes up the western ridge. The hike will travel down this trail later on your trip. Continue straight on the Red Creek Trail without crossing Red Creek.

3.1 Reach a junction with the Fisher Spring Trail (TR 510), coming in from the right. Turn left and follow the Red Creek Trail down to Red Creek. The trail fords Red Creek and travels north along the creek bank. (**FYI:** A highlight in the valley is a cascade in Red Creek over a large slab of sandstone.)

3.8 Pass the junction with the Rocky Point Trail (TR 554) on your left. Continue straight on the Red Creek Trail. (**Option:** You can make a 9.4-mile loop by turning left on the Rocky Point Trail and hiking directly to Rocky Point. Continue on to the Big Stonecoal Trail, turn left [south], and walk directly back to the Red Creek Trail.)

5.2 The Red Creek Trail reaches the Breathed Mountain Trail (TR 553). Turn left at the junction. The Breathed Mountain Trail crosses stretches of open plains separated by stands of forest. (**FYI:** North of this intersection, at the confluence of Red Creek and the Left Fork, aka The Forks, there are many campsites, along with swimming holes. If you plan to camp, instead of turning left on the Breathed Mountain Trail, continue straight about 0.2 mile on the Red Creek Trail to these sites.)

7.6 The trail crosses a small stream and then exits the wilderness boundary onto a gravel road. At this junction is an information kiosk and the trailhead for the Big Stonecoal Trail (TR 513). Take a left onto the Big Stonecoal Trail.

10.0 The Big Stonecoal Trail passes the Dunkenbarger Trail (TR 558) on the right. Continue straight.

10.5 The Big Stonecoal Trail intersects with the Rocky Point Trail. Take a left here and follow the trail to an obvious side trail at a cairn that takes you up a short, steep jaunt to the top of Rocky Point.

11.5 Hang out at the top of Rocky Point, with its views of the Red Creek Valley.

12.5 Return the way you came to the junction of the Rocky Point and Big Stonecoal Trails. Take a left onto the Big Stonecoal Trail.

15.5 Cross Red Creek and arrive at the junction with the Red Creek Trail, near where you began your hike. Take a right.

16.2 Arrive back at the trailhead.

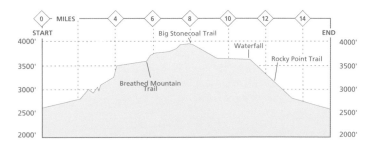

HIKE INFORMATION

Local information: Tucker County Convention and Visitors Bureau, (800) 782-2775 or http://canaanvalley.org; Randolph County Convention and Visitors Bureau, (304) 636-2780 or (800) 422-3304, www.randolphcountywv.com/

Camping: Free backcountry camping is permitted throughout the Dolly Sods Wilderness. Red Creek Campground is located on FR 75, just outside the boundary of the wilderness. The campground has 12 fee campsites that are filled on a first-come, first-served basis.

Organizations: West Virginia Highlands Conservancy, www.wvhighlands.org

44 NORTH FORK MOUNTAIN TRAIL

Spruce Knob–Seneca Rocks National Recreation Area

WHY GO?

Encompassing more than 100,000 acres, the Spruce Knob–Seneca Rocks National Recreation Area contains two of the most popular outdoor attractions in West Virginia. Spruce Knob is the highest point in the Mountain State, and Seneca Rocks has some of the best rock climbing in the East. North Fork Mountain forms the eastern boundary of the recreation area full of high ridges and steep cliffs. The North Fork Mountain Trail is an excellent two- to three-day backpack, offering some of the most scenic vistas in the entire state as well as a unique dry ridge ecosystem. The major drawback to this trail is a lack of water along the crest. For a day hike, begin from the northern terminus and hike up the ridge to a view of Chimney Rock, then return the way you came.

THE RUNDOWN

Start: Southern terminus for a backpacking trip or northern terminus for a day hike
Distance: 24.2 miles one way
Hiking time: About 2 to 3 days
Difficulty: Difficult due to distance
Trail surface: Dirt trail and forest roads
Best season: Spring through fall
Other trail users: Mountain bikers, horseback riders
Canine compatibility: Controlled dogs are permitted

Land status: National forest
Nearest town: Franklin
Fees and permits: None
Schedule: The wilderness is accessible 24/7 year-round.
Maps: USGS quads: Circleville, Franklin, Upper Tract, Hopeville, Petersburg West
Trail contact: Potomac office of the Cheat-Potomac Ranger District, Monongahela National Forest, (304) 257-4488 or www.fs.usda.gov/mnf

FINDING THE TRAILHEAD

Southern terminus: From the intersection of US 220 and US 33 in Franklin, take US 220 north/US 33 west 0.5 mile and turn left on US 33 west. Travel 8.3 miles to the summit of North Fork Mountain. Parking is on the right. There is a small green metal building with a tower and a gate across the road. This is private land. Do not block the gate. **GPS:** N38 42.64'/W79 24.12'

Northern terminus: From the intersection of WV 28, WV 55, and US 33 in Seneca Rocks, take WV 28 north/WV 55 east toward Petersburg. Proceed 15.3 miles to CR 28/11 (Smoke Hole Road) and turn right. Cross the bridge and travel 0.3 mile to the parking area on the right. **GPS:** N38 58.96'/W79 13.85'

Fall colors along the North Fork Mountain Trail

THE HIKE

This hike follows most of the 34-mile backbone of North Fork Mountain. The Nature Conservancy has identified this mountain worthy of protection due to its relatively dry, fire-prone ecosystem that is home to paper birch, dwarf pine, red pine, and a virgin red spruce forest. It's also home to natural grass bald as well as rock outcroppings that allow unobstructed views of the North Fork Valley to the west. You're so high that you might spot eagles (both bald and golden) flying below. Listen for the *zee-zee-zee-zoo-zee* of the black-throated green warbler. Spend a night here and you may get lucky and encounter a black bear, fox, or bobcat.

This trail description begins at the southern trailhead and proceeds north. It is highly recommended to hike the North Fork Mountain Trail (TR 501) in this direction, especially if the hike is tackled as a multiday hike, because the elevation gain is minimal. The elevation at this trailhead is 3,592 feet. The elevation at the northern end of the trail is 1,300 feet.

From the road, hike past the gate and into the woods. There are NO TRESPASSING signs posted at the beginning of the hike; remember to stay on the trail, which is marked with blue blazes. The trail is wide and easy to follow as it travels an old road grade along the ridge crest. Rock outcroppings provide exceptional views of Germany Valley and Spruce Knob to the west. After a few miles, the road ends and the trail becomes a footpath.

The path is narrow but easy to follow. The North Fork Mountain Trail hugs the eastern slope of the mountain just below the ridge crest. Even on very windy days, there is little wind on the trail, which contours the eastern slope. The ridge is steep along this section. The trail then descends to a narrow saddle and again contours on the leeward side of the mountain. The trail reaches a wide, level region known as High Knob. Pines dominate the canopy, and mountain laurel crowds the trail. Many short side trails lead to the western ridge. There is an excellent view of Seneca Rocks.

Not far beyond this area, the trail drops over to the western side of the mountain. It can be very windy along this short section of the hike. Another descent is followed by a long moderate climb along an old road. At 10.1 miles, the trail reaches a gas pipeline. There is a sign for US 33 to the south and Chimney Rock to the north. The road climbs at an easy grade to the highest point of the hike (elevation 3,895 feet). A metal building is located on this high point, along with one of the few clear views to the east.

After the summit, the trail descends and follows FR 79, a gravel road. The middle parking area is at a sharp right bend for the North Fork Mountain Trail. The distance is 11.9 miles, the halfway point of the trail.

The trail reenters the forest and leaves the road behind, again becoming a narrow path. An easy climb leads to a pleasant campsite, and the trail begins a series of easy climbs and descents, staying near the 3,100-foot level. About 2.5 miles past FR 79, a sloping stone slab lies west of the trail. At the top of this slab is a view of Champe Rocks, the Dolly Sods region, and the North Fork of the South Branch of the Potomac River.

The final section of the North Fork Mountain Trail is a steep descent, dropping 1,750 feet over 2.5 miles to CR 28/11. At the beginning of the descent, the canopy is dominated by small scrubby pine. Near the end of the descent, tall second-growth hardwoods reign supreme. There are several switchbacks during this descent. A sign marks the trailhead at an elevation of 1,300 feet.

MILES AND DIRECTIONS

0.0 START the North Fork Mountain Trail (TR 501) at the southern trailhead off US 33. The trail is marked with blue blazes; you will not see these blazes immediately, as the first portion of the trail goes through private land.

3.5 Cross under power lines and angle slightly right to stay on the trail.

3.8 Pass around a green metal gate.

4.5 Come to a four-way intersection. Continue straight.

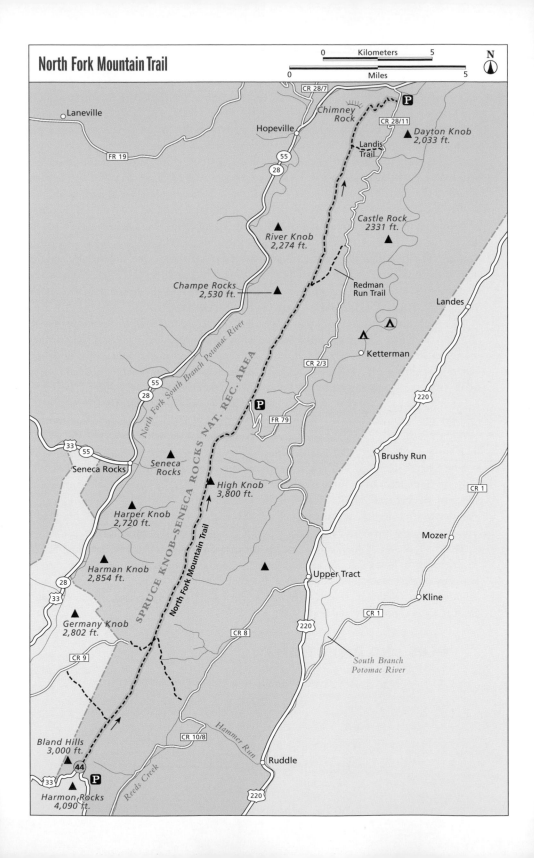

North Fork Mountain Trail

Kilometers
0 5
Miles
0 5

N

Laneville

Hopeville

Chimney Rock

CR 28/7

CR 28/11

P

Dayton Knob
2,033 ft.

Landis Trail

FR 19

55
28

River Knob
2,274 ft.

Castle Rock
2331 ft.

Champe Rocks
2,530 ft.

Redman Run Trail

Landes

North Fork South Branch Potomac River

CR 2/3

Ketterman

55
28

SPRUCE KNOB–SENECA ROCKS NAT. REC. AREA

P

FR 79

220

Brushy Run

33
55

Seneca Rocks

Seneca Rocks

High Knob
3,800 ft.

CR 1

Harper Knob
2,720 ft.

Mozer

North Fork Mountain Trail

Harman Knob
2,854 ft.

Upper Tract

Kline

28

33

Germany Knob
2,802 ft.

CR 8

220

CR 1

CR 9

South Branch
Potomac River

Hammer Run

Bland Hills
3,000 ft.

CR 10/8

Ruddle

44

33

Reeds Creek

220

P

Harmon Rocks
4,090 ft.

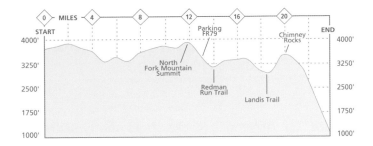

8.2 A short side trail to the left takes you to a campsite and a view of Seneca Rocks. The main trail continues straight.

10.4 At the T intersection with FR 79, turn right and follow the road for less than 0.5 mile.

10.9 Arrive at a fork at a metal tower. Take the left fork and descend on the road.

12.4 At a sharp right bend, leave the road, hiking straight into the woods. There is a brown TR 501 sign and a blue blaze. (**FYI:** A small parking area off FR 79 is at this bend; you can use this to park a shuttle vehicle or to stash a resupply of water.)

15.0 An unmarked trail enters from the right. Continue straight.

16.4 The Redman Run Trail (TR 507) comes in from the right. Continue straight. (**FYI:** There are campsites around this junction with views to the west.)

20.4 Come to a fork. Go left to stay on the North Fork Mountain Trail. (**FYI:** The right fork is the Landis Trail [TR 502], which is also blazed blue.)

21.4 Get a view of Chimney Rock to the north.

24.2 End at the northern trailhead.

HIKE INFORMATION

Local information: Grant County Convention and Visitors Bureau, (304) 257-9266 or (866) 597-9266, www.grantcountywva.com; Pendleton County Guide, www.pendleton county.net

Camping: Backcountry camping is permitted along the North Fork Mountain Trail; an overnight stay will require stashing water beforehand.

Organizations: The Nature Conservancy, www.nature.org or (304) 345-4350; West Virginia Highlands Conservancy, www.wvhighlands.org

The North Fork Mountain Trail is an International Mountain Bike Association Epic Ride.

45 SENECA ROCKS TRAIL

Spruce Knob–Seneca Rocks National Recreation Area

WHY GO?

The thin quartzite "fin" of Seneca Rocks soars nearly 900 feet above the clear, fast-flowing North Fork of the South Branch of the Potomac River (simply known here as the North Fork) in the Spruce Knob–Seneca Rocks National Recreation Area. Seneca Rocks is usually crawling with climbers, while the river below is a favorite for anglers. After a challenging and satisfying hike to the top of these rocks, end your day at what may be one of the best swimming holes in the world.

> ### THE RUNDOWN
>
> **Start:** Sites Homestead parking lot trailhead
> **Distance:** 2.8-mile out-and-back
> **Hiking time:** About 1.5 hours
> **Difficulty:** Moderate due to steepness
> **Trail surface:** Gravel path with some wooden steps
> **Best season:** Spring through fall
> **Other trail users:** Rock climbers
> **Canine compatibility:** Leashed dogs permitted
>
> **Land status:** National forest
> **Nearest town:** Seneca Rocks
> **Fees and permits:** None
> **Schedule:** Trails are open daily year-round; the Seneca Rocks Discovery Center is open mid- to late Apr through Oct 9 a.m. to 4:30 p.m.
> **Map:** USGS quad: Upper Tract
> **Trail contact:** Potomac office of the Cheat-Potomac Ranger District, Monongahela National Forest, (304) 257-4488 or www.fs.usda.gov/mnf

FINDING THE TRAILHEAD

At the intersection of US 33 and WV 28/WV 55 in the town of Seneca Rocks, go north on WV 28/WV 55 about 0.2 mile and turn right into the Seneca Rocks Picnic Area parking lot. When the access road forks, continue right into the parking lot. The trailhead is well marked on the east side of the parking lot. **GPS:** N38 50.14' / W79 22.3'

THE HIKE

People have been awed by Seneca Rocks for ages before a formal trail was built to the top. Native Americans lived in and passed through the area, as did the Seneca Trail, an old Native footpath extending from what is today New York to Alabama. In its more recent history, Seneca Rocks was host to the 10th Mountain Division in World War II, where troops trained for mountain warfare in Europe. Today, Seneca's dramatic history is just that: history. But the dramatic scenery draws hikers, anglers, and rock climbers who come to scale one of the East's premier climbing destinations.

The trail to the observation deck leaves the parking lot and heads to the North Fork, crossing the river via an arcing steel footbridge. On the opposite shore, the trail turns

Crossing the North Fork on the Seneca Rocks Trail

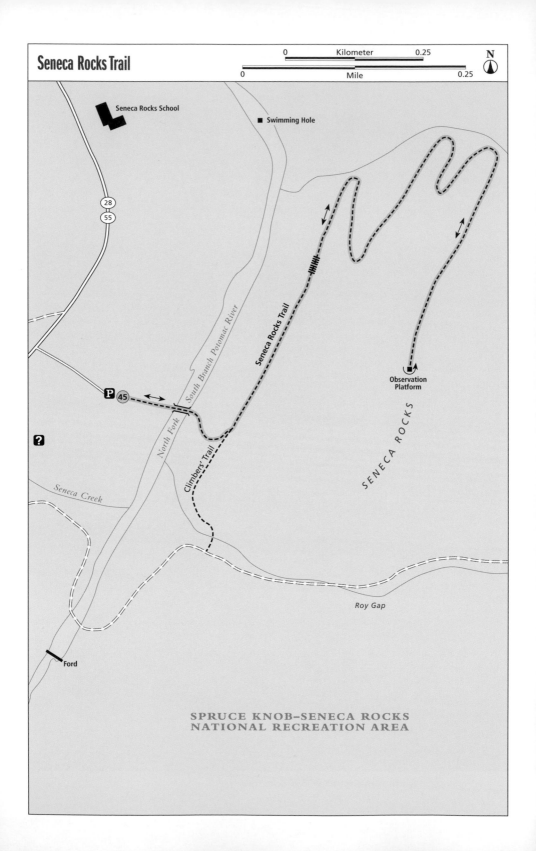

Seneca Rocks Trail

Kilometer

0   0.25

Mile

0   0.25

N

Seneca Rocks School

■ Swimming Hole

28
55

South Branch Potomac River

Seneca Rocks Trail

P 45

North Fork

Climbers' Trail

Observation Platform

S E N E C A   R O C K S

Seneca Creek

Roy Gap

Ford

SPRUCE KNOB–SENECA ROCKS
NATIONAL RECREATION AREA

right and briefly parallels the river upstream, then bends left at the creek that runs through Roy Gap. At the T intersection, climbers take the right fork and hikers take the left fork. Wildflowers bloom along the trail from spring through fall. In the spring, look for Dutchman's breeches, miterwort, and trout lily. In the fall, keep an eye out for asters.

The wide gravel trail climbs gradually for about 0.25 mile. The trail starts flat, but this flat section quickly ends and the grade becomes more moderate. As the trail gets steeper, switchbacks help with the grade. The halfway point is followed by another easy stretch and then more switchbacks under a stand of towering hardwoods. After another set of switchbacks, the trail climbs to a small saddle. A short set of stairs leads to the observation platform. The view to the west is absolutely worth the climb. The North Fork River far below leads the eyes to the Dolly Sods region farther north. After taking in the view, retrace your route along the trail to the parking lot.

MILES AND DIRECTIONS

0.0 START from the Sites Homestead parking lot north of the visitor center. The trail enters the woods, heading east toward the rocks, and then crosses over the North Fork on a footbridge.

0.2 After crossing the creek, the trail curves right (upstream), then left, and comes to a T intersection. Take a left. (A sign for the observation platform is here.)

0.5 Climb two sets of wooden stairs.

0.8 The trail switches back to the left. A faint trail goes off to the right/straight. Stay on the main gravel path.

1.2 The trail forks at a stone wall. Take a right, following the wall.

1.4 Wooden steps lead up and then down to the observation platform. This is a great lunch spot. Turn around and return to the trailhead. (**FYI:** Heed the warnings to go no farther. There is a great deal of loose rock here, and it is dangerous to walk along the rock above the climbers, who are below.)

2.8 Arrive back at the trailhead.

HIKE INFORMATION

Local information: Pendleton County Guide, www.pendletoncounty.net
Camping: Seneca Shadows, the national forest campground, has 80 sites; the walk-in tent camping has a view of the rocks, (304) 567-3082.
Local events/attractions: Seneca Rocks Discovery Center, (304) 567-2827 or www.fs.usda.gov/attmain/mnf/specialplaces
Organizations: West Virginia Highlands Conservancy, www.wvhighlands.org

46 SENECA CREEK TRAIL TO SPRUCE KNOB SUMMIT

Spruce Knob–Seneca Rocks National Recreation Area

WHY GO?

Sure, you could drive to within 900 feet of the highest point in West Virginia. But creek-to-peak is the only honorable way to summit Spruce Knob, and the Seneca Creek to Huckleberry Trail is your ticket. Parallel Seneca Creek—this backcountry trail is on the beaten path, and for good reason—and then hike a steep section of trail through a dense forest to the Huckleberry Trail, which takes you along the ridge all the way to Spruce Knob, West Virginia's highest point at 4,863 feet. This 11.3-mile trail plus a shuttle might take all day, which allows you to end it by watching the sunset from Spruce Knob. Alternately, you can do it as an overnighter and enjoy pitching your tent in the high meadow backcountry sites, where you can fall asleep under the stars.

THE RUNDOWN

Start: Seneca Creek Trail trailhead, off FR 112

Distance: 11.3 miles one way, plus a 4-mile shuttle

Hiking time: About 5 to 6 hours, plus lunch and a shuttle

Difficulty: Difficult due to length and elevation gain

Trail surface: Rocky dirt trail with stream crossings

Best season: Spring through fall when the roads are reliably passable

Other trail users: Horseback riders, mountain bikers

Canine compatibility: Controlled dogs are permitted

Land status: National forest

Nearest town: Seneca Rocks

Fees and permits: None

Schedule: The wilderness is accessible 24/7, but access roads may be impassable in winter due to snow.

Maps: Seneca Creek Backcountry map (available from Forest Service); USGS quads: Circleville, Onego, Spruce Knob, Whitmer

Trail contact: Monongahela National Forest, Potomac office of the Cheat-Potomac Ranger District, (304) 257-4488 or www.fs.usda.gov/mnf

Special considerations: The long hike plus a shuttle might take all day; be sure to allot enough time to complete it. Also be prepared for several stream crossings. Snow may make the road impassable in winter.

FINDING THE TRAILHEAD

From the town of Seneca Rocks, follow US 33/WV 28 south 10.0 miles to CR 33-4 (Briery Gap Road). Turn right (west) and head up the mountain 2.5 miles to where the road becomes FR 112. Continue up to mile 9.7 and the intersection with FR 104. Turn right onto FR 104 and travel 1.7 miles along the ridge crest of Spruce Mountain to the summit parking lot. Leave a car or bicycle here. **GPS:** N38 42.12' / W70 31.88'

Watching the sunset from Spruce Knob

From the summit parking lot, take a car to the starting trailhead. Follow FR 104 back to FR 112 and turn right. Go 4.0 miles to the Seneca Creek trailhead parking lot on the right. **GPS:** N38 42.70′ / W79 32.99′

THE HIKE

With more than 60 miles of trails through beautiful northern hardwood forests, it's easy to understand why the Seneca Creek Backcountry is a favorite among West Virginia backpackers. You can dance across the cold, clear water of Seneca Creek, muscle your way up steep ridges, rest in mountain meadows, and travel through spruce forests near the summit of Spruce Knob, the highest point in West Virginia at 4,863 feet. The thick forests of birch, beech, maple, and cherry offer cool shade in the summer. Deep snows blanket the area in winter, and often in the fall and spring! Give yourself extra time when visiting the backcountry—there's no need to rush through this beautiful area.

Begin on the Seneca Creek Trail, a relatively level, old road grade. Ferns crowd the trail, and the forest is made up of some deciduous trees and red spruce. Birds and wildlife are abundant. Seneca Creek is a high mountain creek that begins as a small trickle but picks up water as it slowly descends and side runs enter it. You will need to cross the creek a number of times. If you elect to do this hike as an overnighter, plan to bed down in the campsites in the high meadows so you can stargaze.

At mile 5.0, the Seneca Creek Trail reaches the junction with the Huckleberry Trail. Take a moment before you begin the Huckleberry Trail to continue downstream along Seneca Creek about 75 feet to the largest waterfall along the creek and a swimming hole. This would make a good lunch stop.

After checking out the waterfall, return to the junction with the Huckleberry Trail. The rest of the hike is almost entirely uphill. You are, after all, hiking to the high point of West Virginia. The Huckleberry Trail along the ridge crest of Spruce Mountain is invigorating. The climb becomes a mere predecessor to reaching this picture-postcard landscape. The ridge crest is open to the sky and covered with grasses, wildflowers, blueberry, huckleberry (a cousin to the blueberry), azalea, mountain ash, and spruce. The trail passes from open sky to deeply shaded spruce forest in a matter of steps. Often rocky, the trail is nevertheless a delight to hike. Views are primarily to the west.

The Huckleberry Trail widens and the path is covered in gravel just before it reaches the civilization of the summit parking lot. Follow the paved road to the trail that leads to the lookout tower at the 4,863-foot summit of Spruce Knob. The 360-degree views from the summit tower are worth the day's effort. Stay to watch the sunset before shuttling back to the trailhead.

MILES AND DIRECTIONS

0.0 START at the Seneca Creek Trail (TR 515) trailhead. Walk north, past the trailhead bulletin board.

0.9 Come to the junction with the Tom Lick Trail (TR 559) on the left. Continue straight.

2.3 The Swallow Rock Trail (TR 529) comes in from the left. Continue straight. (**FYI:** There are campsites in this area.)

3.5 Come to a junction with the Judy Springs Trail (TR 512) on the right. There is a cascading waterfall across the creek. (**FYI:** Good campsites can be found along the next half mile.)

4.5 An unmarked trail is on the left. Continue straight, following the creek.

5.0 Arrive at the junction with the Huckleberry Trail (TR 533). Cross the creek by a cascading waterfall. The trail forks; take a right and walk uphill. (**Option:** Before beginning the Huckleberry Trail, take a left at this junction and go about 75 feet to the 25-foot-tall waterfall and swimming hole.)

5.5 Come to a T intersection with the High Meadows Trail (TR 564). Go right to stay on the Huckleberry Trail.

6.2 The Judy Springs Trail enters from the right. Continue straight.

6.5 Come to a four-way intersection with the Lumberjack Trail (TR 534). Turn left to stay on the Huckleberry Trail, following the sign marked SPRUCE KNOB.

7.3 Come to a T intersection. A small, unmarked trail goes straight, but take a right to stay on the Huckleberry Trail.

7.5 Take a left at a campsite to stay on the Huckleberry Trail.

10.9 Arrive at the Huckleberry Trail trailhead and parking lot. Turn right and walk through the parking lot toward a brown sign pointing to the observation tower at the summit of Spruce Knob. Follow a gravel trail.

11.1 Reach the Spruce Knob observation tower.

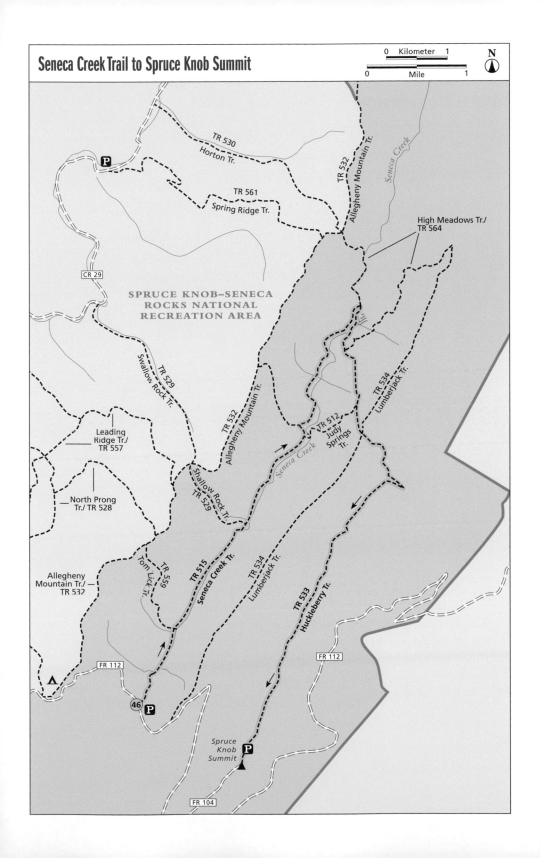

Seneca Creek Trail to Spruce Knob Summit

0 Kilometer 1
0 Mile 1

N

TR 530
Horton Tr.

TR 561
Spring Ridge Tr.

TR 532
Allegheny Mountain Tr.

Seneca Creek

High Meadows Tr./
TR 564

CR 29

SPRUCE KNOB–SENECA
ROCKS NATIONAL
RECREATION AREA

TR 529
Swallow Rock Tr.

TR 532
Allegheny Mountain Tr.

TR 534
Lumberjack Tr.

TR 512
Judy
Springs
Tr.

Seneca Creek

Leading
Ridge Tr./
TR 557

North Prong
Tr./ TR 528

Shallow Rock Tr.
TR 529

Allegheny
Mountain Tr./ —
TR 532

Tom Lick Tr.

TR 559

TR 515
Seneca Creek Tr.

TR 534
Lumberjack Tr.

TR 533
Huckleberry Tr.

FR 112

FR 112

△

46 P

Spruce
Knob
Summit
▲

P

FR 104

11.3 Return to the parking lot for your car or to meet the very good friend who came to pick you up.

HIKE INFORMATION

Local information: Pendleton County Guide, www.pendletoncounty.net

Camping: Camping is allowed in the backcountry. Seneca Creek Backcountry should be treated in a manner similar to wilderness. There are no developed or designated campsites. In high-use areas it is best to camp in sites that have been used before, while dispersed camping is recommended in low-use parts of the wilderness. If backcountry camping is not your cup of tea, the Gatewood campground has 6 sites, and the campground at Spruce Knob Lake has more than 40.

Organizations: West Virginia Highlands Conservancy, www.wvhighlands.org

47 HIGH FALLS TRAIL

Monongahela National Forest

WHY GO?

High Falls of the Cheat River seems like a misnomer. At 100 feet wide and barely 15 feet tall, it seems they should be called Wide Falls of the Cheat River. However, the falls are at nearly 3,000 feet in elevation, making them one of the highest, in that sense, in the Mountain State. You'll notice the elevation as you make the 3.9-mile hike over Shavers Mountain for the payoff, but the trail is not too steep and is quite varied, making the entire route enjoyable. Be forewarned—after all of your hard work, you might happen upon a crowd of people who arrived by tourist train. That's okay, you'll have the satisfaction of knowing you earned the view.

THE RUNDOWN

Start: High Falls Trail trailhead, off FR 44
Distance: 7.8-mile out-and-back
Hiking time: About 4 hours
Difficulty: Moderate
Trail surface: Rocky dirt trail with a section on gravel paralleling the railroad tracks
Best season: Spring through fall
Other trail users: Horseback riders
Canine compatibility: Controlled dogs are permitted

Land status: National forest
Nearest town: Elkins
Fees and permits: None
Schedule: Forest trails are open year-round, but the roads leading to the trailheads may be impassable during the winter.
Map: USGS quad: Horton
Trail contact: Greenbrier Ranger District, Monongahela National Forest, (304) 456-3335 or www.fs.usda.gov/mnf

FINDING THE TRAILHEAD

Take US 33/WV 55 east of Elkins 11.9 miles to Glady Road (CR 27) and turn south. Drive 9.3 miles to Glady and CR 22. Turn left (east) onto CR 22 and go 0.2 mile to Beulah Road (CR 22-2). Take a right. At mile 2.9, CR 22-2 changes to FR 44. Continue to mile 3.8 and find a small pullout on the right side of the road to park. The trailhead is quite easy to miss; look for a trailhead sign on the right and down the slope. **GPS:** N38 45.01'/W79 45.16'

THE HIKE

The High Falls Trail (TR 345) is named for its destination. But in this case, the journey is just as important as the destination. The trail begins in an inconspicuous place off FR 44. Look down the embankment for the trailhead sign and blue blazes. Dip down toward the valley bottom as you begin your hike. The forest in this area is filled with hardwoods as well as spruce and hemlock. In about a half mile, the 330-mile Allegheny Trail (TR 701) joins the High Falls Trail and the trail crosses the West Fork Trail (TR 312), a gravel doubletrack road that's great for a flat hike or bike ride (see honorable mention R). After crossing the West Fork and walking through a break in the fence, the landscape becomes

The High Falls of the Cheat

more meadow than forest. There is a stand of hawthorn trees in the meadow that you will walk through.

Soon the trail comes to the ascent of Shavers Mountain. Topping out over 4,000 feet, Shavers Mountain is imposing, but the trail itself is well graded, with enough switch-backs to make the hike moderate. In the spring, look for wildflowers like trout lily, wood anemone, and violet. As you reach the saddle of Shavers Mountain around mile 1.5, you will see a dry backcountry campsite on your right. After that, the Allegheny Trail turns south, leaving the High Falls Trail. This is an unusually moist mountaintop; hemlocks and spruce tower over a forest floor covered in ferns and moss-covered rocks. Depending on the time of year, you may be able to find a spring producing enough water to make that backcountry campsite not a dry one after all.

In the saddle of the ridgetop, the trail continues and turns to the right as it joins an old road grade. After briefly following the road grade, the trail takes a left off the ridge and begins a descent to Shavers Fork, a tributary to the Cheat River.

At the bottom of the west side of the mountain, the trail crosses over railroad tracks. These are actively used tracks, so be careful when crossing and do not walk on the tracks. You have the option of turning right to parallel the tracks to the north, following the blue blazes. You can also continue straight and descend down to the river (just a stone's throw away) and parallel the river downstream. After nearly a mile, you'll see a train stop.

High Falls Trail

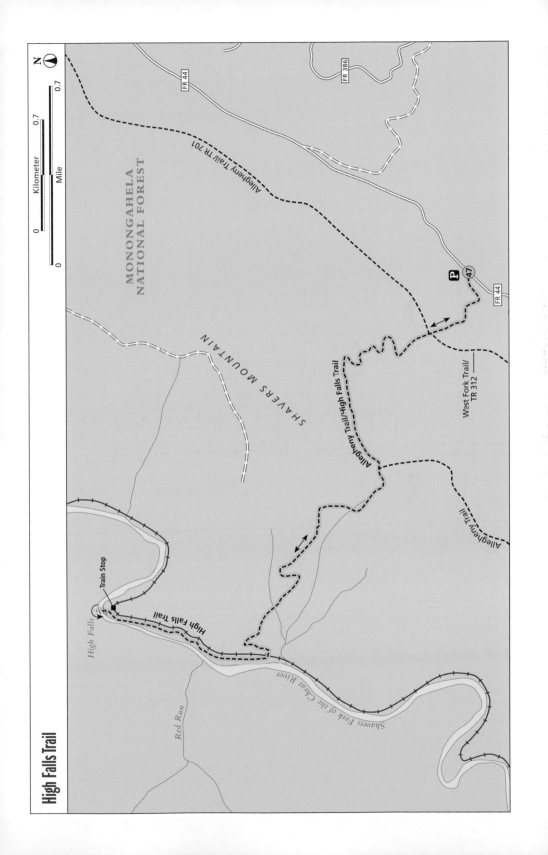

N

Kilometer
0   0.7

Mile
0   0.7

MONONGAHELA
NATIONAL FOREST

SHAVERS MOUNTAIN

FR 44

FR 386

Allegheny Trail/ TR 701

West Fork Trail/
TR 312

Allegheny Trail/High Falls Trail

Allegheny Trail

FR 44

P
47

High Falls

Train Stop

High Falls Trail

Red Run

Shavers Fork of the Cheat River

This is a stop on a tourist train taking people directly to the falls. Pass the shelter and follow the sign and gravel trail down to the falls, which you will hear before you see.

The High Falls of the Cheat are magnificent—you can see, hear, and even feel this force of nature as you stand next to or beneath the falls. There is a boardwalk to an overlook and a rocky "beach" below the pools under the falls. Plan enough time to enjoy the falls and have lunch before your return journey.

MILES AND DIRECTIONS

0.0 START at the High Falls Trail trailhead, off FR 44. Drop down from the road, heading west.

0.4 Cross the West Fork Trail (TR 312), a doubletrack gravel road. The Allegheny Trail (TR 701) joins from the right. Continue straight across the road.

1.5 After climbing Shavers Mountain, arrive at the saddle. The Allegheny Trail splits off to the left, marked with a sign. Continue straight.

2.0 After the trail joins an old road grade in the saddle, it takes a left at a giant rock cairn and begins the descent of the other side of Shavers Mountain.

3.0 Arrive at a set of railroad tracks. Carefully cross the tracks and take a right, paralleling the tracks for the rest of the hike. There is a trail here with blue blazes. (**Option:** Aesthetically, it might be worth your while to continue to descend another 50 feet or so to the river and just follow the river downstream the rest of the way.)

3.8 Come to a train stop shelter. Pass the shelter and see a signed gravel path on the left leading down to the waterfall, which is now within earshot.

3.9 Arrive at the High Falls of the Cheat. Turn around and return the way you came.

7.8 Arrive back at the trailhead.

HIKE INFORMATION

Local information: Randolph County Convention and Visitors Bureau, (304) 636-2780 or (800) 422-3304, www.randolphcountywv.com/

Camping: Backcountry camping is permitted throughout the Monongahela National Forest; the nearby Laurel Fork Campground is a nice primitive campground in the Mon. The Forest Service also runs the Middle Mountain Cabins; make cabin reservations at (877) 444-6777.

Local events/attractions: Mountain Rail Adventures makes trips to the High Falls of the Cheat, (877) MTN-RAIL (686-7245) or www.mountainrailwv.com.

Organizations: West Virginia Highlands Conservancy, www.wvhighlands.org; West Virginia Scenic Trails Association, www.wvscenictrails.org

48 LAUREL RIVER TRAIL SOUTH

Laurel Fork South Wilderness

WHY GO?

Fall asleep to the sound of the babbling Laurel Fork of the Cheat River and awaken to so many stellar day-hiking opportunities, you'll barely know where to begin. For starters, try this: The 7.5-mile Laurel River Trail South parallels the clear-running Laurel Fork through dense forest and open meadows. Eventually hike away from the river valley up a side stream and then to the mountaintop. You can tackle this as a one-way day hike with a shuttle or an out-and-back in a day or two since the Laurel Fork Wilderness provides practically endless backpacking options as well.

THE RUNDOWN

Start: Northern trailhead for the Laurel River Trail
Distance: 7.5 miles one way
Hiking time: About 4 hours
Difficulty: Moderate
Trail surface: Dirt trail with stream crossings
Best season: Spring through fall
Other trail users: Horseback riders
Canine compatibility: Controlled dogs permitted
Land status: National forest
Nearest town: Elkins
Fees and permits: None
Schedule: The wilderness is accessible 24/7 year-round, but access roads may be impassable during the winter.
Maps: Monongahela National Forest Laurel Fork Wilderness map; USGS quad: Sinks of Gandy
Trail contact: Greenbrier Ranger District, Monongahela National Forest, (304) 456-3335 or www.fs.usda.gov/mnf
Special considerations: This hike requires several stream crossings; make sure you have waterproof boots or sandals or are ready to go barefoot. Additionally, groups larger than 10 are not permitted in the wilderness.

FINDING THE TRAILHEAD

This is a one-way hike; transportation is needed at both trailheads. From Elkins, take US 33 11.9 miles to Alpena and turn south on CR 27. Travel 9.3 miles to Glady and turn left onto CR 22 (Bemis Road). Continue 2.1 miles and continue straight on FR 422 another 2.4 miles to a stop sign. Take a right on CR 10 (Middle Mountain Road) and go 0.2 mile to a fork. Take the left fork onto FR 423 and travel 1.5 miles to the Laurel Fork Campground. Parking is in first campground loop, on the right. Go to the back of the campground, by the pit toilets. This is the trailhead for the Laurel River Trail, and there is some parking here. For additional parking, park across the road at the maintenance lot. **GPS:** N38 44.37'/W79 42.96'

To reach the southern trailhead to leave a shuttle car, return to Middle Mountain Road and turn left. Travel 8.0 miles to FR 179 and the Laurel River trailhead. There is parking on the left. Do not block the gate. **GPS:** N38 40.94'/W79 42.39'

THE HIKE

Laurel Fork South is the southern half of the Laurel Fork Wilderness. Middle Mountain forms the western boundary of the wilderness, while Rich Mountain forms the eastern boundary. Between these two high ridges runs the fast-flowing Laurel Fork. This clear-running river is the centerpiece of this masterpiece of nature. Hardworking beavers have altered the upper portion of the river basin significantly, and tall grasses thrive in the former backwaters of their old dams.

The Laurel Fork Wilderness (both North and South) is a prime backpacking area with loops of any size when the trail system is combined with Middle Mountain Road. Or simply make a base camp at Laurel Fork Campground—one of the loveliest, most remote campgrounds in the state—and take your time exploring the area through day hikes, made easier if you are able to do a car or mountain bike shuttle between the campground and the trailheads along Middle Mountain Road.

The trailhead for the Laurel River Trail (TR 306) is located behind the pit toilets in the campground. After leaving the campground, the trail passes a spring on the right, with good, clear, cool water. The trail follows an old grade on the right side of the creek, climbing gradually through a forest dominated by black bark cherry and yellow birch.

The Laurel River Trail intersects with a number of trails, beginning with the Forks Trail (Trail 323). The Laurel River Trail continues straight and parallels the Laurel Fork. After dropping into an open glade, the trail crosses a small feeder stream. Hemlock and

Riverside campsite overlooking the Laurel Fork

spruce occupy the canopy of the forest. The trail hugs the river a short distance before crossing it. Within 150 yards, cross the river again. It can be possible to do both crossings without taking off your boots.

After the second crossing, the trail becomes a footpath. Running cedar covers the forest floor. The trail climbs the right side of the hollow, then drops to a large creek. Cross the creek to the junction with the Beulah Trail (TR 310).

The Laurel River Trail continues straight, climbing gradually. After crossing a small feeder, the trail drops back to the creek and rejoins the old logging railroad grade. Climb away from the creek again to a junction; take the left fork and begin to descend. The trail is now a footpath that wraps around the end of a finger ridge then drops into a small glade. There is some trail confusion in this area; rock cairns mark the way. The trail crosses two small creeks and eventually drops to the river's edge and parallels the river a short distance.

Climb up away from the river again and pass through a thicket of young red spruce. The trail drops back to the river. There is a forest of tall pines on the right. Enter a wide boggy area and cross Camp Five Run. Parallel the run upstream a short distance to the junction with the Camp Five Run Trail (TR 315). The Laurel River Trail bears to the left and drops down to the river. Cross the river, taking off your boots if necessary. An old logging road leads up into a stand of widely spaced red spruce. Follow the trail to a small clearing where a little stream comes down the mountain from the left, then follow the stream toward the Laurel River to an old road. Turn left on the road, which climbs gradually through a stand of tall pine. There are several blue blazes as the road leads out of the woods and into a grassy beaver flat. Follow the trail to the river and cross. This crossing is too wide to jump and too deep to cross without taking off your boots.

The trail soon hits an old road and begins an easy climb away from the Laurel Fork River. The road parallels a small stream, climbing gradually to the crest of the ridge. As the trail bends right, there is a small sign for the Laurel River Trail and the Laurel Fork Campground at FR 179. Turn right on FR 179 and continue an easy walk to Middle Mountain Road. A locked gate blocks the road. Pick up your shuttle here or retrace your steps back to the Laurel Fork Campground.

MILES AND DIRECTIONS

0.0 START on the Laurel River Trail (TR 306) behind the privies in the campground. (**FYI:** After leaving the campground, the trail passes a spring on the right, with good, clear, cool water.)

0.5 The Laurel River Trail intersects the Forks Trail (Trail 323). A post marks the trail numbers at the junction. The Laurel River Trail continues straight and parallels the Laurel Fork.

1.5 Come to the junction with the Beulah Trail (TR 310) on the right. The Laurel River Trail continues straight, climbing gradually.

4.0 After walking through a wide boggy area and crossing Camp Five Run, parallel the run upstream a short distance to the junction with the Camp Five Run Trail (TR 315). Laurel River Trail bears to the left and drops down to the river. Cross the river and follow the cairns along this section, staying on the same side of the stream.

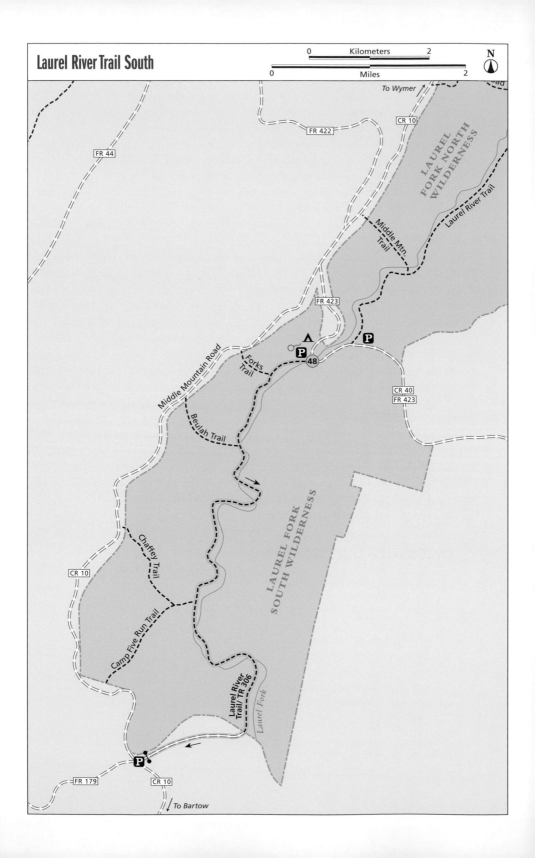

Laurel River Trail South

0 — Kilometers — 2

0 — Miles — 2

N

To Wymer

CR 10

FR 422

FR 44

LAUREL FORK NORTH WILDERNESS

Laurel River Trail

Middle Mtn. Trail

FR 423

Forks Trail

P

P

48

Middle Mountain Road

Beulah Trail

CR 40
FR 423

LAUREL FORK SOUTH WILDERNESS

Chaffey Trail

CR 10

Camp Five Run Trail

Laurel River Trail/ TR 306

Laurel Fork

P

FR 179

CR 10

To Bartow

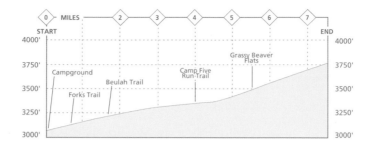

5.0 After walking through a stand of evergreens with blue blazes, come out to a meadow. Cross the stream again at this point and pick up the trail on the other side. (**FYI:** Cairns may not be present here, as it is a floodplain.)

6.3 After ascending the mountain, pass the trailhead register and in about 150 yards (trending right), come to FR 179. Take a right on this gravel doubletrack.

7.5 The hike ends at a gate near Middle Mountain Road.

HIKE INFORMATION

Local information: Randolph County Convention and Visitors Bureau, (304) 636-2780 or (800) 422-3304, www.randolphcountywv.com/

Camping: Backcountry camping is permitted throughout the wilderness. The primitive Laurel Fork Campground has 16 spaces filled on a first-come, first-served basis. You can filter or boil water from the Laurel Fork, and there is a spring near the curve in the road just before it arrives at the campground. Look uphill for a plastic pipe and follow it up to the spring. It is advisable to filter this water, but plenty of people drink it without incident.

Local events/attractions: The Gaudineer Scenic Area, located on the Gaudineer Knob of Shavers Mountain, contains stands of virgin red spruce forest; contact the Greenbrier Ranger District of the Mon at (304) 456-3335 or www.fs.usda.gov/mnf.

Organizations: West Virginia Highlands Conservancy, www.wvhighlands.org

49 MIDDLE FORK TO BIG BEECHY TRAIL LOOP

Cranberry Wilderness

WHY GO?

Wallace Stegner viewed wilderness as "a part of the geography of hope." You can understand what Stegner meant in the Cranberry Wilderness. Traveling from stream bank to ridgetop, this hike delivers all of what is wonderful about the Cranberry Wilderness, including spruce-covered ridgetops, hillsides carpeted in ferns, valleys alive with the chatter of streams, and solitude that only wilderness can provide.

THE RUNDOWN

Start: North-South Trail trailhead
Distance: 16.75-mile loop
Hiking time: About 2 days
Difficulty: Difficult
Trail surface: Dirt trail with stream crossings
Best season: Spring through fall
Other trail users: Hikers only
Canine compatibility: Controlled dogs are permitted
Land status: National forest
Nearest town: Marlinton
Fees and permits: None

Schedule: The wilderness is accessible year-round but access roads may be impassable in the winter due to snow.
Maps: Recreation Guide for the Gauley District; USGS quads: Hillsboro, Lobelia, Webster Springs SE, Woodrow
Trail contact: Gauley Ranger Station, USDA Forest Service, (304) 846-2695 or www.fs.usda.gov/mnf
Special considerations: Groups larger than 10 are not permitted in the wilderness area.

FINDING THE TRAILHEAD

From US 219, turn west on WV 39 near Mill Point. Travel up the mountain to the intersection with WV 150, the Highland Scenic Highway. Turn right on WV 150. The trailhead is on the left 8.7 miles from the intersection of WV 39 and WV 150. A sign at the small parking area announces the North-South Trail (TR 688).
Traveling east on WV 39 from Summersville, follow WV 39 to the intersection with WV 150, the Highland Scenic Highway. Turn left onto WV 150 and follow the road 8.7 miles to the trailhead and parking on the left. **GPS:** N38 16.35′ / W80 14.15′

THE HIKE

Unlike other popular wilderness areas in the Mon, the Cranberry Wilderness is not home to expansive vistas. But it is home to red spruce forests, moss- and fern–covered forest floors, cascading waterfalls, and seasonal solitude that characterize just part of the experience you can have in the Cranberry Wilderness. The dense canopy of red spruce and yellow birch filters out most of the sunlight and leaves the forest floor in cool shade. The combination of foliage and dark shade creates a scene of rich, saturated greens.

Marsh marigold at Cranberry Glades Botanical Area

Start on the North-South Trail (TR 688). The wide and grassy trail sometimes becomes overgrown, which, on rainy days, will drench your legs. The trail travels slightly downhill and reaches an intersection at the 1.5-mile mark. Turn left and follow the Middle Fork Trail (TR 271) downhill to the left. The trail travels downhill at an easy angle to its namesake, the Middle Fork of the Williams River. Upon reaching the stream, turn right and follow it down the valley. There are numerous campsites on both sides of the creek along the Middle Fork Trail, which is wide and easy to follow. As the trail continues to lose elevation, maple begins appearing in the canopy.

At about 5.0 miles from the parking area, cross the Middle Fork the first of several times. You pass several "stair step" waterfalls on the Middle Fork Trail, but the most notable are those at Slick Rock Run, a small feeder stream that intersects the Middle Fork from the right. Just past the confluence of these two streams, at about 6.25 miles, the Middle Fork slides and cascades down an inclined slab of sandstone. This is wonderful summer fun.

The trail continues on its way to the Big Beechy Trail (TR 207). At 7.75 miles, the Hell for Certain Branch can be seen cascading into the Middle Fork to the left. There are campsites in this area. The trail is as wide as a road here and is lined with hemlock and rhododendron.

At 8.5 miles, reach Big Beechy Run and the intersection with the Big Beechy Trail. A gorgeous 10-foot waterfall at Big Beechy Run makes a pleasant backdrop for lunch. The

Big Beechy Trail begins at a sign on the southeast bank of Big Beechy Run. Take a right off the Middle Fork Trail and hike uphill to the east. The trail wraps around the ridge and immediately starts to gain elevation over the stream valley that lies to the left. Make sure your water bottles are full before leaving the stream; the moderate incline will last for about 3 miles, turning a not-so-difficult hike into a burner. Some respite is along the way, as short easy sections break up the climb. The forest here begins with hemlock, beech, and tulip poplar dominating, but as you gain elevation, these species give way to ridgetops thickly covered with spruce.

> There are no developed or designated campsites within wilderness areas. In high-use areas, it is best to camp in sites that have been previously used; dispersed camping is recommended in low-use parts of the wilderness.

As the Big Beechy Trail nears the ridgetop, tall sandstone pillars are surrounded by spruce and the forest floor is covered with ferns. The trail bends around the ridge to the right and starts to travel in a southerly direction. The Big Beechy Trail reaches the crest of the shoulder, then the trail climbs and drops as it travels across the ridge crest. The forest varies from bright, open-canopied beech to dense, shady spruce where little light reaches the forest floor. The Big Beechy Trail weaves through a rhododendron jungle and passes through a thick stand of young spruce at 12.0 miles. Route finding can be difficult in this area, as the spruce chokes out the path. The trail starts a final descent to the North Fork Trail at 14.25 miles. The descent is moderate and lasts for about 0.5 mile. The Big Beechy Trail reaches the North Fork Trail (TR 272) by an open meadow.

At the junction a sign—Highland Scenic Highway—points left. To continue the hike on trails, turn right at this junction and follow the North Fork Trail south. The trail is wide and flat, which is welcome this late in a long hike, but portions of the trail are choked with young spruce. At 15.25 miles, the North Fork Trail reaches the intersection with the Middle Fork Trail. Take the left fork at this Y intersection and hike uphill. This portion of the hike backtracks the earlier part of the hike. At 16.25 miles, reach the junction with North-South Trail. Turn left and hike the short distance to the information stand and parking lot.

MILES AND DIRECTIONS

0.0 START at the North-South Trail (TR 688) marked with a sign. The trail leaves the parking area and passes a small meadow and an information stand. A wide trail that appears to be the remnants of an old logging road branches off to the right. The North-South Trail enters the forest straight ahead (west).

0.5 Turn right and follow the North Fork Trail (TR 272) north. (The North-South Trail continues straight.)

1.5 Come to a junction and turn left to follow the Middle Fork Trail (TR 271) downhill.

5.0 Ford the Middle Fork for the first of several times.

6.25 Just past the confluence with Slick Rock Run, arrive at a cascading waterfall along Big Beechy Run.

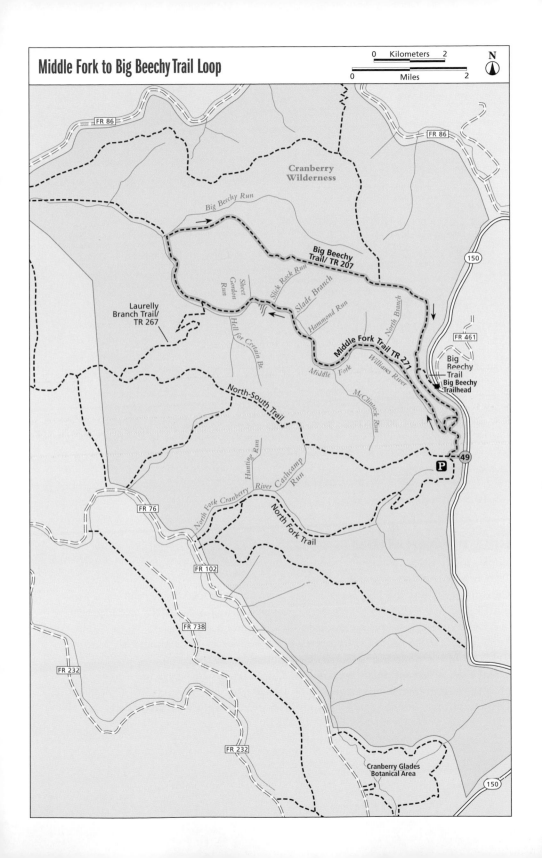

Middle Fork to Big Beechy Trail Loop

0 Kilometers 2
0 Miles 2

N

FR 86

FR 86

Cranberry
Wilderness

Big Beechy Run

Big Beechy
Trail/ TR 207

150

Laurelly
Branch Trail/
TR 267

Sheet
Gordon
Run

Stick Rock Run

Slade Branch

Hammond Run

North Branch

FR 461

Big
Beechy
Trail

Big Beechy
Trailhead

Hell for Certain Br.

Middle Fork Trail TR 271

Middle Fork

Williams River

McClintock Run

North-South Trail

49

P

Hunting Run

North Fork Cranberry River

Cashcamp Run

FR 76

North Fork Trail

FR 102

FR 738

FR 232

FR 232

Cranberry Glades
Botanical Area

150

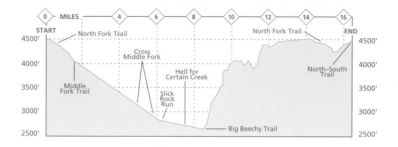

7.8 Pass the Laurelly Branch Trail (TR 267) on the left. Continue straight, remaining in the creek valley. (***FYI:*** There are good campsites in this area.)

8.5 Reach Big Beechy Run and the intersection with the Big Beechy Trail (TR 207). The Big Beechy Trail begins at a sign on the southeast bank of the creek. Take a right off the Middle Fork Trail and hike uphill to the east. (***FYI:*** This trail is blazed with double blue blazes, albeit infrequently. A double blaze on this trail does not indicate a trail junction as it normally would. Stock up on water here before you head up the mountain. This is a good place to camp before finishing the hike on day two.)

13.0 Pass the District Line Trail (TR 248) on the left. Continue straight.

15.0 Come to the junction where the North Fork Trail reaches the intersection with the Middle Fork Trail. Take the right fork at this Y intersection to continue on the North Fork Trail to the south. (To the left is a spur trail to the Big Beechy trailhead.)

15.25 Arrive at a fork. The Middle Fork Trail junction is on the right, where you began the trail. Take the left fork to take the North Fork Trail back to the trailhead.

16.25 Reach the junction with North-South Trail. Turn left and hike the short distance to the information stand and the parking lot.

16.75 Arrive back at the trailhead.

HIKE INFORMATION

Local information: Pocahontas County Convention & Visitors Bureau, (800) 336-7009 or www.pocahontascountywv.com

Camping: Because this hike is in designated wilderness, backcountry camping is permitted throughout the area. There are 4 developed campgrounds in the area managed as Cranberry Backcountry: Summit Lake Campground has 33 sites, Big Rock Campground has 5 units next to the Cranberry River, Cranberry Campground has 28 single and 2 double sites, and Bishop Knob Campground has 49 single and 6 double sites.

Local events/attractions: Check out the Cranberry Mountain Nature Center, open mid-Apr to mid-Oct, Thurs through Mon from 9 a.m. to 4:30 p.m.; (304) 653-4826.

Organizations: West Virginia Highlands Conservancy, www.wvhighlands.org

Honorable Mentions

P TURKEY RUN TO OTTER CREEK TRAIL LOOP, OTTER CREEK WILDERNESS

Shuttling to do the whole length of the 11.8-mile Otter Creek Trail can be a bear (figuratively), so an alternate is a day hike making a loop out of the Turkey Run and Otter Creek Trails. Start on the 3.8-mile Turkey Run Trail (TR 150), and be sure to wear long pants because you have probably never seen stinging nettle like this before. Follow the Turkey Run Trail to its end at the Moore Run Trail (TR 138). Take a left and go about 2.0 miles to a four-way junction. Go left here to hop on the Otter Creek Trail (TR 131), and follow it upstream about 4.3 miles to the junction with the Big Springs Gap Trail (TR 151). Take a left and go 0.8 mile up to the parking lot for Big Springs Gap. Turn left on the road and walk 0.2 mile back to your car. This makes an 11.1-mile loop, not saving you mileage over an Otter Creek hike one way, but saving you the shuttle. For more information, contact the Potomac office of the Cheat-Potomac Ranger District at (304) 257-4488 or go to www.fs.usda.gov/mnf.

From the stoplight in downtown Parsons, take US 219 0.2 mile across the Shavers Fork bridge, then take a right followed by an immediate left. Brown Otter Creek signs are here where the road becomes Billings Avenue. Parallel the Allegheny Trail bike path and Dry Fork upstream. At mile 2.6, the road forks; there is a sign for the gravel FR 701 here. Take the right fork. At mile 5.3, the road forks again (unmarked). Take a left and head uphill. At mile 5.9, come to the Otter Creek Trail trailhead. There is a bulletin board here (though signs may be ripped down) and a wooden sign for the Zero Grade Trail. Continue 0.2 mile to the Turkey Run trailhead on the left, marked with a trailhead sign and bulletin board. GPS: N39 02.62' /W79 39.90'

Q PLAINS CIRCUIT, FLATROCK AND ROARING PLAINS BACKCOUNTRY

Just south of the Dolly Sods Wilderness is the similarly scenic Flatrock and Roaring Plains Backcountry. Northern hardwood forests with cascading streams at lower elevations give way to spruce forests, heath barrens, and mountain plains at higher elevations. Many hikers who descend on Dolly Sods largely ignore Flatrock and Roaring Plains. This 14.5-mile hike climbs steeply up the side of Mount Porte Crayon to Roaring Plains, with gorgeous views of the surrounding countryside and north into Dolly Sods. The descent back to Red Creek is steeper than the climb up but a little shorter. The last portion of the hike follows FR 19. It's lightly traveled and scenic, but the dust vehicles leave in their wake can be an annoyance. For more information contact the Potomac office of the Cheat-Potomac Ranger District at (304) 257-4488 or www.fs.usda.gov/mnf.

From the junction of US 33/WV 55 and WV 32 in Harman, drive north on WV 32 for 3.7 miles to Bonner Mountain Road (32-3). Turn right (east) and go 4.2 miles to the trailhead on the right, marked with a sign; continue to mile 4.4 to the trailhead parking on the left. From the parking area, walk back along the road to the trailhead. GPS: N38 58.50'/W79 25.98'

R WEST FORK TRAIL, MONONGAHELA NATIONAL FOREST

There are few places in the Mon where you can find an easy trail with relatively easy access yet without the crowds. The 22-mile West Fork Trail (TR 312) is one of these, but here's the trick to finding solitude: For a day hike, access the northern end of the trail in Glady (rather than the southern end in Durbin). But come prepared: There are no crowds here because there are no amenities either. Enjoy relatively long views for this part of the forest combined with classic Monongahela hiking, paralleling a swift-flowing river (the West Fork of the Greenbrier) in a deep, densely forested mountain valley. Because it's a rail trail, the wide swath will leave you in the sun, so bring your hat. Do an out-and-back at your own pace, or try to make a loop with the Allegheny Trail (TR 701) or High Falls Trail (TR 345). For more information, contact the Greenbrier Ranger District at (304) 456-3335 or go to www.fs.usda.gov/mnf.

To find the trailhead, take US 33/WV 55 east of Elkins 11.9 miles to Glady Road (CR 27) and turn south. Drive 9.3 miles to Glady and CR 22. Continue straight on Glady Road to mile 10.1, where the road ends at a parking area by a trailhead map and a gate. GPS: N38 47.52'/W79 43.31'

S CRANBERRY BOG BOARDWALK, CRANBERRY GLADES BOTANICAL AREA

Get in touch with your inner botanist at Cranberry Glades Botanical Area. Located in the high mountains of the Monongahela National Forest, this National Natural Landmark conserves a unique West Virginia feature—mountain bogs that are home to unusual plants including the carnivorous sundew and pitcher plant. This 0.6-mile boardwalk loop takes you through the heart of the area. Bogs are dark, acidic soil wetlands that are more commonly found in northern boreal forests. The ecosystems found here are holdovers from the glacial age of 10,000 years ago. Here you will also find plants such as sphagnum moss, orchids, and, yes, cranberries. The open bogs also allow for views of the valleys and mountains beyond. The bog ecosystem is very fragile, so please stay on the boardwalk.

The Cranberry Mountain Nature Center is open mid-Apr to mid-Oct, Thurs through Mon from 9 a.m. to 4:30 p.m., and offers guided hikes during the summer. Call (304)

653-4826. The rest of the year, contact the Gauley Ranger District (304-846-2695 or www.fs.usda.gov/mnf) to make sure the roads to Cranberry Glades Botanical Area are passable.

At the intersection of WV 219, WV 39, and WV 55 south of Marlinton, turn west on WV 39/WV 55. Proceed 7.0 miles and turn right on FR 102. There is a sign for the botanical area at this intersection. Proceed 1.5 miles to a parking area on the right. GPS: N38 11.87'/W80 16.50'

T FALLS OF HILLS CREEK TRAIL, FALLS OF HILLS CREEK SCENIC AREA

This is a bang-for-your-buck hike if ever there was one. Three sets of falls are on Hills Creek, the (creatively named) 25-foot upper falls, 45-foot middle falls, and 63-foot lower falls, on a trail that's a mere 0.7 mile (1.4 miles round-trip). Shoulder your tripod and head out in the morning or evening for even light conditions, and get ready for a lot of steps. The trail to the upper falls is actually wheelchair accessible and paved. Past that, a combination of dirt path and boardwalks (and lots of stairs) takes you down to the middle and lower falls. Hills Creek is surrounded by sandstone walls, and the forest is composed of hemlock, rhododendron, river birch, magnolia, nettle, and fern. It's a lovely hike any time of year, from the high-flowing water of spring through the ice and snow of winter. Check with the Gauley Ranger District (304-846-2695 or www.fs.usda.gov/mnf) to make sure the road is passable in winter.

From I-64 exit 169 in Lewisburg, take US 219 north 31 miles to the junction with WV 39/WV 55. Go west (left) on WV 39/WV 55 and drive 11.7 miles to Hills Creek Falls Road (FR 1632), marked with a brown scenic area sign. Take a left and drive 0.2 mile to the parking lot. The trailhead, located on the east side of the parking lot, is marked with a big trailhead sign and map. GPS: N38 10.41'/W80 20.09'

U NORTH FORK MOUNTAIN TRAIL TO LANDIS TRAIL LOOP, SPRUCE KNOB-SENECA ROCKS NATIONAL RECREATION AREA

The 24.2-mile North Fork Mountain Trail is all about the views, and some of the best are found within a few miles of the northern trailhead. For a day hike, start at the northern trailhead and take the (steep) North Fork Mountain Trail up to views of Chimney Rock and the valley below. Hike 3.8 miles to the junction with the Landis Trail. Take a left and descend the eastern side of North Fork Mountain down to Smoke Hole Road (CR 28-11). Take another left and return on the gravel road back to the trailhead for about a 7.2-mile loop. You can always do an out-and-back to Chimney Rock, too. For information contact the Monongahela National Forest, Potomac office of the Cheat-Potomac Ranger District at (304) 257-4488 or www.fs.usda.gov/mnf.

To reach the northern trailhead, at the intersection of WV 28, WV 55, and US 33 in Seneca Rocks, take WV 28 north/WV 55 east toward Petersburg. Proceed 15.3 miles to CR 28-11 (Smoke Hole Road) and turn right. Cross the bridge and travel 0.3 mile to the parking area on the right. GPS: N38 58.96'/W79 13.85'

V GAUDINEER SCENIC AREA TRAILS, MONONGAHELA NATIONAL FOREST

Gaudineer Scenic Area is known for its virgin red spruce forest. Like most other remaining bits of virgin forest, this small tract remains thanks to surveying errors back when the surrounding area was clear cut. There are two short trails in this area. Be sure to bring a lunch and plan to eat it at the Gaudineer Knob/Gaudineer Overlook picnic area. There are several picnic tables along the trail that may be the most beautifully sited ones you'll ever see. The half-mile trail winds through an enchanting forest of dense spruce with a thick carpet of emerald moss and includes an overlook at about the halfway point. Then head to the trailhead for the Gaudineer Old Growth Trail. This half-mile loop takes you through the virgin forest of red spruce and yellow birch. The trees are not huge (these species simply don't grow as big as others) but the forest is a great lesson in forest growth, decay, and regeneration.

To find the trailhead, start at the railroad depot in Durbin and take US 250 north 4.9 miles to Forest Road 27, which is marked with a brown GAUDINEER SCENIC AREA sign. Take a right onto FR 27 and continue 1.7 miles to a fork. Take a left at the fork onto Forest Road 27A and continue 0.5 mile to the Gaudineer Knob/Gaudineer Overlook picnic area and trail. After you complete the Gaudineer Overlook trail, return to this fork and take a left this time, continuing on Forest Road 27 another 0.5 mile to parking for the virgin red spruce trail on the right, marked with a sign. GPS: N38.615 / W79.844

GEORGE WASHINGTON AND JEFFERSON NATIONAL FORESTS

The George Washington and Jefferson National Forests tip just slightly into West Virginia from Virginia. Management of the two separate national forests was combined into one administrative unit in 1995. The former Jefferson National Forest dips into West Virginia along Peters Mountain in Monroe County. The former George Washington National Forest occupies two landmasses in West Virginia: one just east of the towns of Mathias, Lost River, and Baker in Hardy County, and the other east of the towns of Sugar Grove, Brandywine, and Fort Seybert in Pendleton County. The GW-Jeff occupies more than 123,000 acres in West Virginia, approximately 7 percent of the forest's 1.8 million acres.

Don't underestimate the difficulty of even a short trail. The surrounding areas are very rural, so make sure you are well supplied before you begin your trip. Finding supplies near the trailhead may be difficult, if not impossible. Camping is available in campgrounds and by dispersed camping in the forest.

As with all national forests, hunting is allowed in the George Washington and Jefferson National Forests. Although hunting seasons tend to be in the fall and early winter, check local hunting calendars any time a hike is planned in the forest. If planning a hike during a hunting season, wear blaze orange and stick to well-marked trails.

Azaleas grow wild in this region.

50 ROCK CLIFF LAKE TO TROUT POND TRAIL LOOP

Trout Pond Recreation Area

WHY GO?

The Trout Pond Recreation Area is located in the West Virginia portion of the George Washington and Jefferson National Forests on the western slope of Long Mountain. This area of the state is marked by 50-mile-long ridges, bucolic farm valleys, and tall mountains. A popular destination for fishing—trout and other species—the Trout Pond Recreation Area is also home to a dozen miles of trail. This loop takes you along the shores of azalea-lined Rock Cliff Lake and past Chimney Rock before bringing you back to the lake again.

THE RUNDOWN

Start: Rock Cliff Lake Trail trailhead

Distance: 2-mile loop

Hiking time: About 1 hour

Difficulty: Easy

Trail surface: Dirt trail

Best season: May and June for flowering shrubs

Other trail users: Mountain bikers

Canine compatibility: Leashed dogs permitted

Land status: National forest

Nearest town: Baker

Fees and permits: Fee required to enter the recreation area

Schedule: The recreation area is closed from Dec to Apr. The trail system is open year-round for day use from 8 a.m. to sunset.

Maps: Lee Ranger District map; Trails Illustrated Map 792; USGS quad: Wolf Gap

Trail contact: Lee Ranger District, George Washington and Jefferson National Forests, (540) 984-4101 or www.fs.usda.gov/gwj

Special considerations: A gate before the entrance station is closed from 10 p.m. to 8 a.m. You cannot pass the entrance gate at night or in the off-season. If you arrive and the gate is closed, park in the gravel lot just before the gate and look for the trailhead with blue blazes. This is the 0.4-mile Fisherman's Trail, which leads directly to the Rock Cliff Lake Trail. When you arrive at Rock Cliff Lake, turn left and continue walking around the lake.

FINDING THE TRAILHEAD

At the intersection of WV 55 and WV 259 in Baker, turn south on WV 259 and travel 7.1 miles to CR 16. There is a sign for the Trout Pond Recreation Area at this intersection. Turn left (east) on CR 16 and proceed 4.5 miles to the campground sign. Turn right and continue 1.5 miles to the entrance station. There is a fee to enter the day-use area or to camp. Past the entrance station, take a left, following signs for the pond. Park at the second parking area, which is on the left. The first gravel trail toward the lake takes you to the Rock Cliff Lake (Doris Agnew) trailhead, just a few feet from the parking lot. It's marked with a trailhead sign. **GPS:** N38 54.15' / W78 54.97'

THE HIKE

Starting at the 17-acre Rock Cliff Lake, walk around most of the lake on the Rock Cliff Lake Trail. Although this is technically the Rock Cliff Lake Trail, a sign at the trailhead identifies a portion of the trail as the Doris Agnew Trail, named in memory of a volunteer campground host (the Lina Constable Overlook is also named in memory of a volunteer host). The first section of this hike takes you halfway around the lake, which is lined with azaleas and stocked with trout, though brook trout are native here as well. A lovely rock outcropping in the lake hosts a lone pine tree near the dam.

After arriving at the dam, the trail goes away from the lake, picking up the Chimney Rock Trail. Follow the orange blazes through a lush forest, paralleling Trout Pond Run. Cross the run and dead-end right into Chimney Rock, a surprising sand-

Chimney Rock

stone rock outcropping that is indeed tall and narrow. Take a right at Chimney Rock and immediately cross another run. Take the Chimney Rock Trail to the junction with the Trout Pond Trail, marked with a sign and blazed purple. As you take a right turn onto the Trout Pond Trail, you might hear ducks nearby; the "pond" just out of sight on the right is a water treatment plant. You're now walking on a gravel road and will soon walk past the maintenance sheds for the area.

Past the maintenance area, there is a trail to the right, which leads up to the power lines. A sign marks this trail, but only from the other side. It's the Burger Knob Trail. Take a right and join the power-line cut. Follow this cut all the way back to Rock Cliff Lake. You can cross the parking lot to the restrooms. The trailhead where you began is on the other side of the restrooms.

MILES AND DIRECTIONS

0.0 START at the Rock Cliff Lake Trail trailhead; a sign marks it as the Doris Agnew Lake Trail. It's between the parking lot, lake, and restrooms. Follow the gravel trail into the woods and across a footbridge. It soon becomes a dirt path. Cross a second footbridge. (*FYI:* If you started on the Fisherman's

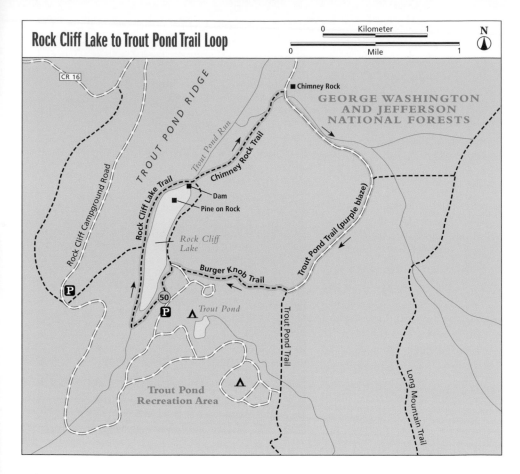

Rock Cliff Lake to Trout Pond Trail Loop

0 — Kilometer — 1

0 — Mile — 1

N

CR 16

Chimney Rock

GEORGE WASHINGTON
AND JEFFERSON
NATIONAL FORESTS

TROUT POND RIDGE

Trout Pond Run

Chimney Rock Trail

Rock Cliff Lake Trail

Dam

Pine on Rock

Rock Cliff Lake

Trout Pond Trail (purple blaze)

Rock Cliff Campground Road

Burger Knob Trail

P

50

P

Trout Pond

Trout Pond Trail

Long Mountain Trail

Trout Pond
Recreation Area

Trail near the entrance station, walk to the lake and take a left, then continue with the directions below.)

0.1 A blue-blazed trail comes in from the left; this is the Fisherman's Trail. Continue straight, paralleling the lake.

0.5 Come to the earthen dam and a sign for the Trout Pond Store (the store is closed) as well as the junction with the Chimney Rock Trail, blazed orange. Do not cross the dam; continue straight, following orange blazes.

0.6 The trail switches back to the right, then the left. Keep following the orange blazes.

0.9 Ford a stream and arrive at Chimney Rock on the other side. The trail hits a T intersection. A sign marks the Trout Pond Store to the left. Go right and ford another stream.

1.3 Come to a junction marked with a sign for the Trout Pond Store, dam, and campground. Take a right, picking up the purple-blazed Trout Pond Trail.

1.4 The trail joins a gravel road. Continue straight and walk past a maintenance storage area.

1.5 Come to the Burger Knob Trail on the right; there is a sign but it is only marked on the other side. Take a right and walk into the woods up to the power lines. Follow the power lines all the way back to Rock Cliff Lake.

1.7 Pass a side trail on the left; continue straight, under the power lines.

2.0 Arrive at a parking lot on the east side of Rock Cliff Lake. Take a left to cross the parking lot to your car.

HIKE INFORMATION

Local information: Visit Hardy County WV, (304) 897-8700 or www.visithardywv .com

Camping: Trout Run Recreation Area has a thirty-eight site developed campground open from the third Tues in Apr until the end of Nov.

Local events/attractions: Lost River Artisans Cooperative, (304) 897-7242 or www.lostriver crafts.com

Organizations: A number of organizations work with the George Washington and Jefferson National Forests; contact the Lee Ranger District for information about how to get involved.

> Near the trail is the name-sake Trout Pond, West Virginia's only natural pond—it's actually a sink-hole that holds water except in times of drought.

51 ALLEGHENY TRAIL TO HANGING ROCK RAPTOR OBSERVATORY

WHY GO?

Record numbers of birds of prey are found near the Hanging Rock Raptor Observatory. Once you arrive at this spot, you'll know why they hang out here: A refurbished fire tower sits atop the "hanging" rocks at 3,800 feet and affords 360-degree views. Not only will you have a chance to see hawks and eagles, you can also take in long, narrow mountain ridges as far as the eye can see. You can even use what may be the world's most scenically located outhouse.

THE RUNDOWN

Start: Trailhead parking lot off Limestone Hill Road
Distance: 1.8-mile out-and-back
Hiking time: About 1 hour
Difficulty: Easy
Trail surface: Rocky dirt trail
Best season: Sept and Oct for eagle and hawk viewing
Other trail users: Birders, horseback riders, mountain bikers, hunters during hunting season
Canine compatibility: Controlled dogs are permitted
Land status: National forest

Nearest town: Gap Mills
Fees and permits: None
Schedule: Hanging Rock is a day use area, open 6 a.m. to 10 p.m.; the road is usually closed in the winter due to snow.
Maps: "Hiking Guide to the Allegheny Trail" available online at www.wvscenictrails.org; USGS quads: Ronceverte, Waiteville
Trail contact: Eastern Divide Ranger District, George Washington and Jefferson National Forests, (540) 552-4641 or www.fs.usda.gov/gwj

FINDING THE TRAILHEAD

From the junction of CR 8-1 and WV 3 in Gap Mills, take WV 3 east 0.5 mile to Zenith Road (CR 15). This junction is marked with a brown national forest wildlife-viewing sign. Take a right (south) and travel 3.4 miles to Limestone Hill Road (CR 15), also marked with a brown wildlife-viewing sign. Take a left on Limestone Hill Road and go 1.7 miles to a parking area on the right. A trailhead sign is located on the southwest corner of the gravel lot. The trail is marked with yellow blazes. **GPS:** N37 30.59'/W80 26.29'

THE HIKE

Hanging Rock Raptor Observatory is a unique West Virginia treasure—one that almost fell by the wayside due to neglect. There are some variations on the story, but generally it goes like this: The state of West Virginia built the original fire tower in the 1930s, and it was in use for decades. In the 1970s the tower was abandoned as a fire lookout when aerial fire surveillance began. By this time, Hanging Rock was a well-established raptor observatory, though the tower itself was in disrepair and at risk of being demolished.

Enter the Brooks Bird Club, which worked with the Forest Service to keep the tower in use. The tower was fully refurbished by the 1980s, but then in 1996 arson destroyed

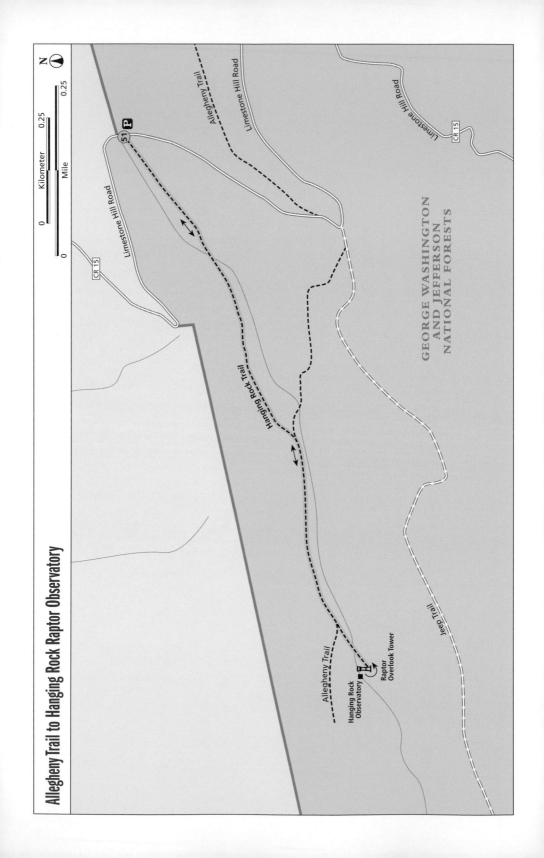

Allegheny Trail to Hanging Rock Raptor Observatory

it. The Forest Service, supplied with many hours of elbow grease from Brooks Bird Club volunteers, got the tower built again. Today, Hanging Rock Raptor Observatory is a wildly popular destination among birders: Some 1,500 people visit the tower from mid-August to the first of December, many of them in September when broad-winged hawks can circle in kettles of up to 200.

The hike to Hanging Rock Raptor Observatory is an exercise in anticipation, knowing of the payoff that's coming. The grade is alternately gradual and steep. At first, the forest is young and part of the path travels under power lines. You'll see a lot of invasive plants, such as garlic mustard, but also attractive spring wildflowers like trillium and wild geranium. Listen for songbirds in the forest, including catbirds and ovenbirds. Yellow blazes are frequent, and the path is easy to follow. As you approach the very top of the ridge, the forest gets nicer, with mossy sandstone boulders and oak and buckeye trees.

Just before reaching the tower, the trail forks. The Allegheny Trail continues on to the right, and the left fork is a spur to the Hanging Rocks—dramatic slabs of rock creating a tilted peak at the top of Peters Mountain—and the observatory, which has a wraparound porch giving you views of the mountains, valleys, forests, and, of course, the raptors that you are likely to see when they migrate through here in the fall. Information inside the observatory includes bird count lists going back to the 1970s. Sightings of hawks and eagles have increased steadily over the years.

MILES AND DIRECTIONS

0.0 START at the trailhead from the gravel parking area. Begin ascending as the trail enters the woods, following the yellow blazes.

0.8 Come to a fork, marked with a trail sign. The Allegheny Trail goes to the right (yellow blazes), and the final section of trail to the tower is to the left, blazed blue.

0.9 Arrive at the Hanging Rock Raptor Observatory. Return the way you came.

1.8 Arrive back at the trailhead.

HIKE INFORMATION

Local information: Visit Southern West Virginia, (800) 636-1460 or www.visitwv .com

Camping: Nearby Moncove Lake State Park has a 48-site (both electric and nonelectric) campground. Campsites are on a first-come, first-served basis, (304) 772-3450 or www.moncovelakestatepark.com.

Hike tours: Organized tours from nearby Moncove Lake State Park are sometimes offered. Call the park at (304) 722-3450 to inquire.

Organizations: Brooks Bird Club, www.brooksbirdclub.org; West Virginia Scenic Trails Association, www.wvscenictrails.org

Honorable Mention

W TROUT POND TO LONG MOUNTAIN TRAIL LOOP, TROUT POND RECREATION AREA

The Trout Pond Recreation Area is located on the western slope of Long Mountain. The Long Mountain Trail is an 8.4-mile strenuous loop hike to the top of the mountain, with wonderful views from the Lina Constable Overlook and sections on gravel roads and wide grassy trails. The trail offers great rock formations and quiet solitude. The Long Mountain Trail joins the trail system around Trout Pond Lake, popular for fishing and swimming. Trail Illustrated Map 792 includes a map of the Long Mountain Trail.

A spur trail heads from the parking area to the campground. At the campground, pick up the Trout Run Trail by site 27, blazed purple. Walk uphill 1.0 mile to the Lina Constable Overlook. (This is a good place to turn around if you want a shorter hike.) Continue up to the ridge another 1.0 mile to CR 59 and take a left onto the gravel road. After 1.0 mile, pass the orange-blazed North Mountain Trail on the right. Continue another 0.9 mile and take a left off the road onto the Long Mountain Trail, traveling north. The Long Mountain Trail, blazed yellow, gradually descends 2.5 miles to the Trout Pond Trail. Take a left here and walk south, following the purple blazes back to the campground. For more information, contact the Lee Ranger District at (540) 984-4101 or go to www.fs.usda.gov/gwj.

To reach the trailhead, at the intersection of WV 55 and WV 259 in Baker, turn south on WV 259 and travel 7.1 miles to CR 16. There is a sign for the Trout Pond Recreation Area at this intersection. Turn left (east) on CR 16 and proceed 4.5 miles to the campground sign. Turn right and continue 1.5 miles to the entrance station. A fee is charged for the day-use area or camping. Past the entrance station, the road forks. Take the left fork and park in the first parking lot, on the right. GPS: N38 57.36' /W78 44.29'

APPENDIX

USGS 1:24,000 QUAD MAP LIST

NORTHERN PANHANDLE

Tomlinson Run State Park—East Liverpool South

Oglebay Resort—Wheeling

Grand Vue Park—Moundsville

Panhandle Trail—Steubenville and Steubenville East

MOUNTAINEER COUNTRY

Valley Falls State Park—Fairmont East

Coopers Rock State Forest—Bruceton Mills, Masontown, and Lake Lynn

Cathedral State Park—Aurora

Watters Smith Memorial State Park—West Milford

EASTERN PANHANDLE

Cacapon Resort State Park—Great Cacapon and Ridge

Harpers Ferry National Historical Park—Harpers Ferry

POTOMAC HIGHLANDS

Jennings Randolph Lake Project—Kitzmiller and Westernport

Blackwater Falls State Park—Blackwater Falls

Canaan Valley National Wildlife Refuge—Blackwater Falls and Davis

Lost River State Park—Lost River State Park

Kumbrabow State Forest—Adolph, Pickens, Samp, and Valley Head

Snowshoe Mountain Resort—Cass

Seneca State Forest—Clover Lick and Paddy Knob

Droop Mountain Battlefield State Park—Droop

Watoga State Park—Denmar, Hillsboro, Lake Sherwood, and Marlinton

Beartown State Park—Droop

MOUNTAIN LAKES REGION

Cedar Creek State Park—Cedarville, Glenville, Normantown, and Tanner

Audra State Park—Audra

Holly River State Park—Goshen and Hacker Valley

Stonewall Jackson Resort State Park—Roanoke

NEW RIVER/GREENBRIER VALLEY

Babcock State Park—Danese, Fayetteville, Thurmond, and Winona

New River Gorge National River—Meadow Creek and Prince

Twin Falls Resort State Park—Mullens and McGraws
Camp Creek State Park—Odd
Pipestem Resort State Park—Flat Top and Pipestem
Bluestone National Scenic River—Flat Top and Pipestem
Greenbrier State Forest—Glace and White Sulphur Springs
Greenbrier River Trail—Cass, Cloverlick, Edray, Marlinton, Hillsboro, Denmar, Droop, Anthony, White Sulphur Springs, and Lewisburg
Pinnacle Rock State Park—Branwell

METRO VALLEY
Kanawha Trace Trail—Barboursville, Glenwood, Mount Olive, Milton, and Winfield
Huntington Museum of Art National Recreation Trail—Huntington
Cabwaylingo State Forest—Kiahsville, Radnor, Webb, and Wilsondale
Kanawha State Forest—Belle, Charleston East, Charleston West, and Racine
Beech Fork State Park—Winslow

MID-OHIO VALLEY
Blennerhassett Island Historical Park—Parkersburg
North Bend Rail Trail—(west to east) South Parkersburg, Kanawha, Petroleum, Cairo, Harrisville, Ellenboro, Pennsboro, West Union, Smithburg, Salem, and Wolf Summit
North Bend State Park—Cairo and Harrisville
McDonough Wildlife Refuge—Parkersburg
Mountwood Park—Elizabeth

MONONGAHELA NATIONAL FOREST
Otter Creek Wilderness—Bath Alum, Green Valley, Montrose, and Parsons
Dolly Sods Wilderness—Blackbird Knob, Blackwater Falls, Hopeville, and Laneville
Spruce Knob–Seneca Rocks National Recreation Area—Circleville, Franklin, Upper Tract, Hopeville, Petersburg West, Circleville, Onego, Spruce Knob, and Whitmer
High Falls Trail—Elkins and Glady
Laurel Fork South Wilderness—Sinks of Gandy
Cranberry Wilderness—Webster Springs SE and Woodrow
Flatrock and Roaring Plains Backcountry—Harman, Hopeville, Laneville, and Onego
West Fork Trail—Beverly East, Durbin, Elkins, Horton, and Wildell
Cranberry Glades Botanical Area—Lobelia
Falls of Hills Creek Scenic Area—Lobelia
Gaudineer Scenic Area—Wildell and Durbin

GEORGE WASHINGTON AND JEFFERSON NATIONAL FORESTS
Trout Pond Recreation Area—Wolf Gap
Allegheny Trail to Hanging Rock Raptor Observatory—Ronceverte and Waiteville

INDEX

HM = Honorable Mention

Sidebars

Lower falls on Falls of Hills Creek Trail (hike T)

ABOUT THE AUTHOR

Reviser Mary Reed is a freelance journalist and photographer based in Athens, Ohio. She has been hiking, backpacking, and rock climbing in West Virginia for thirty years. Her work has appeared in *Backpacker, Ohio Magazine, New River Gorge Guide,* and many other publications. She is also the author of *Hiking Ohio* and *Best Easy Day Hikes Fort Collins.* Learn more at maryreed.biz.